FUNDAMENTALS OF DEMOCRATIC EDUCATION

FUNDAMENTALS OF DEMOCRATIC EDUCATION

AN INTRODUCTION TO EDUCATIONAL PHILOSOPHY

BY

ROBERT ULICH
Harvard University

GREENWOOD PRESS, PUBLISHERS
WESTPORT, CONNECTICUT

Copyright © 1940 by American Book Company

Reprinted by permission
of Van Nostrand Reinhold Company

First Greenwood Reprinting 1970

Library of Congress Catalogue Card Number 71-97390

SBN 8371-3015-8

PRINTED IN UNITED STATES OF AMERICA

To

HENRY WYMAN HOLMES

*Interest in education is only
an expression of our whole
interest in the world and in
humanity.*

—HERBART

ACKNOWLEDGMENTS

I wish to express my gratitude to the William F. Milton Fund of Harvard University and to the Carnegie Foundation for the Advancement of Teaching for their financial support of this work. I also gratefully acknowledge the assistance received in the preparation of the manuscript from Mrs. Florence Graves Strong and the interest which Mr. Herbert Snelgrove took in improving the style of the original draft. The exchange of ideas with friends, colleagues, and students has been a constant stimulus for me. For permission to use excerpts from copyrighted sources I am indebted to many authors, associations, and publishers. Acknowledgment for permission to make quotations is made to American Book Company; A. & C. Black Ltd.; Dodd, Mead & Company; Jonathan Cape Limited; Harlem Book Company; D. C. Heath and Company; Henry Holt and Company; Longmans, Green & Co.; The Macmillan Company; McGraw-Hill Book Company, Inc.; The Nation; New Education Fellowship; W. W. Norton & Company, Inc.; Oxford University Press; A. Picard & Cie.; Progressive Education Association; Charles Scribner's Sons; Simon and Schuster, Inc.; and Yale University Press. Specific credit for quotation is given in the footnotes to the text. In the sixth chapter, "Education and Society," I have drawn freely upon an article of mine originally published in *Social Research, An International Quarterly of Political and Social Science,* September, 1937.

ROBERT ULICH

Harvard University

vi

TABLE OF CONTENTS

INTRODUCTION.   1

  I. WHY DO WE EDUCATE?   3
    A. The Biological Point of View.   4
    B. The Sociological Point of View   10
    C. The Ethical Point of View   19
    D. The Emotional Point of View   42

  II. WHOM DO WE EDUCATE?   51
    A. Historical Introduction   51
    B. The Need for a Total Explanation of the Human
       Being.   59
    C. The Predicaments of Psychology   66
    D. The Structure of the Personality   70
       1. Environment. Self-identity. Vital Urges . .   70
       2. Abilities and the Problem of Freedom   75
       3. Constitutional Endowment   77
       4. Feeling. Will. Intelligence   80
       5. The Directional Character of the Personality .   85
       6. Conflicts in the Personality and the Need for
          Values   89
    E. Growth, Form, and Metaphysics of the Person-
       ality   94

  III. TOWARD WHAT ENDS DO WE EDUCATE?   101
    A. Stating the Problem   101
    B. The Quest for Ethical Criteria   134

IV. THE STRUGGLE OF THE EDUCATOR WITH THE PROBLEM OF VALUES (EDUCATIONAL POLICY) 153

A. The Major Factors Influencing Education . . . 153

  1. The Dependence of Education upon the General Character of a Period 153

  2. The Disintegration of Religion 157

  3. The Disintegration of the Humanistic Ideal . 162

  4. Relativism 164

  5. The Disintegration of the Social and Economic Foundations of Civilization 165

    a. Social 165

    b. Economic 170

B. The Operation of the Major Factors in the Theory of Education 171

  1. Comenius 171

  2. Pestalozzi 172

  3. Herbart and the Victorian Era 176

  4. Modern Eclecticism, Pragmatism, and Nationalism 183

C. Educational Practice 185

  1. The Necessity of Decision 185

  2. The School as Social Environment 190

  3. The School as a Place of Instruction and Mental Discipline 194

  4. The Humanities 196

  5. The Organization of Instruction 202

  6. New Ways toward Educational Values . . . 205

    a. Social Studies 207

    b. Natural Sciences 210

    c. The Modern Organic Curriculum 213

V. POSTULATES OF TEACHING 217

A. The Postulate of Individualism of Method 220

B. The Postulate of Totality 221

C. The Postulate of Adequateness 223

D. The Postulate of Diversity of Subject Matter . .   225

E. The Postulate of Mental Order.   227

F. The Postulate of Correlation of Subject Matter   234

G. The Postulate of Self-activity   236

H. The Postulate of Ethical Direction   238

VI. EDUCATION AND SOCIETY   243

A. Contrast and Interaction of Social Components   243

B. The Groundwork of Social Life   250

C. The "Unconscious" and the "Conscious" in Social Life   252

D. The Educator and the Opposing Demands of
Society   255

E. Responsibility and Freedom in Education   266

VII. EDUCATION AND THE STATE   271

A. The Importance of the State   271

B. The Role of Guide Words in History   272

C. The History of the Concept of Freedom   275

D. The Crisis of Freedom   279

E. The Conditions of Freedom   287

VIII. EDUCATION AND RELIGION   295

A. The Antagonism between Religion and Reason .   295

B. Present Forms of Religious Experience   303

    1. The Fundamentalist Point of View   303

    2. The Religious Philosophy of Identity (Hu-
manism)   304

    3. Kierkegaard's Religion of Paradoxicalness . .   308

    4. Religious Symbolism   311

C. The Transmission of Religious Values   313

D. Critical Evaluation of Religious Education . . .   318

E. The Fundamental Difficulty in Religious Education   323

F. The Role of Religion in Modern Civilization . . .   326

G. The Idea of Reverence   328

IX. THE MISSION OF AMERICAN EDUCATION 335
    A. The Essentials of Civilization 335
    B. The American Responsibility 341

SELECTED BIBLIOGRAPHY 345

INDEX 355

INTRODUCTION

Modern scientific thought displays at first glance a striking antinomy. On the one hand, the scholar finds himself impelled toward specialization; on the other hand, he is forced, even in his specialization, to draw on an increasing number of sciences, thus helping to efface the lines of demarcation between the different fields of research. This contrast is, however, only apparent and not fundamental. It results from the fact that intensified specialization makes more and more explicit the complexity of problems that earlier generations considered relatively simple. Consequently, every modern specialist who is not satisfied with the description of surface phenomena within his own small field needs the assistance of other sciences for the development of his theories.

In this book, written for the purpose of discussing the principles by which democratic civilization regenerates itself, we bring together aspects of sociology, psychology, education, and philosophy, in the hope that each may help to elucidate the questions we have in mind.

That an inquiry into our problem needs sociology and psychology as the sciences concerned with the communal life of man and his mental development requires no specific justification. The science of education must take

1

part in the examination of the ways of civilization, since education is to a large extent an analysis of, and a prerequisite to, human and social development. The success of society, furthermore, depends upon individuals who learn to understand the conditions of their own growth and who put their personalities to the test by voluntary acceptance of their obligations to the community.

But the combination of the different fields of knowledge just mentioned, instead of helping us to investigate the fundamental principles that make for human advancement, may result in a merely descriptive account of the give-and-take between various areas of life. If, however, we want not only such description but also guiding criteria for judging the value of the diverse expressions of democratic civilization, we need philosophy, not as a history of ideas, but as a way of thinking radically and comprehensively about the problems of humanity. The results of such an effort are always open to dispute and to the charge of subjectivity. Nevertheless, philosophy must risk such a charge. For a civilization does not deserve its title unless it constantly attempts to become aware of its inherent postulates and its deeper responsibilities for the liberation of humanity.

During the final stages in the preparation of this book the European war has broken out. There are few principal considerations in these pages which could not, in one way or another, be related to this event, so decisive for the future of our Western Christian civilization. The outbreak of the war, unfortunately, verifies some of my pessimistic remarks about the future of Europe; moreover, it makes a fundamental reconsideration of the democratic problem and the role the United States will play in the future of democracy all the more important.

Chapter I

WHY DO WE EDUCATE?

Man has civilization because, among other reasons, he possesses the capacity of asking the question "Why?" This is not only a stimulating but also a complex little word. It asks both "From what cause or motive?" and "For what purpose?" It expresses, in other words, that kind of wonder from which, according to the ancient Greeks, all inquiry starts.

Therefore, at the beginning of our attempt to understand civilization by analyzing one of its main constituents—namely, education—the question "Why do we educate?" has its proper place. We shall first interpret this question as asking not so much for the final purpose of education as for its causes. The answer will be found in the fact that education has something to do, firstly, with our physical organism; secondly, with our communal life; thirdly, with the ethical motives inherent in culture; and, fourthly and finally, with our ability to project ourselves into the interests of our children. We ask, consequently, for the reasons for education from the biological, the sociological, the ethical, and the emotional points of view. But in speaking of these several components of education we must never forget that they are interconnected parts of a great living complex and that the divisions we propose are logical categories, not separate departments of reality.

A. THE BIOLOGICAL POINT OF VIEW

All human activities depend on physical function and thus civilization and education are also traceable to a biological foundation. From the time that human beings first began wondering about themselves, explanations of man's rise above the animals have been offered. His physical peculiarities have been singled out: his upright walk and the dexterity of his hand, for example. His memory, his power of generalization, and his language, essential to his relations with his fellow men and to time and space, have also been designated. Even these higher faculties, it must be noticed, have a physical basis, though we are today fully aware of our ignorance of the subtle processes that conjoin soma and psyche. William Healy, in his recent *Personality in Formation and Action*,[1] though he is particularly pessimistic about our understanding of the relations of mind and body, nevertheless represents in the following passage the point of view of many of his colleagues toward this significant problem:

> The age-old problem of the nature of the bonds between body and mind we would like desperately to have answered for the sake of knowing better the structure of personality. Our usual phrases, "mind is a function of the brain," "brain is the organ of the mind," give little illumination. As the matter stands we have not the slightest comprehension of how our simplest mental processes are represented in terms

[1] Norton, 1938. Page 20.

of physiology. What occurs in the storing up or release of even visual and auditory memories is quite unknown from the standpoint of brain cell components or activities. The greatest neurologists and biologists readily admit the limitations of our present knowledge. Not long since, Sherrington said of brain-mind connections, "As for me, what little I know of the how of the one, does not even begin to help me toward the how of the other. The two, for all I can do, seem to remain disparate and disconnected." And again, "Strictly, we have to regard the relation of mind to brain as still not merely unsolved, but still devoid of a basis for its very beginning."

One of the reasons for the psychophysical complexity of man, or one of the conditions that accompany it, is his relatively long period of maturation. It allows for an extended nurture and schooling, during which not only is the body growing, with its bones and muscles, its nervous and glandular systems, but also the psychic powers are developing. These powers develop to a degree which sometimes seems slight when we realize fully our weakness and our want of knowledge about ourselves and the universe in which we live, but which is great in comparison with the mental capacities of animals. Though some species of animals are far superior to men in physical strength and acuteness of senses, they are inferior in their total behavior and in their control of environment, which they neither understand nor influence to any considerable extent and therefore cannot master.

Since Darwin expounded his theory of evolution and Herbert Spencer transferred it to philosophy and sociology, many of us have been inclined to attribute the cause of all our strivings, and therefore of education also, to the desire for survival, a biological trend supposedly underlying all animal life. But the desire for survival and other related urges have in normal life little of the psychological equivalent in feeling and consciousness which the weight of scientific terminology sometimes leads us to assign to them. Almost all human activities can, of course, be reduced by force and by tricks of logic to a survival tendency, but that does not prove that self-preservation is the primary and really felt motive of all our actions.

Let us, for the purposes of exposition, imagine a mother and father watching their children at play. Their feelings are compounded of sympathy and pleasure in their children's happiness and of concern for their future welfare, when they shall be left entirely to their own devices. Their thoughts turn naturally to the preparation of their children for that future independence and to the familiar subject of education. What can they do to make John and Mary independent and happy and familiar with the values and utilities of civilization?

We have here in a simple form the natural conditions that lead to education: parents as the creators of new life which has become part of their own and which, nevertheless, they must someday leave, and youth who will someday take the place of the older generation—vitality, sex, love, solicitude, survival, death.

All these elements of the common situation must be considered in their own right. We do not live only in order to survive and do not educate only in order to further survival; the essence of man lies in his desire for life, not only as a mere biological datum, but as something which is worth having and which provides a reality that he can love for its inherent values. We seek and find self-realization through the medium of innumerable motives, attachments, actions, and the feelings that accompany them. Many of these factors apparently contradict the tendency of self-preservation and survival of the fittest. There is love of danger and adventure or voluntary commitment to great superpersonal purposes. At the apex of vitality, in early manhood and womanhood, the most richly endowed are often exposed to a gamut of feelings in which the tendency toward survival is perhaps less perceived than any other urge, even the urge toward danger and death. The history of literature shows that at no other age do the poets write more intensely about death than in youth, and in war no one goes into action more recklessly than the volunteers of student regiments. And this is not simply ignorance, youthful levity, and irresponsibility, but a tendency deeply rooted in the very grounds of existence.

The problem of survival rises above the level of consciousness generally only if something is wrong, if the normal vitalizing powers are depleted or endangered, if we suffer pain or have to defend ourselves. We all appreciate values most when we have lost them. Only an old man, in a retrospective mood, can fully relish the saying that "youth is drunkenness without wine." A young man does not feel himself to be drunk with energy or to be in need of more energy. He simply uses his energy or even wastes it thoughtlessly.

Nor must such a biological generalization as self-preservation lure us into the opinion that it represents mechanical or automatic laws active in the social sphere. Human society presupposes not merely passive reaction to natural "laws" but spontaneous co-operation and, on the higher levels, will and choice. Perhaps it would be better to avoid the term "law" completely and to speak rather of permanent tendencies and directions. It reveals too simple an interpretation of life to think that even being cared for successfully requires only a passive attitude. The newly born baby, though at an almost unconscious stage of life, would not know how to take suck unless vital energy invited him to use the muscles of his mouth and throat. Although this is a form of unreflective behavior and although the mother also nurses her child without the need of much thought, neither the baby nor the mother is a mere machine. They are motivated by an inner and personal drive, accompanied by strong emotional coloring. Here, and not in a scientific generalization such as the survival tendency, are the primary felt realities of life.

The necessity of active co-operation rather than passive reaction increases with every new, though perhaps still elementary, step in a child's breeding. And not all activities are as pleasant as getting food. They are, on the contrary, sometimes very uncomfortable. For however much we try to reconcile education with the nature of the child, it is often connected with some sort of sacrifice on his part and with artificial and externally imposed processes. The constant formation and discouragement of his inclinations need admonition and correction, and the child does not yet fully understand his own interests and the conditions of his development.

All the biological factors that we have stated to be basic to culture and education—energy, growth, love, survival— defy further scientific explanation. They are inherent in life, and life, although it is our most immediate experience, is inexplicable. According to our mental disposition we may accept it simply as given, as something the ultimate nature of which is beyond our interest, or we may wonder about it and revere the mysteries arising out of its inexhaustible sources.

But whatever our attitude may be, one fact has emerged from our foregoing discussion. Biological factors are basic to our existence and consequently also to our culture and education. But taken in isolation they are a completely inadequate explanation of civilization. Wherever man creates, educates, and is educated, he transcends the merely biological sphere and reaches into other areas of life.

At the end of an article on "Society as a Biological Experiment," contributed by J. B. S. Haldane to a symposium on human affairs,[1] the author writes as follows:

Two things stand out, I hope, from this discussion. Most human problems are not biological problems. They are psychological, economical, or technical problems. And even within the biological sphere the questions which we ask, and the answers ·we get to them, depend on our economic and political orientation.

We shall see in the course of this book that Haldane is correct. But we have already seen something that he does not mention; namely, that human affairs depend also upon cosmic or metaphysical forces of which we must be aware even though we are unable to explain them scientifically.

[1] *Human Affairs*, planned and edited by R. B. Catell, J. Cohen, R. M. Travers. Macmillan, 1938.

B. THE SOCIOLOGICAL POINT OF VIEW

Education, in the widest sense of the word, is going on everywhere, whether or not we are aware of it. Both children and adults are educated by the landscape and architecture they see; by the people they meet; by their treatment of one another; by their play, their work, and their leisure; by the disguised and open propaganda that surrounds them; and by the latent and overt ideals and ideologies of the society in which they live. If we take education in this large sense, all life is education and nothing is exempt from it. It is the constant interactions among people and between people and the objective world. It is, to a large extent, identical with culture, and its history with the history of the advances and regressions of humankind. Whether or not, driven by our concern for clear scientific categories, we abhor the arrogant comprehensiveness of this concept, it is true and irrefutable. Life shows in this, as in many other instances, that it is not, from its very beginning, intended to fit nicely into the vocabulary of thought.

If we forget the dependence of education upon its environment, we are likely to cherish mistaken opinions of what the school can contribute to the future of the nation. We are then mostly too optimistic because we overlook the large number of uncontrolled factors that influence our formal educational efforts. And, as often happens with such vague optimism, when results are disappointing, teachers begin to doubt the use and value of their work or are attacked for their lack of accomplishment by outsiders whose exaggerated expectations have not been fulfilled. J. W. Adamson, in the introduction to his work on

English education,[1] is justified in saying that "the cardinal sin of schools has always been the creation of a world for themselves."

How education is embedded in the community is most obvious in primitive societies. Here the individual is so completely merged with the corporate body that he seems to possess no life that is not the will of this greater unity. As the habits of the tribe may prescribe, the family and the whole group transmit inherited customs and ways of behavior to the younger generation, who at a very early age begin to take part in the common activities and undergo almost ritualistic forms of apprenticeship. All this, at first glance, is surprising to the stranger, but perfectly understandable the moment he projects himself into a primitive village with its reciprocal dependencies and responsibilities, its necessary lack of privacy, and its absence of specialization.

The more instinctive tribal collectivism—which must not be thought simple, being, on the contrary, often very complicated—turns in the course of history into a more self-conscious and more distinctly articulated order. With the development of tools and agricultural methods, with growing control over nature and the consequent increase of free time, what we call civilization finally arises, with all its good and bad ways, and culture, with its possibilities for mental and emotional enrichment. Men invent signs and symbols that enable them to communicate between distant places and to succeeding generations. They build gradually an ideal world of form and order around the endless flow of their ephemeral sense impressions. With the growing importance of these symbols, particularly

[1] *English Education, 1789–1902.* Cambridge University Press, 1930.

letters and numbers, education emerges from the close natural intercourse of primitive societies and becomes a salient and institutionalized business, and the profession of teaching takes its place beside the other occupations and professions of a many-sided community.

The new profession is not in the rank and file of the others, each of which has its allotted part in the social, political, and economic organization of society. The teachers do not contribute directly to economic welfare, they do not defend the country against external enemies, nor do they administer the oracles and the sacrifices of the community to the gods. Only where learning is related to the divine mission of the race and where the priest himself becomes the teacher, as the rabbi became the teacher in the Jewish community, does the occupation of the teacher acquire high social prestige. Where it is a more utilitarian affair, as in Roman society, slaves are employed as instructors. But with the adoption of the superior Greek culture, the teaching class spreads over all social strata; slaves teach the three R's, and highly esteemed members of the aristocracy share with slaves and freedmen the teaching of law and philosophy. Learning has always had an equalizing effect upon caste differences.

The teaching profession's lack of an established position in society still continues. In spite of the immense importance of public education in modern society, the teacher in a primary school has to fight for fair recognition. The secondary-school teacher has, in some countries at least, risen into a more estimable status, and the university professor occupies a somewhat more elevated position, which still, however, varies greatly in different parts of the world. The situation shows that even modern society has not yet arrived at an equal appreciation of learning and the transmission of culture. In many parts of South America the profession of university teaching is still in the making. Many citizens of other countries consider the humanities more or less useless and put higher value upon those fields where the students learn how to make money or to secure social prestige by preparing themselves for influential positions. Some of the older universities have raised their members very high in the social scale, and in some European countries university professors enjoy, or have enjoyed, exceptional privileges. Unfortunately, one must confess that this was not always conducive to their open-mindedness toward the social problems of the time.

Generally speaking, the importance of the teaching class has always increased in proportion to the awareness of society that history has woven around the transient joys and afflictions of its everyday life a fabric of wisdom and values too complex to be conveyed to youth through his natural apprenticeship in the activities and affairs of his elders.

So the general trend of division of labor also affects education. Just as the factory increases productivity by the concentration of energy and the development of special techniques, so the school and the university increase teaching efficiency in various respects by a planned organization. Centralization makes possible the provision of adequate buildings, with laboratories, libraries, and better equipment of all kinds; the full-time services of trained teachers and workers can be utilized; and the whole educational project can be organized to produce at the highest level the greatest economy of time and effort. These advantages are possible because the schools, in contrast with the family, deal with large numbers of pupils and have means to enforce order and discipline among them.

Particularly during the past century society has been increasingly compelled to delegate the responsibility for formal education to specialized institutions because of the rapid accumulation of knowledge and the multiplication of skills and techniques. More and more occupations have been transferred from the natural life of the family or group to independent trades and professions with codes, methods, and traditions of their own. So education could have been retained as a common responsibility only by the development of the old "organic" community into a covenant of men willing and able to share their work and experience with the young. But with modern society as it is, most of our children, if deprived of the care of special educational institutions, would be exposed to greater moral danger and neglect than the children of medieval peasants.

In consequence of this development modern life consists less than in earlier times in immediate relationships between men and more in duties in the discharge of which a person cannot tell who may finally profit from his efforts. Therefore, it is not one of the least contributions of the school that it takes the child from an atmosphere of privacy, free play, and naturally selected comradeship into more public and impersonal surroundings. No one who has observed a child's first days in school or who remembers his own initial school experiences will forget the deep impression that the introduction into the objective world makes upon the young mind, however little it is able to rationalize its feelings. In place of the house and yard and the neighboring streets, there is a public building owned and constructed by the community. There are children and teachers brought together, not because they are friends and relatives, but because they are united by a common task. And what is done and said is not only in the interest of the individual child but in the interest of all the children and of the community in which they live, this community representing the town and nation of which the child will become a citizen, and finally all of humanity, whose future depends on the spiritual unity of its members.

So we see that society has given to the school tasks that are more complex than those usually implied in teaching and learning. Schooling means also teaching the child to recognize interests that transcend the individual, to know his duty within the community and his part in co-operative undertakings. In learning to respect children of different social classes, all of whom are given a fair chance to learn and to compete with one another, the child grows socially as well as individually.

As a corollary to harmonizing the child with society, the school serves also as an equalizer of environmental differences. Children from unhealthy or uneducative surroundings are brought into a school that may need improvement in many respects but that nevertheless guarantees shelter to the less fortunate.

The school is furthermore a selective agency that begins the process of sifting the fit from the less fit. The latter need to be given an equipment that helps them to lead a dignified life and to combine the protection of their own interests with those of society. With rising problems of overpopulation, overcrowding of professions, unemployment, and delinquency, this service grows in importance. We cannot, however, boast of having made much progress in this respect. From times when the family one happened to be born into largely determined his future in life or when schools were inclined to put competitive acquisition of merely intellectual material above true personal development, we have now not infrequently arrived at a sort of equalitarianism and a contempt for serious learning that dodges the hard responsibilities inherent in the task of selection and sacrifices quality for mediocrity and democracy for uncreative collectivism. It is this tenderness in the face of hard immediate duties that often flatters itself by prating about such qualities as sympathy and understanding. In reality, it is the beginning of unprincipled pitying and of a kind of passing of the buck which finally gets out of everybody's control. Much of our modern social unrest is due to lack of selection, and almost all modern revolutions have had, as the most negative part of their following, the dissatisfied intellectual. Unfit to compete with the best or even the average of his group and yet, through a long, though in his case an inadequate, training, out of touch with practical life, he finally lands in a position far below his aspirations and without any rewards for his long and painful efforts. It is no wonder that the most active of these people, losing their equilibrium, become bitter and use their uprooted intellectual skill for destructive propaganda.[1]

With these considerations we have passed from the advantages to the less inviting features of public schooling. One could generalize and say that the compulsory public-school system shows the shortcomings which all institutions develop in the change from private initiative and individual conditions to a collective enterprise. A process

---

[1] Compare Walter M. Kotschnig, *Unemployment in the Learned Professions. An International Study of Occupational and Educational Planning.* 1937.

of depersonalization takes place. Red tape and inflexibility prevent or hinder the adaptation of the relatively fixed curriculum and aims of instruction to justified individual claims. In the daily routine there is often very little incentive for either teachers or children. And there is waste of time and talent. A talented child, with good private instruction, could easily cover the course of a typical public school in half the allotted time. And though this fact must not be used to deprecate good public instruction—which, as we have said, fulfills the important function of socializing the child while he learns—it is nevertheless doubtful whether the retardation of active and intelligent children by mediocre public schools can be justified. Absorption into the community at the expense of personal fulfillment makes some lazy and indifferent and others obstinate, critical, and conceited. Such results are the contrary of true socialization. Hence we should have, in flourishing school systems, a ceaseless struggle to combine the consistency and universality of the compulsory public school with elasticity and individuality of instruction, tradition with inventiveness, and caution with experimentalism. Here, in the desirability of a constant healthy tension between individualistic and collective interests, lies the right of private schools to exist in a democracy, and not in the more comfortable conditions and the social privileges they may provide.

There is further the disadvantage that formal schooling in specialized institutions unduly separates the process of education from the normal life and work of the outside world and creates an artificial remoteness of spirit. This danger is all the greater in that the teacher, brought up in a school, apprenticed in schools, and bound for a lifetime to textbooks and classrooms, has, or finds for himself, little chance to educate his personality through exposure to the conflicts and troubles that mold men in business and public life.

It is evident, however, that it is not sheer necessity that has made the school rather than private tutoring the dominating factor in our educational life. Apparently the advantages outweigh the disadvantages, even for those who could afford to educate their children privately. Montaigne in his essays and, later, Locke in his *Thoughts on Education*, following a tradition that had prevailed during antiquity and during the Middle Ages, showed that they considered the private tutorial system superior to public education. But since the seventeenth century the wealthy and aristocratic classes have gradually changed from teachers working within the family to the institutionalized school, in which they see, particularly for the older children, richer educational possibilities.

Our view would, of course, be partial if we considered the schools alone as representative of institutionalized education. Besides these there is the Church, one of the oldest agencies of conscious education; and there are medical and welfare agencies, and various kinds of adult education. For the growing complexity of our society has made man increasingly aware that his mental development must not end when he leaves school but ought to be a lifelong process. In addition, he sees that his interests cannot be expressed only in terms of immediate and tangible practicality but that in his daily work and during his leisure he also takes part in the great business of civilization and culture.

C. THE ETHICAL POINT OF VIEW

All of man's history can be thought of as converting into fact the old Persian myth of Ormazd, the spirit of good, and Ahriman, the spirit of evil, fighting with each other for rulership over the world. However we explain this experience of positivity and negativity, whether we are "monists or dualists," it accompanies human life in both its individual and its social aspects. Men have always been divided into good men and bad, lovers of truth and liars, fighters for freedom and slaves. Moreover, each of us has in himself something of all these contrasting types. We are, if we examine ourselves realistically, a mixture of opposites, forced to choose again and again between the positive and the negative. Here, apart from all dogmatism and theological speculation, lies the concrete meaning of the religious idea of original sin and grace. Life has given us the sense of duty, the desire to enhance and perfect our lives, but it has left with us the constant temptation to indifference and failure. And the great issue is whether, even if we decide for the good, we can achieve it by our own powers or whether, in order to be free, we need the help of something that is greater than our perishable individual existence. However obscurely the belief in the struggle between good and evil is expressed in the writings of the divines, it is, nevertheless, more realistic than the creed that we have only to follow our nature to develop toward perfection. This optimism of the Renaissance and the following centuries was of the greatest historical significance, perhaps through the very extremism of its formulation, and it has given the greatest incentive to education up to modern times. But it is a dangerous doctrine. It can imply an ethical *laissez faire*, a *laissez aller* of the potentialities immanent in human beings; it then would release the worst along with the best. It depends upon good luck and circumstances whether men who have been educated and who educate according to such a doctrine will be able to follow the laws of civilization or whether they will be thrown back to barbarism.

Now education is the organized attempt of mankind to develop skills and criteria, knowledge and values, that will help us not only to discriminate between good and evil, freedom and bondage, but to decide actively for the positive and to reject the negative. We would also say that it is the way of man from primordial and unrestrained to self-conscious and directed energy. Parents and teachers, therefore, implant in the minds of the younger generation loyalty to those ideals which they consider consonant with their ethical principles.

These ethical principles are, as we shall argue later on, fluctuating; they progress or regress with the passage of time. Of all historical factors, however, that have molded the moral standards of our civilization, none has proved so persistent as Christianity. In spite of all doubts we may feel concerning our right to do so, we think of our civilization as Christian and our education as directed by a Christian spirit.

The motives behind Christian ideals and the reasons for their propagation have been subjected to very critical analysis. In modern times Friedrich Nietzsche gave an enormous impetus to the re-examination of the ethical problem through his books *The Will to Power*, *Genealogy of Morals*, and *Beyond Good and Evil*. According to him there are no absolute determinants for the true, the good, and the beautiful. These ideals, cherished since Plato as the highest expression of civilization, are in Nietzsche's view ideological concepts disguising the ultimate motive behind all creation of real values; namely, the will to power and the self-assertion of the ego.

Nietzsche was not the first critic to advance ideas of this sort, which, like most penetrating philosophic ideas, have their roots in Greek thought. They are similar to the arguments of the Sophists. According to one of them, Thrasymachos, the laws are the products of the powerful for the subjection of the people. According to another, Kallikles, the laws are invented by the masses for protection against the encroachments of the strong. Nietzsche combined these apparently contradicting theories. With the mixture of profundity and radicalism that makes him both fascinating and irritating, he expounded the theory that the good was originally, and ought still to be, the heroic, the bold, the vigorous, and the cruel. Of course (Nietzsche's argument runs), the powerful want and have the right to use the weaklings for their purposes. But, alas, the latter are in the majority, and with their victory—the victory of the resentful poltroon and the herd of slaves—the good became identified with the cautious, the clever, and the humble, and the term "bad," originally meaning the timid, was insidiously applied to the actions of the daring and valiant man. By means of this inversion of values the weak succeeded in defeating the courageous. The *misera plebs*, incapable of defending itself in a fair battle, and yet eager to gain the rewards and joys that the brave have won only by danger and exposure—the *misera plebs* has transvalued all values for its own advantage.

The main historical instrument of this inversion of values (said Nietzsche) was the Jewish invention of Christianity, which led to the insurrection of slave morals. Christianity, therefore, is the final defeat of the wonderful, though dangerous, beasts of prey to whom the aristocratic thinker belongs just as much as a Cesare Borgia or a Napoleon. Being a menace to timid mediocrity, they are persecuted and tortured, since the vulgar invariably distinguishes himself by hating and ostracizing the exceptional. The salvation of mankind requires that the supermen, those who dare live dangerously, arise and prepare a revaluation of values. They will leave to the meek the perverted religion of humbleness because he needs it. But they will set themselves up as the masters and as liberators of the slandered instincts of greatness, hitherto held in check by the enemies of all that is noble and audacious.

The excitement that Nietzsche's ethical philosophy has aroused, not only in his own country, but also in France, Italy, and to a lesser extent in England, and the role that his theories play in modern political philosophy show that he has hit some sensitive spots in our customary morality. Doubtless many laws and customs have been formulated in the course of time and praised as ethical achievements which have merely helped the timid and weak to suppress the courageous. Doubtless the accepted codes of behavior have often fostered hypocrisy instead of frankness, the young have been taught optimistic ideologies while the world itself was full of suppression and cruelty, and the modern political machine has often tended to give privileges to the weak and to restrict the liberty of the strong even though the latter might have served the true interests of the whole. Doubtless Christian asceticism and pity have frequently perverted sound human instincts into forms of physical and psychic self-mutilation, and they have done great harm to education, the interrelationships of the sexes, and the growth of harmonious and free personalities.

But profound and brilliant as Nietzsche's philosophy is in some respects, it is in others typically half true or completely in error. It contains one fundamental fallacy, a fallacy that can be rightly accused of being, in Nietzsche's own terms, a resentful and insidious distortion of great feelings. This is the lack of differentiation between a sort of love and *caritas* that are no more than self-love and self-pity extended to others and the love and *caritas* that spring from a hot heart and a generous mind. Such a differentiation is not completely absent from Nietzsche's thought. But if he had given it full consideration, he would have been compelled to admit that the teaching of Christ is built not on the first but on the second kind of love, and that Christianity, that "invention of the Jews," was not a diabolic way of revenging the political humiliation of Israel but the result of one of the most singular developments that a people, perhaps as the result of suffering, but of creative suffering, has ever undergone.

As a consequence of this fallacy, Nietzsche's philosophy is thoroughly unfitted for any applicable theory of society. It is the gospel of extreme individualism for a few with the consequence of herd collectivism for the many. But if privileges for the few are to have any productive reality, they can only be the honestly acquired privileges of real leadership, which in any form of political organization are inseparable from the qualities of sympathy, loyalty, and mutual responsibility in both the leader and those who are led. There is no leader who leads in all fields. To lead in one or several, he must allow himself to be led in others. Even the greatest hero is not a lonely, roving animal, which does not exist even in the African deserts. He, too, needs comradeship and confidence, and in order to receive them he must inspire like sentiments in others. Otherwise he would be cast off to die in loneliness and despair as Cesare Borgia and Napoleon were.

Nietzsche would perhaps answer that he did not want to give any sociological theory but a message for the few great individuals. But there is no such message and certainly no realization of it that would not entail social consequences. Power and control tend to continue, after the individuals who established them have died, in the hands of a group of heirs, who become a stable factor in society. They have, then, the choice of two ways. They may use their privileges wisely, follow principles of mutual respect and tolerance, and develop aims, ideals, and conditions within society that make life worth living for the ruled as well as the rulers. This involves their building a moral code contrary to Nietzsche's and in some way or other similar to the fundamental teachings of Christianity. Or they may exploit their fellow men with all the unscrupulousness characteristic of those hereditary groups that live on tradition but have lost their original greatness and will not risk themselves for any great or far-reaching purpose. Then they are not the heroes Nietzsche praises, but simply mean-spirited egoists. As history shows, the aristocratic classes attendant on the rulers likewise quickly cease to be the true *aristoi;* they abuse their position, the law, and the religion they administer in order to prevent the socially less privileged classes from rising toward a dignified human existence.

Nietzsche, although he glorified unbroken natural instincts, was, in his heart, a disappointed idealist. We must understand him not only in the light of his own words but also in the light of his opposition to trends and forces that he considered to be the enemies of true culture. These forces were represented not only by a socially comfortable form of Christianity but also by the gospel of undiscriminating equality, utilitarianism, and the kind of worship of success that is characteristic of the capitalist era. It was these idols of the vulgar crowd from which the lonely philosopher fled to the grandeur of the Swiss Alps. Here he and his Zarathustra dreamed of the "Superman," who was to be the heroic synthesis of nature and spirit and the realization of the highest and most complete specimen that man may conceivably create.

Nevertheless, the popular forms of utilitarianism to which Nietzsche so thoroughly objected have one point in common with his own theory of the will to power. It may be that it was precisely the unadmitted awareness of this affinity that caused the German thinker to express his distaste for utilitarianism so vehemently. Not infrequently, adversaries who feel themselves inwardly akin hate each other much more than the advocates of totally different opinions. The points in which Nietzsche and the utilitarians are kindred are, in spite of their disagreement as to what kind of success man should aspire to, their acceptance of interest as the criterion of action and their idea of self-assertion as the ultimate principle of life. Both philosophies involve the degradation of the ethical sphere to a condition of relativity with respect to sovereign egoistic drives.

The difference between them is that Nietzsche's ethical relativism limits the privilege of self-assertion to the innately superior man. His world is dangerously heroic, his political ideal an aristocracy of supermen, and his naturalism is overarched, as we have already intimated, by an idealism, perverted though it is. The relativism of the typical utilitarians, on the other hand, does not recognize any hierarchy of human beings. It considers egoism not as the privilege of the few and the strong but as the right of every "useful" member of society. It tries to solve the problem of reconciling social conflicts by introducing the idea of a covenant of individuals co-operating for the sake of guaranteeing the greatest amount of comfort for the least amount of effort. Utilitarianism is, in this regard, democratic, though its hedonism and eudaemonism, as we shall see later on, are not a satisfactory basis for a real democracy. While Nietzsche has a predilection for the exceptional and the unhabitual, the utilitarians lay emphasis upon the training of habits in order to direct the flow of interests along constructive channels. But both revolve about the same axis, the assertion of interests, and both have their predecessors in the Greek Sophists— Nietzsche in Thrasymachos and Kallikles; the utilitarians in Lykophon and his friends, against whose arguments Socrates and Plato sharpened their intellectual weapons.

The criticism of the Sophists as well as the relativism of the utilitarians and of Nietzsche has helped considerably to enlighten our understanding of moral conduct. But whether we lean toward one or the other of these schools, we have to recognize that they all fail to see the deeper sources of social life and consequently of education. They lead either to the glorification of the conquering type, and have to accept the educational consequences of this partiality, or to a cult of happiness which does not take into account the fundamental fact that no happiness is possible without sacrifice, no finding oneself without the readiness to lose oneself, and, finally, no community without acknowledgment of spiritual values.

Therefore, any kind of social organization, whether inclined more to aristocracy or to democracy, must guard itself against an interpretation of its existence that gives primacy to egoism. If it accepts such an interpretation, an aristocracy tends to degenerate into a small group of big exploiters and a democracy into a large group of small exploiters. In either case the commonwealth is no longer felt as a common responsibility and its improvement as a never-ending task, but is regarded as a well from which those who manage to push closest can fill their buckets. With this attitude the whole concept of the nation is changed. Instead of being aware of its cultural mission within the human realm, people think of it as an enterprise for the extension of economic power. Outwardly it then moves toward aggressive imperialism in order to take from colonies or from the control of other nations what its citizens desire but cannot produce for themselves. Inwardly it becomes more and more mistaken for some miraculously inexhaustible resource for common exploitation, a sort of automatic water-supply system which nobody needs to take care of. When the source is dry or the machinery broken down, the time is ripe for revolution. But whatever new system may be tried, it will not lead out of misery if it is only the rulers who change while the spirit remains the same. One does not need to know much history to see how infallibly it proves this statement.

Under such conditions education will be degraded as much as the nation. It may disguise its real character under ideological phrases while in reality becoming no more than practical training in the eyes of the many and a means of learning to rule others in the eyes of the few. As to the truth of this, history also offers sufficient evidence. There is, for example, the constant danger in which the university finds itself of being regarded as nothing but an aggregation of specialized professional schools for the training of lawyers, teachers, physicians, and businessmen, rather than equally a place "for the lifting up of humanity," with professors who are "the living sources of learning and enthusiasm." [1]   There are also the frankly avowed plans of a Napoleon, or of modern dictators, to make the school a medium for the indoctrination of their specific political interests. Here again there is a mixture of truth and error. Just as a university must give professional training but can do so adequately only if it is also a humanistic institution, so a nation needs a certain amount of political inculcation to carry on its ways of life. But this inculcation must defeat its own ends unless it is brought into harmony with the larger goal of man, which is not only to live as subject to a government but to enrich his personality through a growing realization of the general values of mankind.

We shall see later on, but it is good to anticipate here, that none of the naturalistic schools of ethics (and as such we may designate both Nietzscheism and utilitarianism) really carries its own principles consistently to the end.

[1] President Charles W. Eliot's Harvard Inaugural Address. 1869.

We have mentioned already how Nietzsche's philosophy oscillates strangely between the two poles of a merely biological concept of man and an almost religious belief in an ideal mission for man, which the philosopher avowed particularly in his educational writings. And in the typical utilitarianism only a mysterious shifting of motives from ego-interests to social interests can explain how a democracy can arise out of the constant struggle for individual happiness.

We are now sufficiently advanced to see that the sources of social ethics and, consequently, of education are not to be found exclusively in the ideas of self-perpetuation, in the egoism of the few, and in the self-preserving habits of the many. If this were true, how could history show, besides the cruelty and conflict of existence, an uninterrupted record of self-sacrifice for the good of man and for such values as truth and brotherhood? And how could it be explained that even in the naturalistic philosophies themselves the aims they set up and espouse contradict their theory of the sources of morality? It is clear that we must try to arrive at a more synthetic interpretation of ethical energies—synthetic in that it does not simply deny the relative truth in the arguments of the naturalists and relapse into illusions about the intrinsic goodness of the world, but tries to reconcile the insights of naturalism with a more comprehensive understanding of individual and social responsibilities for ourselves and others.

Can we support the supposition that there is in mankind a moral drive that is not simply a disguised form of egoism? Man naturally wants to be happy; only the mentally or physically ill do not want to be so. Yet the great figures of mankind, those who do not simply follow the prescribed codes of moral conduct but who *make* morality, feel in themselves as the primary source of their existence an impetus that has often defied all natural desire for mere self-preservation, or what would normally be thought of as happiness. And we have all sometimes felt a like impetus, though we may not have been able to obey it.

But where is it rooted? We stand here before one of the greatest mysteries of human existence and of all existence. This we cannot explain; we can only attempt to describe it in terms that are necessarily indefinite and symbolic, in some such way as the following: In the depths of our individual being we reach into a larger and superpersonal ground, into something that incloses and encompasses us. We are nourished and sustained by it, as the embryo is sheltered in the womb and nourished by the circulation of the mother's blood; we live in it, at times we sense it, and nevertheless we are unable to define it. It is a *givenness* in the face of which we feel the utter inadequacy of our intellectual and verbal conceptions. Let us, in order to have at least a means of verbal communication, call this inexplicable force behind and within all life "cosmic energy."

The assertion that this energy is material is nothing but a sign of primitive philosophic presumptuousness. The word "matter" is just as arbitrary and as magical as any other term. Nor is it possible for us to say scientifically that this energy is spiritual. The kind of idealism that presses the dynamic richness of the cosmos into philosophic classifications may reach deeper and more reverently into the mysteries of life than the typical materialism; but it is also "uncritical," in the sense of Kant's *Critique of Pure Reason*. Scientifically we cannot conceive of more than an energy, a dynamic, which we see exclusively in those forms of existence in which it appears objectively to the human mind: But there is no scientific guarantee that this form of "appearance" which the mind can seize upon reflects the substance of life as it really is—the "thing in itself," as Kant calls it. If, in our traditional and somewhat obsolete philosophic language, we speak of matter and spirit as opposed aspects of reality, we have to be conscious that we are using concepts and categories such as the human mind is able to manipulate. Some of the observable phenomena of life seem to be tied to material laws that do not allow much freedom of choice. Such is our physical growth; so also are deterioration and death, hunger and thirst. Other phenomena seem to possess a certain amount of freedom and chance. They alone are connected with the spheres of life where morality is possible.

But is there, perhaps, in spite of all our helplessness, a way to venture near to those boundary lines where man passes over from the mere immanence of his individuality into those deeper resources which provide him with the energy to exist as he does: as a being endowed with powers of attachment and detachment, self-interest and solicitude, and capable of education and culture? We are sure that these boundaries cannot be approached if we begin to search, as philosophy has often done, in the highest conscious and most sublimated areas of mental life, where man is most alienated from nature because most elevated above it. We must first search among those activities where he stands most clearly within nature.

Now we all acknowledge the existence of something common in human nature that older psychologists called "instincts," and that modern psychologists, afraid of this often misused term, call "vital, or motivational, urges," "drives," "needs," or "propensities." But in spite of their different vocabularies they are all concerned with the same, or at least similar, qualities of behavior. These qualities are a powerful impetus, unreflective in character, and, in contrast to the qualities found in special "achievements" of man—such as, for example, refined intellectual and artistic qualities—they seem to work in the common groundwork of the human being the moment he feels himself exposed to a certain challenge from the outside, or even before.

Among these vital urges there are merely physical needs, such as thirst and hunger, the elements of physical existence. If not satisfied, they may make a beast of an otherwise sociable creature, or, if the opportunity to fight for them is denied, their neglect may lead to physical death. But in themselves they are neither moral nor immoral, so long as they operate within the normal conditions of life. If they rebel against violation, we do not lay the blame on them but on the situation. We blame a person only if he allows himself to be driven so exclusively by his egoistic needs that he encroaches upon the rights of his fellow men. But if he does so in despair because his honest endeavors to satisfy his own and his family's hunger have failed, then a humanly thinking man will lay the blame first of all at the door of society. He will respect hunger as a fact more fundamental than the special institutions of an organized society, which often do not respect it.

Close to these needs are those urges that we may best designate as "propensities." Among them are to be counted—to take only two examples—the sexual and the parental urges. We usually do not call it an "achievement" if young people mature toward sexual life or if a mother cares for her child, but we call it unnatural if they do not do so.

There can be no doubt that the initial motivation of man toward civilization is largely based on these and similar propensities, the character of which we will discuss more thoroughly in our next chapter. One could perhaps defend with very good reasons the opinion that there is no fundamental and persistent ethical trend in mankind which, though perhaps intensely sublimated, has not its ultimate origin in these propensities.

Now if, for instance, in face of the parental propensity, we ask the old dualistic question: "What is it? Is it matter-bound or spirit-bound? Is it egoistic or altruistic, self-centered or devotional?" then we must answer: "It is, in the very nature of this and any other similar urge, all these things in an inseparable unity." It has, doubtless, a physical side: it means the ties of blood and the preservation of the race through care for one's own offspring; it means the enjoyment of an attachment between parents and child. But it also includes the more abstract ethical feelings of sympathy, responsibility, readiness to serve and to sacrifice. And these qualities can increase to such a degree that under their influence a mother will defend her young at the cost of her own life. The same is the case of the sexual propensity of a normal human being. If, in consequence of conditions destructive to the sound development of human activity, it does not degenerate into mere sensuality, the sexual propensity also includes such feelings as attachment and responsibility for the chosen one.

Are we, consequently, not justified in supposing that our ethical behavior has its origin not in arbitrary human decisions or in isolated desires—such as the will to power, competition, or fear on the one hand, or more spiritual and ideal products of the mind on the other hand—but—since our propensities emerge out of infinite and impenetrable streams of life—in ultimate energies which work at the bottom of our total existence? In their more primitive forms they appear as blind emotional drives; in higher forms of life they rise toward conscience and morality. They are, therefore, egoistic and altruistic, material and spiritual, biological and cultural—all these apparent opposites fused into a complex and miraculous unity.

We could call the theory that results from this synthesis "naturalism," in that the word "nature" has often been used, particularly in philosophic and artistic thought, to signify a great creative, cosmic reality. In this sense of the term Pestalozzi, the Swiss educator and philosopher, would be a "naturalist." In his *Evening Hours of a Hermit* [1] he speaks of the obligation of education to follow nature and of the importance of sound relations with the family and with society for the healthy growth of the child. Then he concludes his enumeration of these relations with the surprising sentence: "But the nearest relation of man is his relation to God." Nature and spirit are, from his point of view, inseparable.

But since the term "naturalism" is connected in the history of philosophy with the notions of materialism and determinism and our theory of the origin of morals is far from such assumptions, we have to look for another term.

---

[1] Unfortunately, L. F. Anderson's translation of *The Evening Hours of a Hermit* in his *Pestalozzi* reproduces only the first part, with little allusion to the transcendental turn in Pestalozzi's thinking that comes later. Another translation, however, may be found in Henry Barnard's *American Journal of Education*. March, 1859 (Vol. VI, No. 16).

Our theory brings us into the field of the Gestalt psychologists but without a substantial right to claim them as supporters of our thesis. It shows also a certain affinity with the physiological and philosophic movement of neo-vitalism, as represented in particular by Johannes Driesch, and with Henri Bergson's philosophy of the *élan vital*. But we mention all these schools only to show that the trend of thought of the last decades is not entirely against such an understanding as ours of the essential problems of human life. We also approach the time-honored theory of the *ius naturale*, defended first by the Stoic philosophers, then clothed in a Christian vestment by the Scholastic philosophy. To use a phrase of Thomas Aquinas, there exists a *participatio legis divinae in creatura humana*, the immanence of a divine law in the human creature. These ideas finally were developed, by such men as Hugo Grotius, Samuel Pufendorf, and others, toward the rationalistic understanding of man as elaborated during the eighteenth century, and most impressively actualized in the Bill of Rights. All these theories would be unthinkable without the assumption that at the very groundwork of our existence certain elements are operative which connect us with constructive powers of the universe and which, therefore, have to be respected as inalienable rights of man.[1]

If we were committed to coining a term, we would call our theory the theory of integralism. These fundamental energies of our being, which are basic to the organism's self-realization, constitute a whole or an integral, the integrants of which are both "material" and "spiritual" in an inseparable primordial unity.

According to this theory of integralism, to repeat, our

[1] Compare H. Rommen, *Die ewige Wiederkehr des Naturrechts.* 1936.

moral qualities result from an energy which transcends the sphere of human autonomy and is neither an individual nor a social human creation. It permeates the total man without man's willing it, as life flows through us without asking our permission. Moral energy as well as life energy is a gift, but not one that we are given "to dig in the earth" and hide, as the "wicked and slothful servant" did, but one that we should use as the "good and faithful servants" used the talents delivered to them by their Lord.

This feeling of possessing something that is at the same time beyond ourselves and possesses us just as much as we possess it has often been suppressed by our emphasis upon the merely physical basis of life. It is true that by operating on his brain we can make an idiot of a genius and a cripple of an athlete, and perhaps sometime we shall be able to help a subnormal person to relative normality by correcting the functions of his glandular system. But that means only that this inexplicable life energy is focused within our physical organs. The most skilled surgeon fails if it does not support his efforts, and he cannot alter the fact that, along with life, decay and death also grow within the shell of our individuality and will conquer it at last whether we are ready or not.

These observations about the "integral" character of ultimate life energies lead to one truth of concern not only to the biologist and the physician but to the ethical philosopher and educator as well. It is the fact that moral education involves responsibility not only for the psychical but also for the physical side of our existence. Though life is not our creation it is, nevertheless, in our power to spoil it, together with all of its moral and spiritual potentialities.

These we can neglect until they die out, as our intelligence and our muscles degenerate unless we exercise them. Parents can prevent normal growth in their children, not only by exposing them to dangerous influences, but also by neglecting in themselves the physical prerequisites of a healthy progeny. It is, generally speaking, not only an "external" question what and how we eat, drink, and breathe. However little we like certain apostles for whom this question has become a kind of substitute religion, it is, nevertheless, of intrinsic importance. It seems as if, in spite of our developed medical knowledge, earlier peoples had in some respects a finer insight into the workshop of the total personality than we have today. In the rites of all religions that have conquered the world, in customs and regulations which our proud positivistic era of specialized science feels the right to ridicule, our most advanced physicians discover profound hygienic wisdom. If we are able, and the beginnings already show themselves, to combine the intuitive sense for essential conditions of human functioning with modern empirical science, we may in the course of time arrive at a systematic knowledge of human hygiene of such comprehensiveness and effectiveness that the whole character of our individual and social life will be changed for the better. So far most of us live still in almost complete ignorance of these matters, and our philosophies of ethics and education are not concerned with them.

On the basis of our theory of integralism we are now able to find the cause of culture and education without running into the futile, though ancient, conflict between egoism and altruism or any of the supposed opposites to which we attended while speaking of the philosophies of Nietzsche, the utilitarians, and their opponents. We are not forced into a merely biological and materialistic interpretation of civilization, education, and morality if we admit that all three are interwoven with material and practical human interests. On the other hand, we are not forced to negate matter and the connection of moral progress with our natural tendencies toward self-preservation if we concede that morality cannot be based on these tendencies alone. The truth is rather that humanity, with all its natural and cultivated qualities, is rooted in sources of energy not reducible to rigid classifications, but best conceived of as integral realizations of universal and encompassing energies.

Of course, we realize that behind our speculations lurks the question as to the ultimate character of life itself and the power which may have created it. But this question is of a metaphysical or theological character and cannot be answered with scientific certainty, unless the development of the natural sciences provides surprisingly new methods and materials for its approach. But if, in full awareness of our limitations, an answer may be ventured, then our theory leans more toward a monistic than a dualistic ontology, if we understand by "ontology" that part of metaphysics which deals with the ultimate nature and characteristics of existence. Our suggested solution would be in harmony with the Christian tradition, which, in spite of a prevalent dualistic character of its traditional ethical philosophy, answers the question about the ultimate source of life in a monistic sense. Our own more detailed ideas about the problem of ethics will be discussed in the third chapter, entitled "Toward What Ends Do We Educate?"

After the previous discussion a question imposes itself upon us. What is the reason for all these misleading labels and for such opposing artificial categories as we found in the philosophies of Nietzsche and the extreme utilitarian and idealistic schools? This question, although not strictly belonging to the present context, nevertheless deserves some consideration in a philosophy of education, since our scientific and public life is full of misunderstandings arising from inadequate generalizations. They can be accounted for if we refer to the nature of the tool of which the mind must avail itself the moment it attempts to order and clarify the world by which it is surrounded. Man has to use words in order to formulate his concepts and bring them to his own and other people's consciousness. But words never symbolize the total, concrete reality of their objects; they give only a faint shadow of the richness of reality.

For example, we may see an apple tree growing in a sunny garden or a pine tree in a dark wood. The moment we speak of these two phenomena simply as "trees," we generalize, thereby abstracting what they have in common from all that constitutes their individuality. We construct an abstract universal because it is necessary for the organization of discrete items of experience into the larger concepts which the mind requires for the purposes of thought and communication. But this abstract universal deprives the individual object of the concreteness and color which are its unique reality; and the apple tree in the garden is no longer distinguished from the pine tree in the dark wood. In other words, in ordering the world by means of our conceptual symbols we constantly falsify. There result only dim pictures in our minds that have no exact counterpart in reality and that would not exist save through the existence of the mind of man.

Now transfer these considerations, already known to the Greeks and of particular provocation to the medieval Scholastics, to the usual discussion of egoism versus altruism or materialism versus idealism as the causes of civilization. In order to explain our behavior and our moral tendencies, one group orders the enormous complexity of life under this classification, and the other under the opposite. This may be quite legitimate for certain purposes, and either group would be justified if it remembered that mental categories can be applied to a total reality which actually is too complicated for our conceptual thinking only for the sake of an abstract order and method. But both are wrong if they mistake a method of thought and a partial truth for the real nature of the substance about which they want to arrive at clarity.

This danger, in which we find ourselves constantly, is intensified by another characteristic of the human mind which is almost a corollary to the first; namely, its tendency to relate verbal symbols within a coherent logical system. This is the second step that the human mind makes in its attempt to generalize its impressions. But with the advantages gained by this process of systematization the danger of losing the sense of reality grows still greater. Therefore, people of outstanding artistic qualities, with a refined, sensuous life and a subtle discrimination, often hate all abstract systems. If they are sharp thinkers, they can readily see how often the materialist, for example, selects only those aspects of life that prove his preconceived theory, while the radical idealist, on the other hand, builds up a hierarchy in which matter is degraded to nonexistence and spirit is elevated to the position of sole reality.

The same processes become particularly dangerous if, in the formation of political doctrines, the tendency toward systematization and simplification is increased by the desire to gain adherents. One-sidedness in emphasis may sometimes focus public attention upon an issue that was unduly overlooked; but it may also cause new evils as great as the first. For anyone who tries to order the world according to categories which are not part and parcel of the total reality but are creations of the human mind in isolation from life endangers his own cause and will sooner or later be disappointed. There is a sentence from Goethe that expresses admirably what we mean: "All controversies between the older and younger generations, up to present times, spring from separating what God, according to his nature, has created as a unity."

Now, of course, we must not fall into the error that we have just criticized and suppose that our theory of the integral and comprehensive nature of unreflective urges is a panacea for all the troubles of the ethical and educational philosopher with the problem of morality. This theory simply asserts that any division of the fundamentals of human life into "self-interests" versus "ideals" is based on erroneous assumptions. Scientifically we cannot explain the ultimate and encompassing energies of life, but we do know that on those shores where our existence reaches into the universal energies of a great unknown all human conceptual classifications break down. Consequently, any theory of culture and education that is based on such one-sided distinctions leads mankind into unrealistic distortions and sooner or later to failure.

Our own theory, however, involves a rather delicate question. If human life in its more "instinctive" phases comprehends ethical impulsion, it also comprehends the contrary; namely, self-assertion at any price, greediness, and passion. Therefore, we are far from the opinion that our theory of integralism offers any criteria for decisions to be made on this level of human development where "freedom" and consequently conflict and ethical reflection begin. To summarize the main idea of the previous considerations: our theory serves only one purpose, on which we had to lay particular stress in the course of this chapter on the causes of education; namely, to show that such trends in us as goodness, responsibility, and solicitude, on which the higher forms of civilization rest, are not merely arbitrary and, therefore, more or less historically reversible factors, but natural and necessary motivations in the life of all normal beings.

D. THE EMOTIONAL POINT OF VIEW

We have seen in the foregoing pages that the question of the origin of education can be answered from many different points of view. Further, we have seen that these different approaches, though hitherto resulting in contrasting opinions, are not irreconcilable if we go to those cosmic energies that we may suppose to be working within the multiplicity of appearances. Thirdly, we have seen how our ways of reasoning tend to distort the true totality of life. In their attempts to achieve an abstract logical coherence of ideas, thinkers often insist on unity in the realm of pure thought, without due regard to the richness of the actual forces which surround us. Mankind, although mostly unable to rationalize its uneasiness, has never been unaware of the shortcomings of the intellectual approach to an understanding of human existence. It is, therefore, continually seeking for symbols of its greatest experiences, the profundity and sublimity of which are beyond the grasp of logical processes. Hence, in spite of all attacks by the rationalists and in spite of all its unquestionable dangers, artistic and religious intuition into the miracles of life has ever played an important part in the formation of our beliefs and has often anticipated ideas at which the scholar has arrived only centuries later.

Such intuition can be found especially in humanity's strange creation of what we call "myth," the work of individuals or of the collective mind of people, or of both. All great cultures and all great religions have expressed much of their insight in mythical form. The moral insights of the early Greeks were symbolized in the legends of Hercules, Oedipus, and the Homeric heroes; and the early Christians expressed themselves in myths springing partly from the Asiatic and partly from the Greek-Neoplatonic backgrounds of Christianity. Modernity saw in these myths at first mere fictions of greater or minor artistic value or documents of merely historical significance. Later, however, those same modern sciences that had seemed to destroy the values of myths—namely, anthropology, the critical analysis of religions, and the various analytical psychologies—began to rediscover in them underlying meanings of human significance. But we do not necessarily have to be trained scientists in order to understand the wisdom which many of the great myths must have conveyed to our ancestors and which education, in order to avail itself of our cultural heritage, must not neglect.

A modern mother with imagination and an intense awareness of her motherhood could interpret the life of St. Mary, the mother of Jesus, in such a way that this most beautiful of Christian myths would restore the original and inherent unity of biological, unreflective, emotional, and moral factors usually destroyed by scientific analysis.

"If I read," she would say, "all the complicated scientific explanations of the origin of education, I am surprised to learn how scholars can make things complicated that are for me the most natural in the world. Giving birth to a child and afterward caring for him are wonderful experiences, probably because they form one of the few occasions in life when we intellectual, egoistic, and sophisticated beings are in harmony with our inmost natures and our inmost natures with the universe. As a young unmarried woman, what did I really understand when I saw a dog or a bird caring for its offspring? I called it sweet and charming; it may even have reminded me, unconsciously perhaps, of my own maternal destiny. But now, as a mother, I am aware of the profound sympathy my motherhood arouses in me for everything in nature that is creative and kindly. I have no sentimental feelings about nature. I know how careless it is of life, how every minute thousands of creatures are destroyed, how sliding mountains can bury whole villages of people, and how the greatest of all dangers can be man himself when he fails to harmonize his inner drives and subject them to his moral will. And yet, through my maternity and my devotion to the care of my children, I feel that there is in the universe not merely a mechanical coming and going and struggle for life but also an endless flow of energy full of love and creativeness.

"If I should describe this mixture of necessity and freedom, of instinct and spirit, of egotism and altruism which I find in motherhood, and from which all education begins, I should like to refer to the legend of St. Mary, not only to those parts of it which are recorded in the Bible, but to its romantic, medieval form, which has inspired poets and painters up to modern times. The legend tells us that Mary received her child by a miracle, and we know that within the Church itself there was much arguing about this magic tradition. But think of the myth as a symbolic expression of meanings deeply rooted in reality, and then you must see that love and conception and all maternal solicitude are things beyond our power, things that come to us as the angel of the Annunciation came to Mary. We do not make love; we are possessed by love. We do not create the life of our children, we are but mediators of their life; and we do not care for them because we decide to do so, but because the spirit of maternity and paternity works in us and compels us to. And that spirit is the same whether it is found in a carpenter's, a cobbler's, or a king's house.

"The mother of Jesus, the 'King of Life,' as he was later called by his disciples, gave birth to her son in a stable among cows and donkeys. Really a strange part of the story. But are not all mothers committed in childbirth, like helpless animals, to the laws of nature, to suffering, and even to exposure to death? How could the biological elements in the parental instinct and in education be more simply expressed than in this story?

"Mary educated her son during his childhood, but, when he was a young boy, presented him to the scribes in the synagogue, who were the custodians of the national and spiritual tradition of the people. So everywhere a time comes when the parents delegate the education of their children to the teacher, and the intimate relations of the family are replaced by an impersonal agent of civiiization. Here you have a conspicuous symbol for one of your theories of the origin of education, the sociological theory.

"When her son had grown up, Mary had to retreat into the background, forgotten by the son, who had found his mission in the world. She experienced the fate of all mothers when their sons separate themselves from the ties of home in order to become men. The narratives of the life of Christ strongly emphasize this process of the son's separation from his parents. St. Luke tells us:

'And when he was twelve years old, they went up to Jerusalem after the custom of the feast. And when they had fulfilled the days, as they returned, the child Jesus tarried behind in Jerusalem; and Joseph and his mother knew not of it. But they, supposing him to have been in the company, went a day's journey; and they sought him among their kinsfolk and acquaintance. And when they found him not, they turned back again to Jerusalem seeking him. And it came to pass, that after three days they found him in the temple, sitting in the midst of the doctors, both hearing them, and asking them questions. And all that heard him were astonished at his understanding and answers. And when they saw him, they were amazed; and his mother said unto him, "Son, why hast thou thus dealt with us? Behold, thy father and I have sought thee sorrowing." And he said unto them, "How is it that ye sought me? Wist ye not that

I must be about my Father's business?" And they understood not the saying which he spake unto them.'

"And when Mary at the marriage in Cana admonished her son to use his magic powers, St. John tells us:

'And the third day there was a marriage in Cana of Galilee; and the mother of Jesus was there. And both Jesus was called, and his disciples, to the marriage. And when they wanted wine, the mother of Jesus saith unto him, "They have no wine." Jesus saith unto her, "Woman, what have I to do with thee? Mine hour is not yet come." Nevertheless, Mary said to the servants: "Whatever he saith unto you, do it."'

According to the medieval legend, she followed his work and his journeyings in her mind and deeply enjoyed his glory. But she also held his hand and suffered with him when the world betrayed him, as in one way or another every man is betrayed who wants to change the world for the better. Where is there a more radical answer than this to the question of the ethical character of education? How narrow and inadequate are all scientific concepts in the face of this simple story!"

Let us now go one step further and ask why the figure of Mary has inspired simple men and great poets from the early Christian period up to modern times. There were many much more exciting subjects to be praised in songs and legends. Why did this one overshadow all others?

In giving an explanation for this we shall simultaneously be answering the question we asked when we left the preceding section of this chapter, dealing with the ethical reasons for education. This was the question: If we advance a theory that tries to reconcile natural as well as ethical trends in a more comprehensive and fundamental concept of nature than we generally find, how can we discover a measure for evaluating these trends? Perhaps we should not need a measure if they were always in harmony with one another. But often they are not, either in our own life or in society. The question will be taken up principally in our later discussion of the problem of values. But in considering the reasons for man's long interest in the myth of St. Mary, we cannot avoid anticipating part of that discussion.

This myth continued to live and was woven round with new legendary adornments by each succeeding generation because it gave mankind one great certainty in an emotionally most attractive and understandable way. This certainty was the conviction that nature, though bound to material things, is more than matter. The human mother becomes in Mary the symbol of life's inherent potentiality for overcoming its merely earthly character and for upholding the spirit of love against conflicting trends of our nature. The fact that this myth comprehends nature and spirit in one symbolic unity explains why painters and poets have been so constantly attracted by the figure of Mary. They have portrayed neither the Saint alone nor the natural mother alone, but the Saint in the symbol of the mother and the mother in the symbol of the Saint. This comprehensiveness of the symbol is the reason also that our folk songs reveal a popular preference for the figure of Mary even to the figure of Christ. There was, at times, even in the Catholic Church itself a certain danger that the cult of St. Mary—that is, the cult of maternity— would overshadow the cult of Christ.

The great systematic philosophers, such as Spinoza and

Kant, and the great experimental scientists, such as Faraday, have had one quality in common with the minds that have created our most profound myths. They have all known that we have not even scratched the surface of life if we think that its energies can be grasped by strictly scientific methods and a technical vocabulary. The things that are most precious and profound in the relations of parents and children, or in the soul of an inspired educator, do not occur in forms liable to rational or measurable approaches. Something grows within them that integrates some elements of their personality and overcomes others; something, as in all great formative events in human life, that they voluntarily obey though they cannot fully explain it. Parents can be divorced from happiness, from home and country, and from each other; but they can never be divorced from their children even if their sorrow in them is many times greater than their joy. The true meaning of this reality is conveyed even in the finest symbols only if we put into them all the emotional wealth of human experience before it has been crystallized into concepts and systematized into thought. Analysis, if applied exclusively, distorts the richness, the intensity, and the totality of the motivating forces of life.

This statement, of course, is not intended to favor a certain kind of modern antirationalism, unbridled and fanciful speculation, or the belief in myths and symbols as such. This would only narrow our vision. What we need is not a relapse into prescientific attitudes. But we must overcome both magical dogmatism, which only conceals the deeper meaning of myth and religion, and scientific dogmatism, which does not see the limits of logic and of the laboratory and which also conceals the deeper realities of life.

Chapter II

WHOM DO WE EDUCATE?

A. HISTORICAL INTRODUCTION

It is rather astonishing to observe that elaborate forms of education were developed long before any systematic inquiry was made into the nature of the being to be educated. There are, of course, many penetrating ideas on this subject to be found in the writings of the ancient Greeks and Romans. The philosophic development from Socrates and the Sophists, through Plato and Aristotle, Seneca, Marcus Aurelius, Plotinus, and Boethius yielded many remarkable insights into the nature of man. But, although their ideas were often based on much more profound experiences in the realm of human behavior than many of our modern educators can avail themselves of, they failed to utilize sufficiently the experimental methods already developed by such a great physician as Hippocrates. Consequently, their speculations remained unverified and never reached the status of a comprehensive science of man.

The thinkers of the Middle Ages took over much of the thought of Greek and Roman antiquity and the great Arabic philosophers. It would be inadequate, however, to consider them simply as disciples, since for this they fell short in some respects and added too much in others. Even more than their masters, they neglected experimentation. But they brought to the understanding of man the message of Christianity. They believed that in order to know the most essential things about himself man ought first of all to recognize his place in the universe and the comparative unimportance of his earthly career. Many of us were, and still are, of the opinion that this point of view is obscure and unscientific. But the growing unrest of modern man, the disaster of the World War, and the breakdown of the old values of civilization have unsettled the feelings of self-sufficiency and certainty in which the age of enlightenment indulged. We are beginning to develop a new insight into the total problem of man and to discover that his psychic life is, in reality, influenced by his ideas about his destiny and his place in the universe. Consequently, the medieval philosophers no longer appear to us so completely erroneous, and parts of Scholastic thought find entrance into modern critical philosophies. We must hope that a more adequate appreciation of the medieval tradition will not prevent us from careful discrimination between its lasting wisdom and its superstitions. Modern irrationalists like to point to the sins of omission of the eighteenth and nineteenth centuries, which undoubtedly were unfair in their judgment of the Middle Ages, but themselves commit a like sin in underestimating the heroic struggle which the empirical era had to undergo in order to liberate humanity from the fetters of obscurantism. If this irrationality spreads, we may again, forgetting how much must still be done to save man from credulity, relapse into magical concepts of life, as we did at the end of antiquity.

The first more comprehensive approach to the problem of the nature of man was made by the pioneering scholars of the Renaissance. With few exceptions they had not forgotten that man's self-interpretation depends not only upon what he is but also upon what he believes. On the other hand, they had freed themselves sufficiently from the ties of tradition to read the ancient authors in a new spirit and to venture enthusiastically along new paths of knowledge and science.

The man of the Renaissance looked into himself not only by means of meditation but, as the physicians of antiquity had done, by means of scissors and knives as well. In 1543, after dissection had become a part of medicine, Andreas Vesalius composed the first great anatomy, *De humani corporis fabrica.* It was still dangerous to devote oneself to experimental research; Vesalius was sentenced to death for sorcery by the Spanish Inquisition and would have been burned if the Emperor had not granted him a pardon. Nevertheless, at about this same time, the Catholic theologian and philosopher Ludovico Vives wrote his book *De anima et vita (Concerning the Soul and Life),*[1] containing a mixture of ancient, Scholastic, and rather modern ideas, which we might call the first modern psychology. That a new aspect of man had been brought to light can also be shown by reference to Vives's main work, *De tradendis disciplinis (Concerning the Teaching of the Sciences),*[2] published in 1531. Here he recommends that the physicians ought, first of all, to understand the structure of the human body and to attend the sessions in anatomy. "They must learn where the

---

[1] *Johannis Ludovici Vivis Valentini Opera Omnia.* 1782 edition. Vol. III.
[2] *Ibid.,* Vol. VI, pp. 373 ff. (Liber IV, caput vi).

veins, nerves, and bones begin and end, how big and how long they are, what use the human organism makes of them, and how they interact." And he also gives the physician valuable psychological suggestions, which, of course, would not have surprised Hippocrates or Galen. "While visiting the patient the physician ought to consider his attitude, constitution, age, and his psychic condition."

In spite of this new emphasis upon observation and experimentation, the centuries following the Renaissance continued to be stronger in introspective than in experimental forms of psychology. Like the Greeks and Romans, the scholars of the Renaissance did not see the possibility of combining the theory of man with medicine and the natural sciences. The seventeenth century and still more the eighteenth possessed a refined feeling for the subtlest emotions and impulses of the human being, far superior to that of our present scientific psychology. But when, for instance, Johann Heinrich Pestalozzi, the greatest educator of his time, tried to attack the problem of learning and of mental growth in more or less scientific terms, he found very little on which to rely, though one must admit that there was already more available than he discovered.

To the nineteenth and twentieth centuries must be given the credit for elaborating the first consistent methods of a scientific blending of physiology, medicine, and anthropology and of attempting a systematic revision of educational theory and practice in the light of this new psychology. In the course of almost a century these new methods have resulted in breaking through many prejudices which up to the nineteenth century had obscured our view of the relation between the human mind and its physical conditions. We can point to the results of modern psychiatry and of remedial psychology, and to our increasing insight into the relations between growth and mind and between age and mentality. We have discovered relationships between physical changes, particularly in our secretory system, and regulatory phases of the psychic maturation and retrogression of the individual. We have reason to believe that the various forms of temperament and even of creative mental activity are influenced by chemical processes and can be affected by medical intervention. Beyond the merely physiological aspects of the human mind, mental hygiene and psychoanalysis, in spite of their one-sidedness, have opened avenues for the understanding of mental disorders entirely unknown to us a generation ago. Our knowledge of the mutual affinity of problems that previously were confined to either physics or chemistry, to either inorganic or organic life, is steadily increasing. The gradual transfer of this knowledge to the fields of medicine, physiology, and psychology may disclose to future generations facts and functions of which we now have not the slightest idea.

On the other hand, the last decades, like earlier times, have not avoided bias and distortion. This has been revealed by our most recent psychological research, particularly by the work of the configurational school, and by new attempts at a philosophic scrutiny of psychological methods. The dominant psychological schools around 1900, in their natural endeavor to achieve the certainty of the exact sciences, relied too exclusively on the methods of physics and mathematics for their research upon the human mind. No fair judge can doubt that this new outlook directed our attention toward important facts that otherwise would have been overlooked. Nevertheless, during the last two decades the initial enthusiasm for the new psychologies has changed to grave disappointment. The reason is that they had lost contact with the humanities and, what is still worse, with the richness of life and the totality of the human being.[1] They liked to boast of their conflict with philosophy. But either they failed to see that the questions they were constantly dealing with had philosophical implications which they had overlooked or, in order to escape the embarrassment of unpleasant speculations, they narrowed the range of their problems and then fell into the error criticized in our first chapter; namely, of absolutizing a partial truth and obscuring in this way the comprehensive character of the issues involved.

John B. Watson, in his *Psychology from the Standpoint of a Behaviorist*, gives ample testimony to the statement that school psychology lost more in breadth of intuition and philosophic wisdom than it gained in improved experimental procedures.

It was an unfortunate coincidence for the development of American education that at the height of this mechanistic psychology the training of teachers became a large-scale enterprise looking for guidance on its way toward academic recognition. In most European countries the

---

[1] It cannot be discussed here in detail but ought, nevertheless, to be mentioned that this development in psychology represents only a partial aspect of a very general process of thought. For a fine analysis of this process see Edmund Husserl, "Die Krisis der europäischen Wissenschaften und die transcendentale Phänomenologie," in *Philosophia*, edidit Arthur Liebert. Ex officina Societatis Philosophia. Belgradi, 1936. Vol. I, Fasc. 1–4.

theory and history of education had grown up with the liberal studies; unfortunately, in America the faculties of liberal arts had never cared much for this important subject and could, consequently, not be of real help. Furthermore, the idealistic philosophies, which in this country had formed the basis for educational thought up to the end of the nineteenth century, were rightly being submitted to severe critical inspection and losing scientific prestige. In another field from which education could have derived inspiration and a wider cultural horizon, in history, a broad philosophic and cultural aspect was still barred by the tendency to accumulate facts, the significance of which was sometimes very doubtful. There was, consequently, nothing the young science of education could turn to except the natural sciences. They were in vogue, they had the advantage of a certain exactness, and they could perhaps help the educator not only to describe and to philosophize but to arrive at exact and reliable laws or methods. In their youthful enthusiasm the leaders of educational thinking forgot to ask the fundamental question, much discussed in Europe by the Neo-Kantian school, as to the extent to which the methods of the natural sciences could really be transferred to the disciplines concerned with the problems of man. On the contrary, educational psychology outran every other discipline in its admiration for mechanical causality and quantitative relations. The result was that American education developed, on the one hand, completely new and, if once purified, promising forms of research; on the other hand, large and pompous edifices were erected on methodologically sandy ground. Rarely in the history of civilization has such an amount of useless literature been permitted to impose itself on the student of man's behavior as during the last few decades.

At the very time that psychology brought the mechanical interpretation of mental functions and education to its climax, the natural sciences themselves became doubtful whether the strict application of Newtonian principles could produce such certain results as the preceding centuries had supposed.

So we are now at a stage where psychology begins to re-examine its presuppositions and its methods. Not that the necessary search for the physical and mechanical causality of psychic functions will ever be abandoned. Within this field of research the schools of behaviorism and reflexology will probably continue to have value with respect to certain partial problems of human behavior. For instance, problems of fatigue, attentiveness, individual defects in reading, and the like, will always offer fertile fields for a behavioristic approach.[1] If aware of its limitations, experimental isolation of stimulus-response bonds will, furthermore, help us in medical fields and will serve as a protective measure against the old danger of speculations about the human soul, which were more often a kind of wishful thinking clothed in a learned vocabulary than real scientific hypotheses.

---

[1] It may be of general interest that modern experimental psychology of the behavioristic type has contributed much more to the understanding of the mentally abnormal, than of the normal, person. The reason is that in the abnormal person the totality of his personality is disturbed by more or less clearly discernible isolated factors, while the normal individual is characterized by the harmonious co-operation of his capacities among themselves and with his environment and his universe. We are grateful for information about the abnormal and the possibilities of helping him. On the other hand, we are convinced that in the exploration of the factors and interrelationships operating in a sound and harmonious life lie the greatest possibilities for the development of a more

B. THE NEED FOR A TOTAL EXPLANATION
OF THE HUMAN BEING

The kind of psychology we need to serve·the interests of culture and education is still in the making. We need much greater awareness of the place and significance of single observations in the total realm of human life. The philosopher and educator are not concerned with the human being in artificial experimental isolation but with his growth into the world of values and conflicts. Hence, we shall need a psychology that describes the human being experimentally as correctly as possible but, in addition, as a unified individual working within collective groups, institutions, nations, civilizations, and even the part of the universe he may consider his own. We must try to know not only how a person acts and reacts but also what he needs and what kind of education and guidance is conducive or harmful to his fullest development.

Whether psychology will be able to encompass this broader science that we envisage depends upon its energy and the scope of its vision. If one considers the dead ends into which it has run for lack of any philosophic outlook, one is inclined to deplore that in our modern times the term "anthropology" has been deprived of its original significance. Up to the eighteenth century it carried all the responsibility its name suggests: it was a *logos* of *anthropos*, a theory of the essence and meaning of man. During the positivistic era, along with the general decline of synthetic thought, such a discipline disappeared, leaving its subject to be dealt with only by specialized sciences.

comprehensive psychology, which then, of course, would have to arrive at a much more total understanding of the human person.

Genuine anthropology, served by such men as Aristotle, Thomas Aquinas, Comenius, Hobbes, Grotius, Condorcet, Goethe, and Carus, became a special historical discipline concerned largely with the study of man's origin and the development of races and customs. The fact that a number of modern thinkers are beginning to revive the genuine meaning of this science, which fortunately has never been completely forgotten in Europe, shows that the break with a great tradition is now felt to be a loss.[1]

In America, Gordon W. Allport, in his highly important work on *Personality*, has certainly opened an avenue toward the understanding of the personality and of the role of psychology in such a new, or if one wants to say, older sense. He sharply distinguishes, to be sure, between psychology and ethics.[2]

> On all sides [he says] one encounters confusion of psychology with ethics. The layman asks the psychologist, "How ought I bring up my child?" And the psychologist is presumptuous enough to tell him; although no psychologist *qua* psychologist can tell how a child ought to be brought up. The most he can do is to disclose human nature as it is, and then, *after a moral code has been chosen*, find out means of incentive and training that will achieve the end desired. Unreflectingly many psychologists, particularly mental hygienists, pose as experts in ethics, for do they not speak with assurance about the desirability of

---

[1] Sombart, *Beitraege zur Geschichte der wissenschaftlichen Anthropologie.* Gesamtsitzung der Berliner Akademie, 3 Maerz 1938. (Sitzungsberichte der Preussischen Akademie der Wissenschaften. 1938. Vol. VII.)

[2] Holt. Pages 51-52.

"mental adjustment"? Strange to say, it is often the Behaviorist, the most "rigidly scientific" in his ideals for psychology who traffics most unguardedly in ethics.

Allport's distinction between psychology and ethics is doubtless very important for the *methodological* elucidation of the relation between psychology and ethics. The psychologist who mixes ethical evaluations into the process of fact finding will never find the facts which we need to know in order to understand the human personality as clearly and fully as possible.

But, on the other hand, one may reply to Allport with good reason that the division of human nature "as it is" and "as it ought to be" presents in psychology a theoretical abstraction. As we have just said, this abstraction is necessary to guarantee the highest possible degree of logical self-awareness; but it is strictly applicable only in physiology, where the human being can be regarded as a merely physical unit and isolated from the frame of humanly significant references in which it lives as a "personality." (Generally one could say that the confusion between psychology and physiology—another point which Allport sees more clearly than many of his psychological colleagues—is just as frequent as the confusion between psychology and ethics. This is a symbol of the fact that psychology is a subject which gives the topographer of the *globus intellectualis* many riddles still to solve.)

It increases the difficulty of a practical separation of psychology and ethics that the process of civilization and of upbringing does not result from a neat interaction of a "moral code" that "has been chosen," on the one hand,

and human "nature as it is," on the other hand. The human being chooses a moral code because such a tendency is inherent in his "nature as it is," [1] and this moral code in turn reflects upon and forms his psychic make-up. Hence there are in the reality of social life only persons related to, and conditioned by, particular modes of civilization, and a psychology which, for the purpose of scientific exactness, leaves out this relativistic factor is not scientific and exact, but unrealistic.

Allport's book itself—in this respect comparable to Wolfgang Köhler's recent work on *The Place of Value in a World of Facts*—shows in a remarkable way how a modern psychologist can combine awareness of the methodological conditions of science with the understanding of the role of the personality in the framework of civilization. And though the psychologist—*qua* psychologist—may think that Allport, particularly in his chapters on "The Mature Personality" and "The Unity of Personality," sometimes offends against his own methodological prescriptions, the educator—*qua* educator—must be grateful that so clear a methodological thinker does not shy from admitting and analyzing the almost inextricable physio-psycho-ethical complexity of the living person.

However, our main interest is one not of methodology and terms but of substance; and, therefore, let us ask whether we can suggest an "anthropological" view which will help to answer the question of this chapter, "Whom Do We Educate?"

Once again we face the fact that education must first of all reckon with the physical side of man's existence.

---

[1] Compare Chapter I, section C.

Therefore, the first issue that arises in this context is concerned with the growth and bodily functioning of the human organism.

If we omit an answer to the problems raised, we may be excused for the reason that the purpose of this book would compel us to deal rather hastily with a subject that is too important to be handled in a perfunctory way. Educators, of course, cannot attempt to be medical experts, but they should have at least as much understanding of the physical prerequisites of education as a physician should have of the role which education plays in the process of molding a person. The co-operation of these two professions most responsible for the healthy growth of the young is not nearly so well developed as it deserves to be nor as modern nations should insist upon for the physical and mental welfare of their people; this is all the truer in that our public and vocational life requires increased energy of everyone.

But in spite of our hesitation to include physiological problems in our considerations, we have to pay attention to some points connected with them which are of importance for our particular concern with a theory of man. Since the end of the nineteenth century physiology, experimental psychology, and medicine have undergone a remarkable change. New discoveries in the fields of neurology, psychiatry, and metabolism, together with the introduction of more comprehensive principles for the interpretation of physical data, have altered our general view of the human organism. It can no longer be understood merely as a conglomerate of cells and atoms interacting according to mechanical laws of cause and effect. Mechanical causality plays a great part in the functions of our body and consequently minute and specialized scientific investigation of this causality will never cease to be an important, perhaps the most important, part of physiological and medical research. But, however advanced the findings of microscopy and other typical laboratory work, the results will not be very useful unless we see the causal relations of isolated factors as part of a dynamic whole of energy, not simply a sum total of many separate functions, but possessing qualities proper to its wholeness. These qualities are necessarily influenced and dependent upon mechanical processes in the brain, the heart, the stomach, the intestines, and all other special organs; but the whole influences and conditions its parts to an equal degree. That this whole is regulated by something which we must call the *soul* is an inference not necessarily arising from the conclusion we have just stated. But although at the end of the nineteenth century many experimenters believed that the steady advance in our knowledge of the detailed functionings of the human organism would gradually allow us to eliminate such unpleasant riddles from a system of physically determinable energies, we are today much more modest. With the refinement of our insight into the functions of the brain and the nervous system, the most advanced of our scientists have come to the conclusion that it is impossible to understand the normal behavior of man by the analysis of isolated reflexes alone.

The neurologist Kurt Goldstein, in his book on *The Organism*,[1] writes as follows:

[1] Kurt Goldstein, *The Organism. A Holistic Approach to Biology Derived from Pathological Data in Man.* With a Foreword by K. S. Lashley. American Book Company, 1939. Pages 158 and 170.

All this shows that in the reflex, so-called, we are dealing with a *special type of coming to terms of organism and environment*—a performance of the whole organism in a peculiar configuration, due to pathological or experimental causes. . . . As a rule, whenever one refers to an event which is confined to a separate part of the organism, one can only do so by disregarding the behavior of the rest of the organism; and then one is forced to make auxiliary hypotheses to explain all the variations of the past reactions. The facts, however, call for another interpretation: the reflex, just like any other reaction of the organism, must be understood as a response of the whole organism. The allegedly *"isolated" phenomenon, which one alludes to by the term reflex, is in fact a "figure" in a reaction pattern of the whole organism. The "reflex" is the figure, while the activity of the rest of the organism is the background. This is clearly confirmed by the fact that any change in the remaining organism at once modifies the reflex, the figure.* . . . All this should go to prove that *normal behavior is not composed of reflex processes.*

This interdependence of the part and the whole and of the organism's various specialized energies is also shown by the fact that in case of the failure of one organ the organism is not seldom capable of filling the gap by a rearrangement of its specific apparatus. Furthermore, a great deal of human behavior can be understood only by supposing the existence of unconscious mental energies that influence our actions. In making this supposition we are not obliged to join any particular psychological school that postulates a so-called subconscious sphere or believes in the existence of a specific determining element, be it sex or the social or spiritual relations of the individual. But, on the other hand, we cannot deny the existence of undercurrents in human mentality.

In consequence of all that we have so far said, it should be clear that a theory of human behavior based upon merely quantitative or mechanical analysis is no longer tenable.

C. THE PREDICAMENTS OF PSYCHOLOGY

But if this approach to the study of man, which (particularly in American psychology) has been dominant in recent years, is incomplete, can we advance a more complete hypothesis? We use the word "hypothesis" because we are sure that whatever we suggest is bound to be tentative and will, let us hope, soon be superseded by more adequate conjectures. But before we can attempt any positive formulation of a hypothesis, there is still further ground to be cleared, in doing which we hope to throw additional light upon the nature of the problem with which we are concerned.

We have first of all to notice that the human being is not describable in any strict or definitive manner. He is, as we have already suggested, the medium for inexplicable energies which, through vital urges and the operation of special organs, arouse him to life and activity. Yet he is related not only vertically to the sources of life but horizontally to his environment in all its variety and complexity.

But conceding this initial limitation, whence do the methodological confusions arise which constantly hinder the psychologist in his attempt to know an object so close to us as ourselves?

The first difficulty results from the structure of our reasoning, which we have also touched upon in the first chapter. Our conceptual thinking is discursive; that is, it passes successively from one topic to the next and does not allow us to depict diverse events in their coincidence. It has to present them as if they happened one after the other, in a sequence. But psychic processes are of astounding coincidency; consequently, all our ways of analyzing them as first, second, third, and so on are fallacious. In addition, analysis always tends to break up coherent wholes or series of events. Since, however, we have no other way of thinking than the discursive, all we can do is to be aware of its inadequacy whenever we use it for the analysis of psychic processes.

The second predicament of psychology is that in all investigations of our mental activities we are both the observer and the observed, the subject and the object. Hence we lack two conditions of great importance for the success of scientific procedures. One is sufficient distance from our object to permit the great sweep which unbiased investigation presupposes. The other is controlled laboratory conditions, to which our particular object is recalcitrant. The latter condition requires that the object must not change in unforeseen ways during experimentation; it must not be exposed or expose itself to conditions that alter the prerequisites of the experiment; it must be submissible a number of times to identical procedures under identical conditions; and the complete experiment must be capable of repetition with several objects so nearly identical as at least to be closely comparable. None of these conditions occur in any complex investigation of the inner creative life of a human being.

The third, and perhaps most fundamental, impediment to a science of man is that the investigating mind finds itself not only both subject and object but that in examining itself it looks into forms of existence which it meets only in this and in no other situation. When a physicist examines a physical substance and a physiologist observes his animals, they have to do with appearances, reactions, or changes; in any case, with end products of life. The life they observe has already materialized and objectified itself by effecting certain events in a given piece of matter—in a piece of metal, a gland, a chemical compound. This effect has been brought about by an inner life energy the essence of which we cannot clearly describe but which we have to suppose still in the stage of becoming and producing. Now, in digging into the grounds of our own existence, we are in a situation similar to that of the physicist when he speaks not of the effects of energy but of the energy itself, seemingly flowing as an invisible force through the visible universe. But though the situation is somewhat similar to that of the physicist, it differs decisively in that in the process of introspection we ourselves are the flow of life force become conscious of itself.

However much a psychologist may distrust mysticism, in examining not only the reactions of his ego, but his ego as such, he is bound to be an intuitionist and a mystic because the creative center of his ego stays within a realm of cosmic forces which are beyond our ordinary categories of thought, our discursive logic, and the grasp of our conceptual language. All these instruments are able to describe, to a certain extent, the surface, but they cannot seize upon the noumena behind the phenomena, or, in Kant's phraseology, the thing as the thing-in-itself. To use a famous phrase of the Neo-Kantian Vaihinger—without accepting his general philosophical conclusions—we may say that all our assertions about the core of our existence can only be made "as if" they were truly representative of the reality which they try to comprehend, when actually they are not and can not be.

All these difficulties, together with the necessarily subjective character of our attempts to understand ourselves, explain also why our psychological schools, all of which have claimed objectivity, show so decidedly the influence of contemporaneous currents of thought about the meaning of life, of religion, of philosophy, and even of politics.

This holds true not only of the "prescientific" psychologies of antiquity and the Middle Ages, but also of the modern ones. In the eighteenth century the progressive thinker was convinced that through his intellectual capacities, as revealed by the works of a Newton and a Leibnitz, man would learn more and more to realize within himself the inner order of the cosmos. He believed that he was ultimately a rational being, that the universe, too, was a rational enterprise, and that, consequently, mankind would be able to reform society into harmony with the permanent laws of the revealed universe. To a certain extent Herbart's psychology and philosophy also share this rational intellectualistic assumption. On the other hand, in periods of disappointment in the power of reason emotion is honored as the source of true humanity, and a more mystic and religious aspect of man prevails. Some thinkers, in such times, emphasize humility and renunciation; others glorify will and action, even desperate action, as the characteristics of the perfect man and the sole fulfillment of life. Today, when Italian Fascism and German

National-Socialism defend a kind of mystical voluntarism, the political philosophy of Fascism is partly prepared for and partly accompanied by a psychology of emotionalism and activism. It is also not far from the truth to see a connection between American behaviorism and Russian reflexology and the mechanistic interpretation of nature and society originating in the nineteenth century and reaching its fullest expression in the twentieth. These examples do not mean that the psychologist is the servant of political or economic powers. Not at all. The relationship between them is the involuntary effect of the incapacity of psychology as of most other sciences to think about man in terms absolute and distinct from the movements and sentiments of the time. So far psychology has not proved to be much of a help in getting rid of the uncertainty of the liberal arts and humanities in their great effort to arrive at the core of the human problem. It has itself been profoundly affected by the tendencies and ideologies of its own times. Philosophy, during recent decades the preferred target of many psychological schools, has a long tradition in the critical theory of methods, and this has made the philosophers often more aware than the psychologists of the snares threatening our scientific endeavors.

D. THE STRUCTURE OF THE PERSONALITY

1. Environment. Self-identity. Vital Urges

Equipped with this armor of self-criticism and the conviction of our own constant exposure to error, let us now revert to our attempt to understand personality.

Man can never be explained as an isolated being, because his physical and mental life is inseparable from the environment in which he lives. But what meaning of the term "environment" must psychology insist upon to serve its purposes adequately? Our environment not only is what we sense in our immediate neighborhood but consists of all upon which we consciously or unconsciously depend. Environment is not something fixed and given but a dynamic system of functions and relations between a person and that person's "world." And since a person has much to do with making his world and this world in turn helps to form the person, both concepts—that of environment and that of a person—are continuously changing and interrelated units in a continuously changing frame. In this sense the things closest to us may not be part of our environment because they do not affect us. But distant things and things of seemingly little concreteness, such as a scientific discovery in the field of our interests or the death of a friend in a remote country, may form the most impressive and immediate details of our environment.

Consequently, since the influences conveyed to us by the environment have such variety and complexity, the next question confronting us is how there can be any unity in this continuous flux of affairs. This is an important point that we have to face in the initial stage of our considerations. A person is a *unitas multiplex;* he changes within a changing environment and persists only by a consciousness of his own coherence in space and time and of a similar coherence in his environment. We may call this primary quality of individual existence our sense of identity. Without this quality our so-called reflexes would be only a chaotic medley; we could not speak of a "sequence of impressions." How it comes about that within the infinite existence surrounding us we feel ourselves to be a unity, a persisting nodal point of forces, a resultant in a parallelogram of energies, to the utmost degree dependent upon other factors yet, nevertheless, a unique psychophysical ego-system, is one of the greatest mysteries of our existence.

The form of self-identity is seemingly different in different persons. Some prefer to remember themselves in these, and others in other, situations. This variety and selectiveness is certainly one of the factors accounting for the richness of human individualities, which makes it impossible to find two exactly identical persons in the whole human world.

We know that the power of self-identification does not appear in the human being before a certain, though modest, stage of maturity has been reached. Whether it disappears after an individual's physical existence is destroyed has so far been neither proved nor refuted. The answer, if we dare to give any, depends not upon reason alone but upon those personal experiences which in the course of our life go to the formation of our ideals and beliefs.

As inexplicable as self-identity in being are the vital urges constantly motivating human beings. We must now revert to them in order to show the extent to which they determine the structure of the human personality. For this purpose we use, with some changes to be mentioned very soon, the enumeration of "propensities" proposed by McDougall in his book on the *Energies of Man*.[1]

He distinguishes the following innate propensities in the human being: food seeking, disgust, sex, fear, curios-

[1] Page 97.

ity, protective or parental feeling; the propensities he calls gregarious, self-assertive, and submissive; anger, appeal, the constructive and acquisitive propensities, laughter, comfort, rest or sleep, and migrating propensities; and finally "a group of very simple propensities subserving bodily needs," such as coughing, sneezing, breathing, and evacuation.

It seems to us particularly doubtful whether such physical urges as the food-seeking propensity, the rest or sleep propensity, and the group that McDougall denotes as "a group of very simple propensities subserving bodily needs" can be placed on the same level with such propensities as the sexual, the protective or parental, or the self-assertive. As we have already indicated in our first chapter, where we had to speak of this whole area of the human personality in relation to the genesis of human civilization, we should prefer for such urges as the food-seeking urge (or hunger and thirst) the term "needs." They seem to us, though to a certain extent adaptable and plastic, so deeply embedded in our physical system that our freedom in handling them is extremely limited—if we do not prefer to harm or destroy our physical existence. They relate also to the sphere of morality and civilization in a form completely different from, for example, the sexual propensity, which, though still physical and dependent upon season in most animals, is, in spite of its physical basis, open to freedom, choice, and the highest sublimation in the civilized human being. And as with the sexual propensity, so may other propensities include, in one fashion or another, a high potential of development. As, without placing much value on nomenclature in such an unexplored subject, we have to find some kind of terminology, we designate the whole sphere of those energies acting from the center of our organism as vital or motivational urges or drives. Within this sphere we differentiate between "needs," [1] denoting the more physical and restricted drives, and "propensities," denoting the more adaptable urges of human nature.

McDougall himself remarks that his list is not put forward as final and, as a matter of fact, he has not hesitated to correct himself. For our part we are convinced that no enumeration of drives, urges, needs, or propensities can be precise. For the motivating forces in man are developing, overlapping, and shifting configurations impossible of strict classification. Nevertheless, McDougall's attempt has its merit in that it shows the richness of the urges at the bottom of the personality.

With a better conscience we follow McDougall in his opinion that the propensities of man would remain latent if it were not for the capacity to materialize their energies through a functional linking with the various abilities innate in man. Without these abilities all his propensities would be nothing but vague potentialities unable to express themselves through action. As a matter of fact, propensities and abilities belong so closely together that only theoretically can one think of the existence of one separated from the other. In life they constantly interact. Two groups of such abilities may be distinguished: the executive or motor abilities, such as those of locomotion, standing and walking upright, manipulation (especially using the hands in the finer forms of skill), the articulation of speech; and the perceptual or, more broadly, cognitive

---

[1] We use here a term which David Katz in his work on *Animals and Men* advocates for a wider range of vital urges.

abilities, among which those of the ear, the limbs and skin, and the eyes have helped man to succeed in competition with animals superior to him in mere physical strength.[1]

2. ABILITIES AND THE PROBLEM OF FREEDOM

We have intimated in our first chapter that man is able to develop longer, and with more complexity, than animals. This is due partly to his more enduring plasticity and partly to his sense of self-identity, but to the latter not only in the sense of the coherence of his personal experiences but also in the sense of his racial or historical memory.

The nature of his development enables him to interlink his propensities and his abilities in the most subtle and admirable way. Similar interlinkings can be observed in animals. In a bird building its nest there seems to be a combination of the protective or parental propensity with the gregarious and the constructive propensities, all linked to such abilities as locomotion, manipulation, and several of the cognitive abilities. In man the combinations of propensities and abilities not only are of the greatest elasticity but also are most flexibly geared to various other qualities to be mentioned later on. We may see, therefore, how the combination of propensities and abilities found in the bird's nest building extends in man to such complex activities as housing and the social and economic organization. In consequence of his historical memory the whole stream of historical experience has flowed into his development. This may also explain the fact that in animals propensities and abilities are confined to a much narrower,

[1] W. McDougall, *The Energies of Man*, p. 100.

predetermined, and fixed range of activities, while in man there is a certain margin of freedom.

From the psychological side we here arrive at a relatively sound and experimental basis for the understanding of one of the most crucial terms in philosophy; namely, the concept of freedom. Freedom is possible because man possesses a rich and flexible system of elastically linked propensities and abilities. Therefore, the range of his immanent potentialities and of his capacity for reacting to outside stimuli is much greater than is the case even in the higher animals, which, though possessing a certain margin of choice in the mingling of propensities and abilities, are less flexible than man and consequently have produced nothing comparable to human history.

We have shown in our first chapter that the vital urges or propensities represent a unity of apparently contrasting integrals. Because of the inadequateness of our conceptual faculties we commonly denote them as being partly material and partly spiritual in character, though we have no right to assume a fundamental reality corresponding to this verbal dualism. A similar conclusion is necessary with regard to the concept of freedom. The old struggle between determinism and indeterminism, or between the doctrine that human action is completely controlled by external forces and the doctrine that man has the power to choose among different possibilities—this time-honored struggle of theologians and philosophers is also shown to have no basis in reality. It likewise results from the incapacity of human language and logic to comprehend apparent opposites in one inclusive term.

Man is a *coincidentia oppositorum*, to use a philosophic term with which Nicolaus Cusanus and Giordano Bruno contrasted man, in whom opposites meet without always being reconciled, to the eternal harmony of God. In man's nature there is to be found both dependence upon forces which, if wise, he can only voluntarily obey and some degree of freedom in the direction and organization of flexible potentialities.

3. Constitutional Endowment

The difficulties of explaining so complex and contradictory an object as the human being increase with every step we take into the riddles of personality. In order to make clear our next considerations, let us use an analogy which, though it oversimplifies, may still be suggestive. Comparing the human organism with a piece of woven material, we may think of the body with its various organs, muscles, and nerves as the material; the propensities as the warp; and the abilities as the woof. Now where do the design and the individual pattern of the texture come from? In other words, what makes for shape and structure, plan and purpose, individuality and personality in the human being?

In trying to answer these questions, we encounter an embarrassing confusion in the terminology applied to the description of the so-called higher mental processes. Every serious psychologist and philosopher has tried hard to find uninterchangeable categories having a single unambiguous meaning. But how can words, having no concrete counterpart in reality, be other than hazy and inexact?

Today the majority of our experts would suppose that the quality of a man's propensities and abilities and his way of gearing the two together depend largely upon his constitutional endowment. This, in turn, depends upon his ancestry, and of this we can never know which of the innumerable trends accumulated in a long lineage may converge in one particular offspring. The famous laws of inheritance discovered by the Abbot Johann Gregor Mendel in the garden of the Austrian monastery at Brünn may play some role in the human race. But how can we be sure, since other factors constantly interfere in their operation? In the first place, a human being is not so simple an organism as the culinary peas that Father Mendel planted in the beds and borders of his botanical sanctuary. Secondly, man is able to modify the quality of the human sperm and ovum through his manner of living. And, thirdly, who can prove that psychic factors in the relationship of mates have no influence upon the quality of their offspring?

His constitutional endowment colors more than man's propensities and abilities. To a large extent it is also responsible for the tonus, strength, and intensity which determine the character and quality of an individual's self-expression and activity. If any additional emphasis is needed on the fact that a personality cannot be understood without seeing the relation of the parts to the whole, then this is the place to give it. For his constitutional endowment really permeates the whole man. Besides influencing the functions already mentioned, it has much to do with what the sense of self-identity accepts and rejects for the creation of a personal world; it is largely responsible for the way in which a person feels and thinks, for the manner of his approach and response to other people, and for his tendency to take life in either a predominantly optimistic or a predominantly pessimistic mood.

This subjective atmosphere in which a person lives and

which colors his relations with the outside world has recently been called temperament, especially by American psychologists (among them Allport, in his work on *Personality*). It would be good if the term in this sense could be naturalized. We should then need only to be aware that we use it in a more inclusive and responsible sense than is common.

A feeling of awe for the innate temperamental basis of our existence caused one of the men who thought most deeply about human nature, Wolfgang Goethe,[1] to take poetic recourse to the Socratic conception of a demon attending us throughout our life and to the old myth of the stars determining our fate:

> Yea, as the sun (that day thy life was lent
> The world) did stand each planet's sphere to greet,
> So throv'st thou erst, obedient to thy bent,
> By that same law which hither sped thy feet.

> Such must thou be. None yet this Self outwent,
> This rede sibyl and seer of old repeat;
> For never time nor might could break asunder
> The shape seed-hidden, whose life unfolds its wonder.

But do not these Orphic words contradict our statement of an empirical basis for freedom in man? They have sometimes been so interpreted, but in reality they do not deny freedom. They assert only that our being is restricted to the particular resources of our individuality. We cannot use more speed and vitality, more abilities, and more intelligence than our individual nature provides. In this respect we are not free. But within these limits there

[1] *Poems and Aphorisms.* Oxford University Press for the Goethe Society, 1932. Pages 139–140.

are choice and chance variation. Our ego-potentials are
often richer than a natural inertia permits us to realize.
And one who masters himself by a proper balance and
utilization of his resources can do more with little than
another with much, just as a small man who knows how
to take advantage of mechanical laws can lift a much
heavier weight than an ignorant athlete. The reason for
this seeming contrast between freedom and restriction is
that we are not a system of given quantities but one of
dynamic energies and that besides our propensities and
abilities many other factors operate in most various combinations within the given complex of a personality.

4. Feeling. Will. Intelligence

Having discussed the most elemental components of
personality, we must now consider what an older psychology called the faculties of feeling, will, and intelligence.
Although every college student has nowadays to recognize
that such a departmentalization of our psychic functions
is invalid, we nevertheless do not yet know the nature of
the psychological reality behind such verbal symbols as
feeling, will, intelligence, imagination, or intuition. Do
all these terms perhaps refer to a single psychic energy
that finds different forms of self-expression according to
the specific task it is focused upon? Just as the power we
call electricity appears to us sometimes in the form of
light, sound, heat, or an electrical shock, so this invisible
psychic energy may appear as feeling when something ex-
cites us without finding release in any particular action,
as will when conflicting drives are to be integrated and
directed toward a specific goal, or as intelligence when a
problem is best overcome by analysis. This energy may

also be the accompanying overtone in all stages of awareness.

Certainly we have here reached the sphere where our mind not only reacts to outer stimuli or combines and gears the potentialities it finds ready-made within the psychophysical organism, but where it passes over into creative construction of the most sublime character. It changes outer facts into personal property; it creates the personal world in which the individual wants to live and overarches the details of life with a personal tissue of feeling, thought, and spirit. We are led to suppose an organizing power constantly establishing relationships among the various elements drifting about on the surface and in the deeper regions of the mind. In earlier times this power was conceived of as intelligence and reason. But whether this organizing power is primarily intellectual, as we often suppose, may rightly be doubted. Such terms as intelligence, reason, and thought connote too much the idea of a conscious effort. What we mean is something more fundamental than reason, and only if intensified through the presence of a proximate problem does it transmute itself into a reasoning energy. What it does, to repeat, is to order new experience by a continuous reconstruction of its creative pattern.

Let us exemplify this process in one instance, which, however, is taken, to be sure, more from the intellectual sphere than from other spheres already suggested. One of the most important processes of ordering our lives is conceptual thinking. Now what is going on if we symbolize an idea arising in our mind through a combination of sounds that serves as an ultimate and independent unit of discourse and that we denote as a word?

Though words are our constant means of clarifying ideas and of communication, few of us have stopped to consider what takes place when, for example, we denote an object as a birch tree. It must be something of the following sort, though there is not so much a sequence as simultaneousness. A sensory experience arouses the mind from a state of nebulous expectancy to awareness; from the potential plenitude of our environment we have selected a field of vision that concerns us. The first dim impression brightens immediately to a percept ready for discrimination. From the field of vision first selected, a more distinct object is singled out. In our case the birch tree emerges from the bushes it stands among, and we see something with white bark and leaves of a particular shape. (We must remember that distinguishing leaves and bark presupposes the accomplishment of the mental processes we are analyzing with respect to the birch tree.)

We probably do next something that is the very opposite of the process of discrimination involved in making a percept. The object singled out is now submitted to a conceptual treatment, to a process of generalization. We conclude that the object perceived is a tree called a birch. We find in our mental store concepts comprehending certain qualities of the object of our attention. The first of the concepts is the universal "tree" and the other the species "birch." We form the conception that our object is a tree by temporarily overlooking some of its peculiarities and emphasizing others. For instance, we do not notice that the bark is white and not brown, that the leaves are ovate and not needle-shaped; but we do notice the trunk, branches, and foliage characteristic of all trees.

In associating our sensation with the species "birch," we emphasize, instead of the qualities common to the genus, the peculiarities of the species. It is difficult to say whether in a single case the individual sensation is related first to the genus and then to the species, whether the reverse is true, or whether with already known objects we omit one or the other process. In any case we subordinate our percept of an isolated and nameless thing to a more general notion, in doing which this conglomerate of wood, branches, and leaves receives its name and a place in our world.

This example may suggest the amount of activity going on in our mind in even its most ordinary operations. Yet it is not difficult to understand that our mental processes are of still greater complexity in the formation of abstract concepts—such as "idea," "ideal," "energy," or "atom"—or of purely transcendental notions—such as God or the "*summum bonum.*"

We may assume, of course, that with habituation these processes become much simpler than they appear in analysis. The accumulation and repetition of experience helps us to associate new impressions very quickly with previously experienced presentations. As Herbart would say, the new impressions adapt themselves easily to our "apperceptive mass," or, in more modern terms, to our "mental set" or "pattern," as modern psychologists would prefer to say.

Although the theory of habituation or conditioning is doubtless true, it does not deliver us from the necessity of presupposing an active creative element in our mind which, at least when faced with new experience to be dealt with, must operate in a way similar to the one we have tried to describe. Nor could it be correctly maintained that this process is a particularly complicated one, incomparable to other functions of the mind. The power of language, it is true, is a great miracle responsible for the richness and distinctness of our psyche; we do not even know whether without verbal concepts clear and consistent ideas could exist. Nevertheless, through our consciousness there flow innumerable acts of willing, feeling, thinking, forgetting, and rejecting that are part and parcel of our psychic life. The complication becomes still greater when we consider that a unique tonus and shape are given to each system of flowing consciousness by the individual ego-organization.

The whole psychic area just discussed has sometimes been referred to as the area of the "higher" mental functions. But these old hierarchic conceptions of the qualities of the human soul, though they may have a place in ethics, are more confusing than clarifying in psychology. What we have already said about the comprehensiveness of vital urges should make us avoid such classifications. The so-called "instincts" contain a whole gamut of potentialities from the lower passions to the noblest sentiments, and the moment they emerge they intermix with emotions, volitions, and intelligence and in this way undergo either an intensification or a leveling of their affective character. Such being the case, where is a higher or lower level of our psychic life to be located? The weakest point in McDougall's theory of propensities is revealed when we ask how many of those he lists are but mixtures of vital urges or drives with emotions, volitions, and thinking. Furthermore, could not our innate desire to feel, will, and think be as validly considered a vital urge as, for example, the parental or protective propensity? Have not the experiments of McDougall and of other psychologists shown emotional, volitional, and intellectual factors even in the propensities of animals?

So it would be easy to accept the pessimistic conclusion that the farther we advance in the analysis of the human being the more we lose ourselves in thickets and marshes. In reality, what we gain through the scientific analysis of the personality is not so much certain knowledge as a constant refinement of our thinking about ourselves as a problem we may learn to appreciate better but never to resolve. A combination of curiosity and resignation is perhaps the profoundest wisdom we can attain to.

5. The Directional Character of the Personality

In consequence of the constant interaction of psychic energies and environment, the mental components of which we have spoken are in perpetual motion and productivity. In every sound person they tend to be channeled according to his individuality. On the other hand, the innumerable differences in individualities and environments cause the ceaseless stream of human activity to branch in the most various directions. There is a multiplicity of interests, activities, callings, inclinations, and aversions. But as the diverse potentialities of an ego are generally integrated toward an individual pattern, so, fortunately, civilization also exposes its members not only to diversity but also to converging and steadying influences, of which education and tradition are the most important. We are all guided toward some, and deflected from other, possibilities of growth; and conformity and convergence constantly work as a check upon diversity, particularly among members of the same cultural units.

The goal-directedness of an individual is identical with the formation of determining tendencies or attitudes leading to the rejection of some elements of experience and the acceptance of others. If this natural development is enforced by consistent training, either self-training or training from the outside, there sets in the factor of habituation, upon which behavioristic psychology has laid such great emphasis.

In time these determining tendencies become molded into a certain pattern of active, adaptive, or expressive behavior. In the mature person we are able to speak of certain personal traits, which not only serve as matrices into which the stream of mental energies flows to receive its form and direction but also play the role of economizers in the human household. The mechanization of psychic functions relieves us of the need of deciding afresh about each new issue that confronts us. Our movements, gestures, vocabulary, judgments—all our reactions to habitual stimuli—become mechanized, under sound conditions, thus conserving energy for the essential activities of the mind.

On the other hand, habituation and mechanization may encroach upon the active centers of personality so deeply that originality and productivity are seriously diminished. The result is a fixed and hardened soul, a Philistine afraid of new ideas, in whose presence we sense stagnation in the midst of apparent health and life. Therefore, we must hope that education understood exclusively as a process of conditioning will never totally succeed. Otherwise, it would mean the end of civilization.

Finding the right proportions of conditioning and free development is a problem of the educator for the solution of which he cannot resort to isolated psychological schools whose tradition is perhaps no older than thirty years. A fine feeling for individual rights and a recognition that at times a free personality must break through the limitations of mechanized organization can best be learned by familiarity with the values of culture and civilization.

It is due to the dynamic nature of life that resultants of forces, as we may call personal traits, do not forever retain their original quality, but tend to be transmuted into driving energies. The human being is, to use an old Scholastic term, not only *opus operatum* but also *opus operari*. The traits of a person are likewise both products and producers; particular configurations of likes and dislikes, capacities and incapacities, are produced which act as patterns of motivation for the production of further characteristic behavior. If this rotation does not take place, the result is the cessation of a person's development, the danger of which we have already described. Generally speaking, one may consider the velocity of this rotating process a measure of the health and vitality of a person: too slow a rotation means retardation of growth and productivity, too rapid a rotation means fickleness or a sterile kind of intensity analogous to a motor doing what an engineer would call "no-load work"; that is, running at a dangerously high speed without a load to slow it down.

The important element of personality that we have called goal-directedness is also influenced by this process of rotation. In case of fatigue it almost loses both propulsion and direction and becomes stiffness and rigidity;

in case of too rapid a rotation it becomes continual goal seeking without directedness, and only with adequate speed will it contain the right mixture of elasticity and purposefulness. However, we must not forget that, particularly in consequence of the differences of temperament or individual endowment, the speed of rotation adequate for different personalities will vary, just as not every motor runs best at the same speed.

If in the course of his development a normal individual becomes more and more goal-directed, a life plan arises out of the variety of his attempts to establish himself in a world full of challenge and danger. Or, if he is more anvil than hammer, he will more or less be forced into a certain coherence and consistency of action. A person who succeeds in making his life plan compatible with the requirements of his temperament, vitality, and traits not only matures harmoniously but, in maturing, also finds himself. Finding one's self takes place if, in mastering the tasks of life, a person simultaneously develops his ego-potentials in a way most natural to him. Life then becomes meaningful; he gains a feeling of self-identity and courage without which no degree of comfort can bring him happiness. At this point it becomes clear that a psychology of man cannot rest content with merely describing his tangible reactions but must include such terms as "plan" and "purpose," since the interrelationships between what a man is and what he aims for and, furthermore, between his aims and his faith are necessary for any complete picture of his development.

We can differentiate four main stages in the individual's psychophysical development. During childhood the individual begins to discover that he is an ego-system; during adolescence he is busy with the formation of a life plan suitable to his ego, and continual repercussions between the developing plan and the growing ego strengthen his personality; during maturity he not only tests his power but transcends the ego through his responsibility for his family, his work, and his community; and, finally, in old age he reflects upon the past and, if destiny favors him, may arrive at the rare accomplishment of dispassionate wisdom, giving of his richness to those who are still striving but mature enough to listen to him. Under organic social and cultural conditions old age has always enjoyed the highest esteem. It is the period not only nearest to death but sometimes also nearest to perfection and beauty of spirit.

6. Conflicts in the Personality and the Need for Values

It cannot be expected that the raw material of the human personality, with its potential heights and abysses, ideals and passions, joys and disappointments, can be shaped into a life plan without conflicts and crises. There may be rare forms of harmony between temperament and circumstances which allow for extensive and intensive growth with a minimum of friction. A healthy body with the capacity to rejoice in the pleasures of life, a moderate amount of ambition and mental intensity mixed with good aptitudes, a fortunate choice in friendship and love, and all this sheltered by a stable and prosperous nation—such combinations exist; and though their bearers may not be particularly interesting or profound, it would, nevertheless, be fine if we had more of them. They generally instill into the community in which they live an atmosphere of physical and mental ease and well-being, and the world is too full of problems and problematic creatures not to be harmed by their loss. William Wordsworth in his *Ode to Duty* says of them:

> There are who ask not if thine eye
> Be on them; who, in love and truth
> Where no misgiving is, rely
> Upon the genial sense of youth:
> Glad hearts! without reproach or blot,
> Who do thy work, and know it not:
> Oh! if through confidence misplaced
> They fail, thy saving arms, dread Power! around them cast.

For most people, however, the finding of direction is accompanied by self-control and the restraint of some of their ego-potentials. Shortly after birth there begins the process of guidance, encouragement, and reproval, the kindly malicious strategy by which the young are steered into the ways of adult life. And one must welcome it as a healthy sort of development if the repressed potentials fit without too much reluctance into the growing edifice of the personality—perhaps even serving to support it, like the hidden girders in a well-built house.

But the more we learn to deal with human personality and the more complex and unstable our civilization becomes, the greater number of adverse factors we discover influencing the formation of the modern personality. Fifty years ago most parents and educators recognized failures in a child's development only when confronted by open disobedience, defiance, or silent obstinacy. To such overt faults the usual educational recourses were either punishment or persuasion by means of promised rewards. There is no doubt that some modern educators have completely misjudged these old ways of directing growth. In denouncing older times they often forget that our ancestors, besides punishment and reward, had not only a healthier, though often a poorer and rougher, environment for their children than our modern cities provide but also well-established beliefs and customs through which the young imbibed an attitude toward the hardships of life other than that which we have today.

Nevertheless, though the pendulum may sometimes have swung too far toward a false complaisance, when we look back into the history of education we find nothing more appalling than the older forms of punishment. If anything is needed to show the ethical and human value of psychology, it is our increasing awareness of the danger of unthoughtful punishment for the symmetrical formation of the personality. It is, we now know, not only conspicuous rage or defiance that deserves our care (which is not identical with punishment); we need to be as much concerned about the contrary behavior, the yielding to unsuitable claims and the consequent development of traits harmful to the individual's psychic make-up and the form and energy of his action. Inactive acceptance of offenses and injustice; defeats in competition resulting in feelings of jealousy, envy, and inferiority; and supine obedience to codes of thought and behavior instead of a forceful synthesis of freedom and self-discipline—all such failures have made millions of individuals unhappy; and not only them, but those who have to live and work with them.

But as we all, with few exceptions, are sometimes offended, sometimes defeated, and sometimes compelled to yield to conditions and prescriptions that we would not voluntarily accept, what means do we have to avoid psychic prostration and disorder and to arrive at the necessary degree of symmetry?

There are, of course, different degrees of sensitiveness; some people are equipped with a stronger constitutional endowment or have lived in circumstances conducive to greater resistance. But this alone cannot explain differences of behavior in critical life situations. Other factors must also be taken into account. When we speak of the symmetrical formation of a personality, what kind of symmetry do we refer to? It is not symmetry in any quantitative or physical sense of the term. It is partly the result of bodily conditions, and therefore we have several times emphasized their importance. But it is also the result of man's power to obtain, through voluntary acknowledgment of life-regulating values beyond himself, the perspective that frees him from the petty concerns of an isolated ego. Those whose energies are not directed toward some transpersonal goal are the ones most exposed to psychic and, through these, to physical troubles. For lack of an objective sphere of thought and action in which his whole energy may be absorbed, he necessarily becomes egocentric and self-concerned and consequently incapable of discrimination between his own trivialities and the great issues of human life. In this connection great does not mean great in extent but great in intensity. One does not need to be a Napoleon to find values worthy of sacrifice and the devotion of his whole energies. On the contrary, the Napoleonic type, with its lust for power and destruction, is perhaps the best example of those who, failing to find the human values to which the greatest energies and talents can be constructively subordinated, turn in despair to conquest and destruction for the satisfaction of their energies.

Here again we face one of the great wonders of human nature: man's wealth of energies, drives, and ideas would be a peril if there were not the safeguard of an ordering principle within him. Not long ago we called this principle "goal-directedness," but only now are we in a position to understand the whole weight of this concept. Just as the term "symmetry," when applied to the human psyche, does not express a merely quantitative equilibrium, so the concepts of plan and purpose are not quantitative but qualitative and, if the term is rightly understood, spiritual in character. The interrelationship of the various mental functions is neither mechanical nor even organic, in the biological sense, but rather it is directional. Whether in the interplay of the various energies one or the other will dominate can never be foretold, because the nature of his action depends on the particular configuration in which a person finds himself and on the goal before him. Generally speaking, the more intensely a purpose is felt and the more it is in line with traits of personality, the more the diverse drives, feelings, and volitions are likely to converge toward the attainment of the goal in view.

In addition, it must be said that the more comprehensive, far-ranged, and objective the goal—provided there is no loss of intensity—the more it is able to harmonize the total personality for its service and to give, by the very reason of its comprehensiveness, a sense of freedom or identity with a transcendent purpose. All of the greatest minds have agreed that the only person who deserves to be envied is the one who has found an aim to which he can devote himself without restriction. On the other hand, nothing narrows a person more or deprives him more surely of freedom than attachment to a passion growing out of the tyrannical power of one particular vital urge not balanced by the healthy pervasion of other psychic functions.

E. GROWTH, FORM, AND METAPHYSICS OF THE PERSONALITY

These considerations show how worthless for the understanding of culture and education is a concept of growth from which so fundamental a principle as goal-directedness has been excluded. Yet this error has been committed in much of our modern educational philosophy. A cultured and educated person, the kind of person frequently referred to as "an integrated personality," must possess both the power of growing and the power of shaping his growth according to the aims which he has set for himself, not only as an individual, but as a social being. For this purpose he must sometimes act against the urges which, if he simply allowed himself to "grow," like an animal, he would naturally indulge.

But instead of losing ourselves in the contrast between growth and aim, we may better conclude our attempt to understand human personality by resorting to the concept of "form," used by Aristotle in order to rationalize the mystery of individuality. If we interpret him according to our own ways of thinking, without adhering strictly to his words, we may best proceed along the following line. Individual becoming or developing is possible only because there exists an interrelationship between two ontological principles, matter and form. Everything that emerges in the world of appearances is matter formed. But form is more than a geometrical or spatial delimitation of matter; it is the total of its properties. Hence form becomes for Aristotle not only something visible and external but also the immanent essence, or idea, of a thing. Only through the medium of form can the essence or idea be realized; without form it would remain simply an immaterial potentiality. Therefore, it is erroneous and in reality impossible to separate the essence of an object from its phenomenal attributes. On the contrary, the essence of an object expresses itself solely by its appearance, and all individual being may be thought of as matter seeking the best form for its immanent energies.

Abstract though this philosophy of form may sound, it is readily understandable the moment we apply it, for example, to the interpretation of a work of art. A work of art exists only through form, which is its beginning, its principle, and its aim, and true form is unthinkable in dissociation from content. For the content of a work of art has as much to do in determining the form as the form in molding and even determining the content. The relation between form and content is not external or rhetorical but functional, in that what an artist wants to say and how he says it are a unity from the very beginning. If a poet has an idea and then decides to mold it into a sonnet because fourteen iambic pentameter lines arranged in octave and sestet with a certain rhyme scheme might fit it better than a *terzarima*, he is not likely to write a good poem. For form is not a cloth to be thrown over something and arranged in any desirable fashion. It is a necessity.

This philosophy is valid not only with respect to a

work of art but also with respect to the making of a personality, which is, after all, the greatest of the arts. The ontological mystery of the individual is that he starts as a dynamic unity of matter and form, and, in consequence, freedom and direction do not contradict but condition each other. Because of the richness and diversity of human potentials this is not a simple, but a dialectical, process. We do not grow into a personality as the seed of an apple necessarily grows into a tree, or into a pre-established harmony with nature of the sort that makes the certainty of an animal's movements so fascinating to watch. As the Paradise myth revealed so long ago, we have to pay for the blessings of richness and freedom with error, unrest, and labor. In other words, our form is not the result of a natural, organic growth but something we achieve. What we call personality is the raw material of the human being when he has arrived at the realization of its inherent form. Therefore, our concept of form must not be confused with a merely aesthetic and amoral interpretation of personality. After all we have said, it must be clear that there cannot be good form without good "stuff" to be molded and to determine the molding process. And this stuff does not consist only of matter in the physical sense, but of the tasks that occupy the individual, his ideas and ideals—all that might be called the contents of a man's life. Hence, the great obligation of a culture is to present man with aims and traditions that will help him in the orientation of his own growth toward form; the special task of education is to guide him in such a way that the materialization of his inherent form goes hand in hand with his growing familiarity with the productive potentialities of civilization.

Modern psychology has shown us that only this convergence of the inherent individual form and the general principles that have led to the formation of civilization can result in the really productive and integrated personality. Since this convergence and harmony mean a constant overcoming of conflicts, the modern educator is aware that his role is not only that of conveying knowledge, as uninformed people even on university faculties still seem to think, but that of a strategist leading those entrusted to him beyond themselves into transpersonal spheres and through this very process to a deeper realization of their own inherent qualities.

This paradoxical task is given to us as educators because human beings are what they are. Let us recapitulate our findings. We saw that, although experimental and medical psychologies have added much to our understanding of man, the educator, the physician, and everyone concerned with the problem of man need more than psychological details. What is needed is an "anthropology," or a theory of man, that, in spite of the errors to which it is exposed, gives a really encompassing idea of the formation of the personality as an active agent within the framework of civilization. For man living within and for a society is more than a bundle of reflexes; he is a constantly selective and creative energy spanning the poles of matter and form, diversity and integration. The person, as we saw, is an individual continuum and totality, consistent in space and time and endowed with qualities that are simultaneously psychic and physical in character. His existence depends upon the unknown energies of the cosmos, which cause him to grow or to decay and even, to a certain extent, to do both at the same time.

His qualities are partly inherited and partly acquired. The lack of exact knowledge and the probably insuperable deficiencies of scientific concepts prevent clear analysis of the individual's constantly interweaving functions as they are called forth by the situations in which he finds himself. Such terms as instinct, propensity, ability, feeling, willing, and thinking are as yet indispensable and not completely incorrect in that they signify functions rising from our psychophysical existence like waves and currents from the flow of a river. Though these terms are very rough tools for depicting the essence of our psychic life, they have proved useful for defining certain qualities of the person—such as elasticity and freedom—and for understanding the part played by the developing traits in the growth of the personality. We saw both the importance and the limits of the concepts of conditioning and habituation and the need of complementing them by the concepts of purposefulness, goal-directedness, and creativeness. And finally we tried to penetrate the ontological secret of personality by resorting to Aristotle's concept of form. With these ideas we are already deep into the problem of ethics, which, as we have several times remarked, cannot be dissociated from an understanding of human personality. We are now compelled to deal with this problem much more thoroughly than our introductory chapter permitted.

But we should not like to leave this chapter without a final remark. Our attempt at an interpretation of personality is intended not only as a methodological discussion for specialized philosophers and psychologists, though it had to deal with some technical material. Rather, we are of the opinion that a new anthropology revealing man as a purposeful and responsible, though necessarily imperfect, agent in the immense business of civilization is imperative not only for the reform of sciences such as psychology and education but also for the maintenance of our whole Western civilization. And we are glad to find support for this opinion from a great American philosopher and psychologist to whom modern empiricists like to refer as a pioneer in their mode of thinking, though one may feel that, as with many heroes in the world of thought, the more his name is mentioned the less his spirit is followed. The man we mean is William James, and we are all the more glad to pay him due respect since in our next chapter we must take issue with some parts of his ethical philosophy.

Ralph Barton Perry, in his lectures *In the Spirit of William James*,[1] writes as follows concerning James's metaphysics of experience:

A writer of the present day has remarked of most of the issues which concerned James that "if they have not been settled," they have "at least paled a little, displaced by more crying problems." At least one of James's issues, not mentioned by this writer, appears at the moment to have become the central issue of philosophy. It was, I think, the issue which James himself, had he been forced to judge, would have deemed the most fateful. The advance of "instrumentalism" and "operationalism" in the experimental sciences, of symbolism in logic, and of logico-experimental positivism in sociology and philosophy, have created a new cult which touches human thought at all points and threatens a profound and epochal

[1] Yale University Press, 1938. Page 121.

change in the intellectual life of the Western world.
It is the fitting philosophical expression of an age of
technology. This cult teaches that knowledge, in the
maximal or preferred sense, deals with signs and experimental operations. Definitions in these terms are
substituted for the originals. Logico-mathematical
theories and experimental projects being elaborated
and verified, knowledge may thereafter proceed as
though there were only signs and operations. I have
no desire to dispute the propriety of this view as a
description or program of scientific method. Still less
do I desire to disparage the achievements of science,
weaken its prestige, or compromise the rigor of its
procedure. I wish only to insist that there is, unmis-
takably and indisputably, a variegated panorama of
qualities and a warmth of emotional response which
formal and quantitative knowledge omits. Their omission is no less an omission for being conscious and
methodical. They are not annihilated when they are
relegated to poetry. The only effect is to give a new
dignity to poetry. And it is at least open to question whether the terms of formal discourse and the
constructions of experimental inquiry are not themselves derived from, and referent to, those very qualities and feelings for which they are substituted. In
any case, he who by discernment or affection is aware
of the field of original meanings knows that for which
there is no other equivalent. It is at least a part of
the purpose of philosophy to invite men to sense and
feel their world. No one has issued this call more elo-
quently, or himself responded to it more fruitfully and
contagiously, than William James.

Chapter III

TOWARD WHAT ENDS DO WE EDUCATE?

According to the definition of man presented in the preceding chapter, we see that he possesses a certain degree of freedom. Within a limited range he is able to choose among the diverse possibilities offered to him by his nature and his environment. He may say yes or no to alternatives confronting him; he is capable of denying himself in the service of an idea that he holds to be greater than his individual existence. This freedom of choice is the necessary prerequisite of man's capacity to act morally, and this capacity, in turn, is the prerequisite of culture and education.

Therefore, ethics has always played an essential part in the philosophy of education, and, as we have already seen in the course of our psychological considerations, it is necessary to clarify our understanding of this subject.

A. STATING THE PROBLEM

Until the time of our fathers, public education was directed by an essentially religious or idealistic philosophy of values. At the turn of the nineteenth century an allegedly more empirical school of thought began to exert considerable influence not only on the theory but also on the practice of our schools. Today we find in most modern countries all these conceptions, in large array, both traditional and antitraditional, either existing peacefully side by side or fighting each other.

If we project on the ethical level the rich pattern of the problems discussed within and between the different camps of thinkers—admitting that we must thereby violate its complexity—then we see on the one side a form of thought which, for the sake of simplicity, we may call naturalistic, and on the other side a form of thought which we may call idealistic.[1]

If an educator leans more toward the naturalistic school, he derives the ethical principles of education from the immediate desires and interests of man. If he leans more toward the idealistic school, he considers these principles to be rooted in, or related to, permanent verities and laws transcending the human being.

If the naturalists prevail, we then have the following educational consequences: a disinclination for abstract premises and ideals, and a tendency toward experimentalism; emphasis on the changing character of civilization; a tendency to adapt education to the immediate needs of the individual and of society; and emphasis on education as growth for the sake of more growth, with a consequent aversion to any definition of aims.

If the idealists prevail, we then find a general sympathy

---

[1] For a more thorough discussion of different ethical schools we refer to R. B. Perry, *Present Philosophical Tendencies; A Critical Survey of Naturalism, Idealism, Pragmatism, and Realism, together with a Synopsis of the Philosophy of William James* (1929). The influence of different philosophic schools on education has been dealt with by R. C. Lodge in his book on *Philosophy of Education* (1937) and, from a different point of view, by Norman Woelfel in his *Molders of the American Mind, a Critical Review of the Social Attitudes of Seventeen Leaders in American Education* (1933).

for the following principles: the necessity of persistent objectives and standards and of introducing the young to the transpersonal aspects of civilization, and emphasis on the values of discipline and authority for guiding growth in the right directions.

It is not difficult to imagine the general purport of these differing views for educational practice and for the whole concept of culture. They have been the subject of a rather heated discussion among educators for several centuries, paralleling similar controversies in the field of abstract philosophy; and, in these days of cultural unrest, there is an increasing concern with them.

About the reasons for the failure of the older tradition to maintain its prevalence in the field of education we shall have to speak later in more detail. It may suffice here to state that since the beginning of the twentieth century in all Western countries progressive educators—to take this term in its broadest sense—have criticized the curriculum, the ways and aims of the older schools. Whereas in other countries the criticism had its source just as much in neo-idealistic thinking and the revival of Pestalozzian ideas as in empiricism, the progressivists of the United States felt themselves particularly committed to a form of empirical thought which is best characterized by the term pragmatism. It is therefore imperative to discuss its ethical views, so far as they bear on education, in some detail.

For this purpose we refer to William James's famous Lowell Lectures, published under the title of *Lectures on Pragmatism*.[1] But before we do so, one qualifying remark is necessary. The work of James is not completely unified

---

[1] Longmans, Green.

or consistent.[1] In first discussing here his *Lectures on Pragmatism*, we do not thereby intend to give a complete account of his thought. On the contrary, later on we will show how much injustice would be done to the genius of this great American thinker if his most popular and least profound book were exploited as the exclusive source of his ideas.

Pragmatism, according to James's lectures, claims to be a theory in its own right, or better, a "method." As such it is not comparable to those religious and philosophic attempts to provide an explanation of life and a direction, in the sense of a *Weltanschauung*, or world view. Pragmatism, according to James, is radical empiricism, but not naturalism. He says, in the lectures on *Pragmatism:* "There is absolutely nothing new in the pragmatic method." It represents "the empiricist attitude." "At the same time it does not stand for any special results. It is a method only." "It has no dogmas, and no doctrines save its methods." "No particular results then, so far, but only an attitude of orientation, is what the pragmatic method means. The attitude of looking away from first things, principles, 'categories,' supposed necessities; and of looking toward last things, fruits, consequences, facts."

It is completely anthropocentric, for which reason the rather vague term "humanism" has also been applied to it. It is critical, in the Kantian sense, in so far as it does not admit the capacity of reason to attain real truth. But while Kant, with his more rational and intellectual attitude, believes in the capacity of reason to attain a certain clarity about its function, pragmatism denies even this possibility. "That is Mr. Schiller's [a leading pragmatic

[1] Compare R. B. Perry, *In the Spirit of William James*, pp. 206 ff.

philosopher's] belief about the sensible core of reality. We encounter it but don't possess it. Superficially this sounds like Kant's view; but between categories fulminated before nature's presence, the whole chasm between rationalism and empiricism yawns. To the genuine Kantianer Schiller will always be to Kant as a satyr to Hyperion." Everything, according to James, exists for me only in so far as it is related to my psyche and is true only in so far as it proves to be of real value *for me*, or as "*it works*" according to my expectations and assumptions. "The pragmatic method is to try to interpret each notion by tracing its respective practical consequences." "But if you follow the pragmatic method, you cannot look on any such word as God, Matter, Reason, the Absolute, Energy, as closing your quest. You must bring out of each word its *practical cash-value*, set it at work within the stream of your experience."

Therefore, all thought is based on personal motives and interests, and pure thought in the sense of Hegel's idealism, let us say, does not exist. Reason does not produce facts; it only orders and classifies them. And if I say something is true, then I always do so on the basis of something more or other than reason; I do it on the basis of a feeling which emerges in me in conjunction with a special stage of my thinking and doing.

This way of reasoning, of course, gives another aspect to the problems of the theory of knowledge, and such conceptions as truth and error are given a meaning different from either the idealistic or the popular ones. The problem of thinking becomes not so much an epistemological as a psychological issue. Truth is neither the agreement of thought with reality nor a copy of an absolute thing-in-itself behind the appearance, but the real difference between a true opinion and a false opinion lies in their application. Conceptions are true if they work and false if they do not work.

As our judgments and convictions are simply guides for behavior, according to James, so our ethical conceptions cannot be said to have any permanent or ideal value; they signify something useful for our conduct. Consequently, the difference between judgments of fact and judgments of value and the difference between theoretical and practical reason disappears. The words "true" and "real" signify disguised forms of value in the sense of usefulness, and the word "good" signifies a disguised form of something which proves to be true because it proves to be useful. It is evident here how much James unconsciously justified Nietzsche's attack upon the alleged utilitarian distortion of the primordial ethical concepts.[1]

In consequence of these presuppositions our religious convictions also cannot claim to say anything about a transcendent and absolute world; they are true for me in so far as they are useful, just as it is more useful to believe in freedom of will than in determinism. The latter cripples my activity; the first gives wings to it. Therefore, the faith attitude, or the "will to believe," a phrase which James later wanted to change to the "right to believe," is a vehicle of progress. The materialist must be blamed, not because he is wrong, but because he is unproductive—or, at least, not so useful as the idealist, who may be wrong but who, nevertheless, can claim that he provides the necessary fuel for the engines of progress.[2]

---

[1] Compare Chapter I, section C.

[2] Several critical "rationalists" of the eighteenth century, also on the basis of empiricism, come to exactly the contrary opinion.

At this point James, against his own initial assertion of the merely methodological character of pragmatism, has trespassed the border between a mere "method" and a "philosophy," in the sense of Weltanschauung. He himself says: "The alternative between pragmatism and rationalism, in the shape in which we now have it before us, is no longer a question in the theory of knowledge; it concerns the structure of the universe itself." "On the pragmatist side we have only one edition of the universe, unfinished, growing in all sorts of places, especially in the places where thinking beings are at work." "On the rationalist side we have a universe in many editions, one real one, the infinite folio, or edition de luxe, eternally complete; and then the various finite editions, full of false readings, distorted and mutilated each in its own way." "Does our act then create the world's salvation so far as it makes room for itself, so far as it leaps into the gap? Does it create not the whole world's salvation of course, but just so much of this as itself covers of the world's extent?" James answers: "Here I take the bull by the horns, and in spite of the whole crew of rationalists and monists, of whatever brand they be, I ask *why not?*"

Nevertheless, "pragmatism can be called religious, if you allow that religion can be pluralistic or merely melioristic in type." "I believe rather that we stand in much the same relation to the whole of the universe as our canine and feline pets do to the whole of human life. They inhabit our drawing rooms and libraries. They take part in scenes of whose significance they have no inkling. They are merely tangent to curves of history the beginnings and ends and forms of which pass wholly beyond their ken. So we are tangents to the wider life of things. But, just as many of the dog's and cat's ideals coincide with our ideals, and the dogs and cats have daily living proof of the fact, so we may well believe, on the proofs that religious experience affords, that higher powers exist and are at work to save the world on ideal lines similar to our own."

Is this agnosticism? The answer to the question depends upon the definition of the term. An orthodox Christian would call it so. A critical thinker might say that there is a glimmer of hope in the comparison of our religious experiences with the dog's and cat's ideals—though he might find the comparison not particularly happy and certainly not very enlightening, since our knowledge of the "dog's and the cat's ideals" is rather limited.

Let us now pass from a more descriptive treatment of James's pragmatism to a critical analysis.

As Josiah Royce, the idealistic friend and colleague of James, has stated in his *Philosophy of Loyalty* [1]—a book that ought to be just as popular as James's *Pragmatism*—"modern pragmatism is not indeed as original as it seems to suppose itself to be in emphasizing such views. The whole history of modern idealism is full of such assertions." We saw that James also made no claim to novelty, but Royce could rightly have referred to other pragmatic writers. He could have added that the pragmatic understanding of truth can be found even in an old Indian philosophic text,[2] which says that a truthful opinion is one that is able to create a successful endeavor. On the scroll of George Washington's arms we find the motto *Exitus acta probat* ("The end proves the deeds"), which he or his

---

[1] Page 325.

[2] E. Hultzsch, *Die Tartakaumudi des Laugakshi Bhaskara.* Zeitschrift der Deutschen Morgenlaendischen Gesellschaft. 1907. Vol. LXI, p. 773.

family probably took from an ancient author. And he who prefers to resort to common sense may quote the old adage that the proof of the pudding is in the eating, and, generally speaking, what there is good in common opinion is the precipitate of a long series of successes and failures.

Moreover, nobody can doubt that there is a practical attitude and a desire for verification on the basis of facts to be found in all truth seeking. We not only modify our opinions but, for ethical reasons, are bound to modify them when they no longer serve to guide us through the dangers of reality.

In addition, we grant James, in contradiction to some idealistic philosophies, that truth is not an independent and real thing or substance, but a value attached to judgments. A judgment or an opinion, as such, acquires for us the character of truth only in so far as it is evaluated and "found to be" true.

On the other hand, in his *Pragmatism* James omits any classification of truth such as the science of logic has developed. What is, for instance, the relation of the formal side of mathematical truth to the empirical truth of which he constantly speaks? But though an analysis of these issues that James fails to mention would have much bearing on the validity of his pragmatic standpoint, it would lead us too far into theoretical considerations. We shall do better to consider the more practical and ethical issue.

In the beginning of his lectures James makes a sharp distinction between "first things" and "last things." But can the last things, or the fruits, of which James speaks be so easily dissociated from the seeds, and what we think of as the essence of life from what we accomplish, or reversely? James also does not give us any answer to the troublesome question as to whether in our strivings for truth and goodness, or for any kind of self-perfecting, we are only trying to meet the ever-changing tasks and contingencies of life or whether we are approximating something with a more permanent value than just the fulfillment of a merely personal ambition.

However much pragmatism may emphasize the usefulness of ideals, the category of usefulness alone does not include all of the aims for which the human mind is laboring, or all of the motives for our strivings. We assume that "truth is itself a cause," and goodness, love, and honesty, too. Is this questioning power within us, which we call our conscience, really nothing but an indicator of success or failure? Or is it evidence of a relation of man to criteria which cannot be subordinated to merely utilitarian concepts, but depend upon a sphere of responsibilities that we never comprehend completely but to which, nevertheless, we feel ourselves committed—even if we do not have success in terms of "cash value"? Is Kant, whose energy of critical analysis no serious thinker will ever deny, really nothing but a dreamer when he says at the end of his *Critique of Practical Reason:* "Two facts fill our soul with ever new and increasing admiration and reverence, the oftener and the more constantly they occupy our mind: the starry sky above me, and moral law within me"?

Another question arises: If the test of "how a thing works" decides about its truth and value, why must the criterion, as James seemingly supposes, include an altruistic as well as an egoistic interest? James would answer: "Because we believe in each other's experiences and because it is profitable for the human being to take into account his character and dependency as a social being."

Yes, but sometimes it is more convenient to forget this and to follow one's own interest against that of the group. What interest, then, decides? Furthermore, when can we know that an experiment has worked, if the success is revealed not immediately, or at least in our own lifetime, but only when generations have passed? The time factor, in other words, offers to pragmatism just as difficult a riddle as the social criterion.

It is the emphasis on change, on testing through experience, and on the pluralistic character of life that also pervades Dewey's famous early work, of the year 1916, *Democracy and Education*,[1] probably the most effective effort to transfer some principles of pragmatism and experimentalism into the actual practice of the school.

According to this work, education is largely identical with growth and development. Development is possible because man possesses plasticity, or "the capacity to retain and carry over from prior experience factors which modify subsequent activities. This signifies the capacity to acquire habits, or develop definite dispositions."[2] These dispositions enable man to exercise "an active control of the environment through control of the organs of action."[3] "The significance of habit is not exhausted, however, in its executive and motor phase. It means formation of intellectual and emotional disposition as well as an increase in ease, economy, and efficiency of action. Any habit makes an *inclination*—an active preference or choice for the conditions involved in its exercise."[4] "Above all, the intellectual element in a habit fixes the relation of the habit to varied and elastic use, and hence to continued

[1] Macmillan.   [2] Page 54.   [3] Page 55.   [4] Page 57.

growth.[1] Therefore, "since in reality there is nothing to which growth is relative save more growth, there is nothing to which education is subordinate save more education." [2]

With respect to this emphasis on growth we must say that it also is not entirely novel in the history of education. Education has been conceived of as growth by such men as Comenius, Rousseau, and Pestalozzi; and even Herbart, the preferred target of progressivism, writes in his *Science of Education:* [3]

How can the teacher assume for himself beforehand the merely *possible* future aims of the pupil?

The objective of these aims as matter of mere choice has absolutely no interest for the teacher. Only the Will of the future man himself, and consequently the sum of the claims which he, in, and with, this Will, will make on himself, is the object of the teacher's *goodwill;* while the power, the initiative inclination, the activity which the future man will have wherewith to meet these claims on himself, form for the teacher matter for consideration and judgment in accordance with the idea of *perfection*. Thus it is not a certain number of separate aims that hover before us now (for these we could not beforehand thoroughly know), but chiefly the *activity* of the growing man—the totality of his inward unconditioned vitality and susceptibility. The greater this totality—*the fuller, more expanded, and harmonious*—the greater is the perfection and the greater the promise of the realisation of our good will.

[1] Page 57.   [2] Page 60.   [3] Heath, 1896. Page 110.

But all great educators have agreed on one point, a point which Dewey also admits in the practical part of his *Democracy and Education* by reference to democracy as the best form of social co-operation. This point of agreement is that growth and education must have an aim. If, in accordance with a merely relativistic interpretation of pragmatism, one sees in man's conduct primarily the effects of habits that have constantly to be modified with respect to ever-changing experiences, then, in critical situations, we can only set habits against habits or experiences against experiences. But where, if this is true, can we find the criterion for making a decision?

We gladly admit that the typical educator under the old "idealistic" system of thought often set up for youth fixed and immovable aims, that he did not ask whether they were suitable both to the nature and to the growth of the particular individual and of a changing society, and that his definition of aims was a narrow pedagogical one. This merely shows that he had succumbed to the temptation of all human beings to allow the stream of mental and moral energy to freeze instead of retaining an unceasing impetus. But against this peril relativism is just as little a safeguard as idealism. For persons who are inclined to a premature crystallization of their ideas are even more likely to escape into fixed habits and dogmas if they see themselves exposed to a world with no other principle than that of chance and change, because such a world offers insecurity without direction, lacks the challenge of a great ideal, and offers the principle of "utility" with its lure to thoughtless acquiescence. Here is the fundamental mistake in the pragmatist's "most charming philosophical fury," as Josiah Royce would call it,[1] against the assumption of persistent intellectual and moral truths. Radical pragmatism is too easily inclined to suppose that an aim is a "static" aim, a form an "external" form, and an ideal a "superimposed" ideal. But is not an aim rooted in and transcending the individual something with the paradoxical quality that it grows greater and more distant the more we seem to approximate it? And it does so for the very reason of its being in focus and, nevertheless, transcendent, "higher than" anything we can ever achieve. So it is with a real scholar's idea of truth, with the Christian principle of love, and with an artist's devotion to beauty.

This understanding of the nature of aims also helps to resolve the dilemma of "pluralism" and "monism" which has so intensely troubled the pragmatic philosophers as well as their adversaries. Of course, he who forgets the pluralistic character of the universe, in that he tries to press the buoyancy and abundance of its appearances into a narrow channel of thought, violates the richness of its potentialities and sins by setting up a narrow principle against the greater principle of development. On the other hand, he who does not dare to give this development a uniting and far-reaching meaning which ever transcends the immediate deprives the individual or the nation of faith and hinders the progress that he wants to foster. Progress and its prerequisites—growth, tolerance, and open-mindedness—need as their complement the power of direction. For lack of an inherent ordering and at the same time continuously transcending energy, movement, and enthusiasm, so necessary for healthy development,

[1] *Philosophy of Loyalty*, p. 323.

begin to absolutize themselves and remain static in the foregrounds of life, as all human attachment is bound to do which no longer sees the criticism and challenge of eternity in the objects of its love. This explains why, from periods of an exceeding richness of energy, actual and potential, there so often emerges, not the blessings of liberty, but a Janus-head, with one face that of inner anarchy and the other that of tyranny and dictatorship.

The danger springing from the incapacity of a merely experimental philosophy to give life far-reaching impetus and direction has not escaped such minds as James's and Dewey's. Both thinkers, to be sure, may be criticized for their lack of a consistent system of ethics which would bind their empiricism and the sometimes hidden metaphysical premises of their thought into a coherent rational unity. And it is due to this lack that under the colors of pragmatism there march today naturalists and relativists, just as well as conscious or unconscious idealists. But if one wants to fight against merely relativistic or naturalistic forms of pragmatism, he can find the most effective support in James and Dewey themselves.

In his essays "The Will to Believe" and "Is Life Worth Living?" and in many other of his shorter writings, James testifies to his acceptance of the right to believe, not only in a world of ever-changing situations, but in a reasonable order of the universe and in the permanency of moral values. In an article on "German Pessimism" [1] he speaks of the contradictions of our existence and concludes as follows:

[1] *Collected Essays and Reviews.* Longmans, Green. Pages 17–18 and 18–19.

Common-sense contents itself with the unreconciled contradiction, laughs when it can, and weeps when it must, and makes, in short, a practical compromise, without trying a theoretical solution. This attitude is of course respectable. But if one must needs have an ultimate theoretical solution, nothing is more certain than this, that no one need assent to that of pessimism unless he freely prefer to do so. Concerning the metaphysical world, or the ultimate meaning of things, there is no outward evidence—nothing but conceptions of the possible. Distinct among these is that of a moral order whose life *may* be fed by the contradictions of good and evil that occur in the external phenomenal order. Those empiricists who are celebrating nowadays with such delight the novel mathematical notion of a fourth or "transcendental" dimension in space, should be the last persons to dogmatize against the possibility of a deeper dimension in *being* than the flat surface-pattern which is offered by its pleasures and pains, taken merely as such. Now if such an order in the world is possibly true, and if, supposing it to be true, it may afford the basis for an ultimate optimism (quite distinct from mere nerveless sentimentalism), there is no reason which should deter a person bent on having some commanding theory of life from adopting it as his hypothesis or working faith. . . .

Now, a hypothetical door like that offered by the notion of a ransoming moral order "behind the veil" is better than no loophole of escape; and to refuse to give one's self the benefit of its presence argues either a perfectly morbid appetite for dogmatic forms of thought, or an astounding lack of genuine sense for the tragic, which sense undoubtedly varies, like every other, from man to man.

With transcendental optimism, on the other hand, it is just the reverse. If it is *true*, why, then, there is the deepest internal congruity in its *not* being mechanically forced on our belief. As a fatalistic *nolens-volens* creed, it would be devoid of all moral character. Or rather we may not talk of its *being* true, but *becoming* true. Its full verification must be contingent on our complicity, both theoretical and practical. All that it asserts is that the facts of the world are a fit basis for the *summum bonum*, if we do our share and react upon them as it is meant we should (with fortitude, for example, and undismayed hope). The world is thus absolutely good only in a potential or hypothetic sense, and the hypothetic form of the optimistic belief is the very signature of its consistency and first condition of its probability. At the final integration of things, the world's goodness will be an accomplished fact and self-evident, but, till then, faith is the only legitimate attitude of mind it can claim from us.

With these considerations, we are no longer in the realm of mere "method." The religion expressed in it is not "pluralistic or merely melioristic in type." In order to accept it we must assume—with the great medieval mystic Master Eckhart—a "divine spark" in us which distinguishes our relation to the universe not only in degree but also in quality from that of our canine and feline pets to their masters, though millions of humans live in such miserable conditions and under such persecution that they might envy these pets their security in comfortable "drawing rooms and libraries."

There is one passage in James's work that may help us to understand more clearly what pragmatism, without trespassing its due limits, can rightly mean—the limits, that is, as James himself says at the beginning of his Lowell Lectures, of "a method only," which is willing always to give up the results gained in one field if the next step of research shows their inadequacy. This passage is to be found in the Epilogue to "Psychology and Philosophy" at the end of his *Psychology*,[1] and bears the title "What the Word Metaphysic Means."

In the last chapter, we handed the question of free-will over to "metaphysics." It would indeed have been hasty to settle the question absolutely, inside the limits of psychology. Let psychology frankly admit that *for her scientific purposes* determinism may be *claimed*, and no one can find fault. If, then, it turn out later that the claim has only a relative purpose, and may be crossed by counter-claims, the readjustment can be made. Now ethics makes a counter-claim; and the present writer, for one, has no hesitation in regarding her claim as the stronger, and in assuming that our wills are "free." For him, then, the deterministic assumption of psychology is merely provisional and methodological. This is no place to argue the ethical point; and I only mention the conflict to show that all these special sciences, marked

[1] *Psychology. Briefer Course.* Holt, 1892. Page 461.

off for convenience from the remaining body of truth
. . . must hold their assumptions and results subject
to revision in the light of each other's needs. The
forum where they hold discussion is called metaphysics. Metaphysics means only an unusually obstinate
attempt to think clearly and consistently. The special
sciences all deal with data that are full of obscurity and
contradiction; but from the point of view of their limited purposes these defects may be overlooked. Hence
the disparaging use of the name metaphysics which is
so common. To a man with a limited purpose any discussion that is over-subtle for that purpose is branded
as "metaphysical." A geologist's purposes fall short
of understanding Time itself. A mechanist need not
know how action and reaction are possible at all. A
psychologist has enough to do without asking how
both he and the mind which he studies are able to
take cognizance of the same outer world. But it is
obvious that problems irrelevant from one standpoint
may be essential from another. And as soon as one's
purpose is the attainment of the maximum of possible
insight into the world as a whole, the metaphysical
puzzles become the most urgent ones of all. Psychology contributes to general philosophy her full share of
these.

The contrast is immediately apparent between these
words and James's statement in the Lowell Lectures that
pragmatism concerns "the structure of the universe itself" and that it requires a "universe, unfinished, growing
in all sorts of places." For the scientist who follows James's
demand at the end of his *Psychology* and turns from his

study of causal determinism to metaphysics and the question of free will is no longer satisfied only with the empirical "edition of the universe" which is "unfinished" and "growing in all sorts of places." In turning to metaphysics, as "an unusually obstinate attempt to think clearly and consistently," he is hoping to find not another unfinished universe in addition to the one he already has as an empiricist but a more unified and uniting principle. And however much, as a good scientist, he recognizes that he will never reach the end of his endeavors, he nevertheless supposes that he can approximate something that is no longer merely "pluralistic" in character, but that approaches a "monistic" explanation of the riddles of the "one" and the "many."

The philosophizing, metaphysically interested, and empirical psychologist, who, according to James, is the only radical thinker, is, consequently, a pragmatist and pluralist in the empirical foreground of his thought; but he does not acquiesce in this situation but goes into an ordering sphere beyond this foreground. James himself does this constantly, as does every real thinker in whatever field he works. It is in the very nature of science and one of its strongest motivating forces to search for ever higher and higher unities behind the plurality of appearances. In this respect science does not differ from religion. The great difference is that man, in his role as scientist, moves toward a higher unity tentatively and rationally, while in his religious role he must experience intuitively the ultimate logos behind or within the phenomena accessible to human reason. Consequently, such terms as those used by James in his Lowell Lectures—the "one" and the "many" editions of the universe, the "real and the infinite folios," the "edition de luxe" and the "pragmatic" edition—such terms are, by the implications involved in James's own thinking, compatible and not mutually exclusive. In any deeper scientific or philosophical pursuit we have before us the pluralistic and unfinished universe, but we try to pierce through this foreground in the direction of an ideal sphere of verities.

Dewey also sets himself in contrast to those who are inclined to interpret his early concepts of growth and experience, as expressed in *Democracy and Education*, in the sense of mere self-preservation or relativistic adaptation. With increasing emphasis he has pointed at the necessity incumbent upon our rather chaotic society of defining the aims to be held in view rather than leaving them simply to chance. Probably under the impact of the breakdown of democratic government in Europe and all of its consequences, he speaks of a "moral foundation," of a "law of life," and of "friendship, beauty, and knowledge" as the great vehicles of social progress. In his article on "Education and Social Change" in *The Social Frontier*,[1] he says:

> No social change is more than external unless it is attended by and rooted in the attitudes of those who bring it about and those who are affected by it. In a genuine sense social change is accidental unless it has a psychological and moral foundation. . . . The trouble, at least one great trouble, is that we have taken democracy for granted; we have thought and acted as if our forefathers had founded it once for all. We have forgotten that it has to be enacted anew in every generation. . . . Democracy also means voluntary choice

[1] May, 1937.

based on an intelligence that is the outcome of free association and communication with others. It means a way of living together in which mutual and free consultation rules instead of force, and in which cooperation, instead of brutal competition, is the law of life; a social order in which all forces that make for friendship, beauty, and knowledge are cherished in order that each individual may become what he, and he alone, is capable of becoming.

The metaphysical element in pragmatism comes to light also if we examine Dewey's religious philosophy, as expressed in *A Common Faith*,[1] a book which is comparable to James's "The Will to Believe." The following passages are to the point:

In his fascinating book, *The Dawn of Conscience*, James Henry Breasted refers to Haeckel as saying that the question he would most wish to have answered is this: Is the universe friendly to man? The question is an ambiguous one. Friendly to man in what respect? With respect to ease and comfort, to material success, to egoistic ambitions? Or to his aspiration to inquire and discover, to invent and create, to build a more secure order for human existence? In whatever form the question be put, the answer cannot in all honesty be an unqualified and absolute one. Mr. Breasted's answer, as a historian, is that nature has been friendly to the emergence and development of conscience and character. Those who will have all or nothing cannot be satisfied with this answer.

[1] Yale University Press, 1934. Pages 55, 56, and 85.

Emergence and growth are not enough for them. They want something more than growth accompanied by toil and pain. They want final achievement. Others who are less absolutist may be content to think that, morally speaking, growth is a higher value and ideal than sheer attainment. They will remember also that growth has not been confined to conscience and character; that it extends also to discovery, learning and knowledge, to creation in the arts, to furtherance of ties that hold men together in mutual aid and affection. These persons at least will be satisfied with an intellectual view of the religious function that is based on continuing choice directed toward ideal ends.

The considerations put forth in the present chapter may be summed up in what they imply. The ideal ends to which we attach our faith are not shadowy and wavering. They assume concrete forms in our understanding of our relations to one another and the values contained in these relations. We who now live are parts of a humanity that extends into the remote past, a humanity that has interacted with nature. The things in civilization that we most prize are not of ourselves. They exist by grace of the doings and sufferings of the continuous human community in which we are a link. Ours is the responsibility of conserving, transmitting, rectifying and expanding the heritage of values we have received that those who come after us may receive it more solid and secure, more widely accessible and more generously shared than we have received it. Here are all the elements for a religious faith that shall not be confined to sect, class, or race. Such a faith has always been implicitly the common faith of mankind. It remains to be made explicit and militant.

Let us finally consider some points in Dewey's recent work on problems of schooling, *Experience and Education*, published in 1938.[1] This book shows perhaps more clearly than any of his other utterances his point of view concerning the relationship of education to the problem of ethics. In spite of all asseverations pointing to the contrary, he has remained the old and not always unbiased fighter against "traditional education" and neglects obvious facts in denying the intimate and necessary relationship of the older forms of education to consistently developed philosophies of education.[2] As a matter of fact, it is the strength of these older forms that they were the very expression of consistent philosophies and that they had clear principles of selection—namely, the Christian, the idealist, and the humanist—and that they were also, for the most part, the outgrowth of rather rigid aspects of a social order.[3] One may doubt whether Dewey's assertion that the "new education" is "in harmony with principles of growth"[4] is sufficient evidence that this new education is, in respect to philosophical foundations, in a position preferable to that of the traditional systems. On the contrary, the very ones who gladly admit that progressive education has many incontestable merits may rightly be longing for a uniting *Weltanschauung* behind it and for more commonly accepted criteria of selection of subject matter and method. Dewey himself states that "conservatives as well

---

[1] Macmillan.
[2] Page 18.
[3] Compare Chapter IV, sections A and B.
[4] Page 20.

as radicals in education are profoundly discontented with the present educational situation taken as a whole,"[1] and it seems to be his main intention in *Experience and Education* to convince his followers that the principles of growth and experimentation, in order to provide a satisfactory theoretical and practical basis, must be connected with selective and organizing ideas. These ideas, of course, must be derived from faith in certain values essential for the sustenance of a dignified and general human civilization. Otherwise, we would have difficulty in explaining sentences of Dewey's to the effect that "freedom of outer movement is a *means*, not an end," or that "every experience is a moving force" the value of which "can be judged only on the ground of what it moves toward and into."[2] And even if we may be inclined to think that Dewey, in this as in other books, defends too intellectual a concept of ethics in stating that "the only freedom that is of enduring importance is freedom of intelligence,"[3] nevertheless we can hardly doubt that in this, his latest book on education, Dewey's pragmatism is, in spite of all disinclination against a metaphysical foundation of ethics, opposed to mere relativistic or naturalistic moral philosophies.

If we ask whence comes the aversion to older forms of idealism which James and Dewey express in certain phases of their thinking, the answer must be based on grounds largely historical. When these two men appeared on the philosophical scene in this country, an obsolete idealism, contrary to the general scientific development and abandoned decades earlier in other countries, prevailed. We do not mean by this the philosophy of Ralph Waldo Emerson,

[1] Page 113.
[2] Pages 70 and 28-29.
[3] Page 69.

which is the confession of a great mind not properly belonging to scientific philosophy, nor the philosophy of Josiah Royce. The case becomes clear if we refer to Dewey's own description of the philosophical and educational impressions of his youth.[1]

> Teachers of philosophy [he says] were at that time, almost to a man, clergymen; the supposed requirements of religion, or theology, dominated the teaching of philosophy in most colleges. . . . It is probably impossible to recover at this date the almost sacrosanct air that enveloped the idea of intuitions; but somehow the cause of all holy and valuable things was supposed to stand or fall with the validity of intuitionalism; the only vital issue was that between intuitionalism and a sensational empiricism that explained away the reality of all higher objects.

The leading authority in philosophy and education in this country was at that time William T. Harris, who, according to his own words, read Hegel's *Philosophy of History* seventeen times. This is undoubtedly a great document in the field of cultural thought, but it was already outmoded when Harris read it so often. In the mind of Harris education was primarily the adaptation of youth to a society with rather fixed conceptions of aims and values. Though a man of undoubted merits and of ideas progressive for his time, Harris thought of the curriculum as a co-ordination of strictly departmentalized disciplines that had nothing to do with one another. What is still more remarkable is the fact that the work of Karl Rosenkranz

---

[1] *Contemporary American Philosophy*. Edited by George P. Adams and W. P. Montague. Macmillan, 1930. Vol. II, p. 15.

enjoyed great repute in the circle around Harris; this was a dry and dogmatic attempt to transfer Hegel's system to the field of education, employing particularly the schematic and formal elements of his philosophy. Rosenkranz's philosophy had already been refuted by the Herbartian school in Germany in the first half of the nineteenth century.

It is natural that under these conditions the new pragmatism, particularly in the field of education, should emphasize growth, experimentation, and empiricism in contrast to fixedness, dogmatism, and a priori theorizing. It is also natural that in contrast to the esoteric and sacerdotal style of Hegel and Fichte and the sometimes too enthusiastic style of Emerson and his friends a more sober and realistic conception of philosophy and of the nature of culture and civilization should arise.

But sufficient time has passed since the beginnings of pragmatism for us to attain a wider perspective. And during this time we have been given great historical experiences calculated to make us doubtful of the blessings of pure dynamic forces with purely practical directing principles. Pragmatism itself has turned from a polemical to a more comprehensive attitude. It deserves to be seen in its totality.

If we judge pragmatism from this more detached point of view, we see that it is a complex cultural movement. Doubtless it has within it elements of relativism and utilitarianism, but in spite of these elements it has never become materialism or skepticism. Even behind the relativistic and agnostic elements of James's Lowell Lectures and Dewey's *Democracy and Education* is a deep faith in a reasonable world order. The typical American pragmatist often shows a confidence in the eternally productive power of growth which reveals in its very unconsciousness of itself a genuine strength. For only the deepest foundations of a personality escape the critical probe of philosophic self-examination. One could venture the paradox that Hegel, because of his radical and ceaseless attention to the problem, felt more doubt about the reasonableness of the universe than either James or Dewey. What distinguishes the latter from the German idealist is not lack of faith in the necessity of realization of spirit in the world but their very understandable disinclination for the Hegelian arrogance of striving to know the most intimate secrets of the ultimate energy behind the pluralistic phenomena of the world. Once their spheres of competence are clearly defined, there is room both for pragmatism, as an attitude necessary for dealing with an ever-changing environment, and for critical idealism, as the belief in eternal intellectual and moral verities.

In general mood and attitude the philosophers of American pragmatism belong to the philosophic tradition whose first great representative was Leibnitz, and which gave the main impetus to the rise of liberalism and progressivism in the modern era. If one should try to suggest the driving spirit behind American pragmatism, an adequate term would be "Directionalism," for the reason that it is dynamic rather than static and believes in immanent rules which give the dynamic process of life meaning and direction. This belief, as a matter of fact, brings pragmatism closer to idealism than to skepticism and materialism, and it may well be that in a hundred years the historians of philosophy will describe William James, John Dewey, and their friends as thinkers who, in a technical and experimental age, tried to replace the more aprioristic, older idealism with a new kind of empirical idealism.

But what is the need then, so the reader might object, for this whole discussion? The answer is that the interpretation of pragmatism, as the leading empirical philosophy in the American democracy, in either a more naturalistic and relativistic or a more idealistic sense, is of greatest bearing on both modern education and the future of democratic civilization. The belief that we have no criteria for our actions but action and no criteria for our experiences but new experiences may be well suited, indeed, to the democratic way of life if we have nothing else in view than its willingness to adapt itself to changing situations and to learn from experimentation. But such a philosophy is incomplete; it does not tell us how and why and where in this continuous change we have the right to set up freedom, friendship, responsibility, beauty, and reason as regulating principles just as necessary for a democracy as change and experiment.

One might answer that the results of our action and habits show us that freedom and other virtues provide a better basis for new experiences than the contrary and that, consequently, we should allow ourselves to be conditioned and form habits in this direction. But if, in accordance with relativistic forms of pragmatism or with behaviorism, the aims of this conditioning process are held to be nothing but a kind of external consensus of opinion resulting merely from our "milieu," then these aims can always be modified or completely rejected according to any changes in the environment. In consequence, democracy would have no essential values independent of any external contingencies that may compel us to change its modes of operation and our "habits" of traditional political or economic thinking. Being but the result of circumstance and habits, it may be overthrown by those with the power to do so whenever it ceases to be conducive to their special interests.

But let us pass from philosophical abstractions to the more colorful field of history, which is the greatest experimental laboratory we possess. It is difficult to refrain from reference to recent events in Europe, but we do so because, as contemporaries, we may still lack the necessary degree of perspective.

There is, however, the example of the French Revolution. Of course, it took more than the philosophers to prepare for it. Like every violent political change, it was preceded by failures of the ruling class and the hatred of the exploited. But the spirit of the French Revolution was decisively influenced by certain philosophies of the eighteenth century which resemble modern behaviorism and utilitarianism, the philosophies of such men as Mandeville, Lamettrie, and Helvetius.

Stephen d'Irsay, former professor of the history of sciences at Johns Hopkins University, in his *Histoire des Universités, françaises et étrangères*,[1] describes the educational consequences arising from the regime of the empiricists and the utilitarian revolutionaries.

We come now [he says] to the government of the Consulate [1799]. The judgment of Chaptal, one of

[1] Published by Picard. Vol. II, p. 157; author's translation.

the leaders of the Revolution, is startling: Public education is eradicated almost everywhere; the generation growing toward its twentieth year is irrevocably
sacrificed to ignorance. Why? Because for ten years
no one has thought of anything except practical appli-
cations for the immediate service of the state . . . no
one has thought of the great and profound mission of
public instruction with respect to morality. The idea
of usefulness is easily perceivable; practical applica-
tions are quickly understood and assimilated. They
are within the reach of everybody. But the subtle
network of ideas which are the moral and intellectual
substance of mankind, whether or not they have to
do with utility, is too easily forgotten by a rapidly
changing society, partly because of prejudices, partly
because of lack of experience. The same process is
going on in our present times.

There is, of course, the danger that Stephen d'Irsay's
judgment of the French Revolution is one-sided, especially since, from his particular philosophic point of view,
he may convey the impression that the whole spirit of the
Age of Enlightenment was primarily destructive. Empiricism and even materialism in the eighteenth century
had their mission: they had to fight against reaction and
superstition combined. Stephen d'Irsay is too disposed
to absolve absolutism and ecclesiasticism of the sins of
omission and commission which finally drove the country into the radicalism of the Revolution. In addition,
these revolutionaries were not simply shallow utilitarians.
The wars of the young republic against the Continental
monarchies revealed great moral enthusiasm. In no other

political upheaval, with the possible exception of that of the English Commonwealth, was there so much serious concern with the awakening of a new morality.[1] And in spite of all its horrors, the French Revolution paved the way for a new form of social organization which, if not absolutely better than the old one, was at least more adequate to the necessities of the eighteenth and nineteenth centuries. The year 1789 had a liberating influence both on politics and the human spirit.

But, in spite of a certain bias, Stephen d'Irsay's criticism of the French Revolution contains much truth, and we have referred to it particularly because it enables us, by the analysis of concrete historical facts, to understand the bearing of certain philosophies on the actual life of nations. It is not the empirical attitude itself that deserves to be criticized, as d'Irsay seems to believe. Sound emphasis on observation and experiment has never harmed humanity. Nor is skepticism of "fixed" values and "ideologies" to be blamed, since a good portion of this mental stimulant is to be found in all great periods from the time of Socrates and that of Christ, through the beginnings of Scholasticism, down to modern times. If we ask what was the failure of thought at the time of the French Revolution, we must answer that it was lack of insight into the universality of man's life, the tendency to submit it to narrow categories of immediate applicability. It does not matter whether this tendency is revealed by a foreground of empiricism or of absolutism; and a wise man can prefer neither, especially since they generally

[1] Compare the "Rapports" given to the National Assembly or the "Débats législatifs" and the work by C. Hippeau, *L'Instruction publique en France pendant la révolution. Débats législatifs publiés et précédés d'une introduction. . . .* 1881.

work hand in hand to make life poorer. The dry and fanatic moralism of Robespierre, with its lack of understanding of the deeper forces in history and in man, was as dangerous as the superficial naturalism and utilitarianism of the French salons, perhaps, indeed, more dangerous. The latter could at least claim to have contributed to the destruction of superstition and prejudice, while Robespierre's moralism was a repetition of the Inquisition in terms of dogmatic, moralistic utilitarianism, eventuating in the militaristic dictatorship and the imperialism of Napoleon.

A tragical impression is given us by reading the description which Daunou, like Chaptal (one of the leaders of the French Revolution), has left of the outcome of the attempts made by the lower middle class of Paris to organize society into a faultlessly functioning and unimaginative machine. He says:[1]

> Finally, the frenzies of the public, the divagations of opinion, the quarrels of the parties, the wars of the factions, the continuous distractions of the mind, all this including the very intention to improve public education, necessarily interrupted progress and led to decadence.

The results of this historical experiment ought to give those who advocate a merely utilitarian understanding of education something to think about. This group confuses the means and the ends, the immediate practical outcome with the final meaning and ethical nature of an ac-

[1] C. Hippeau, *L'Instruction publique en France pendant la révolution.* 1881. Vol. I, p. 476.

tion. It has no basis for blaming anyone who raises his own interests or the interests he represents above all other considerations and makes the accomplishment and success of his activity the sole criterion for judging it. And how can those who possess most power, as the government and its leaders, be forbidden to give to their particular interests the character of a supreme law unless we recognize, to use the phrase of William James, "a deeper dimension in being than the flat surface-pattern which is offered by its pleasures and pains, taken merely as such," or, to use the words of Dewey, "ideal ends to which we attach our faith" and which, in spite of their idealistic character, are "not shadowy and wavering"?

B. THE QUEST FOR ETHICAL CRITERIA

However critical we may be of the relativistic forms of modern pragmatism, they are, nevertheless, the inevitable results of a long and historically necessary development. Since the Renaissance the empirical sciences and some schools of philosophy have shaken a central concept of earlier philosophies; namely, the notion that reason has the capacity, by following correct logical methods, of arriving at the ultimate principles of the universe and deducing from them the meaning of human destiny and the unchangeable rules of ethics. This doubt in the power of deductive reasoning was corroborated by anthropologists, explorers, and historians, who discovered astonishing differences in ethical standards among various races and in different historical periods, thus casting doubt upon the Aristotelian theory of the sameness of man and his experience regardless of differences in space and time.

These various movements of thought, enforced by

other influences, could not fail to undermine the belief in the divinely revealed and therefore absolute ethics of Christianity, based partly on the Decalogue and partly on the teachings of Christ. The result was a deep despair of the catholicity of our ethical concepts, our so-called modern crisis of values, which has long ceased to be simply a philosophic concern. It has led to a rather general skepticism which continues to draw vigor from its struggle with the absolutism of "fixed" values and a priori concepts of existence.

The philosophies of James and Dewey, among many other similar philosophies, are attempts to avoid an inveterate idealism, on the one hand, and a merely subjective relativism, on the other.

If we can now no longer accept the older idealistic forms of ethics and if modern pragmatism has not completely succeeded in its attempts to construct a coherent moral philosophy, must we resign ourselves to drifting like loose leaves before any chance wind? Does it follow that our ethical decisions are nothing but products of circumstances, of habits, or of laws enforced upon us by some ruling group? Did the great religious prophets and the idealistic philosophers do nothing but build comforting fantasies to help man to deceive himself about the ultimate meaninglessness of existence?

In order to answer these questions we must return to ideas elaborated in our chapter on psychology. For we hold that the ethical problem must be brought into harmony with the psychological nature of man. When we spoke of the vital urges that lie at the foundations of human personality and connect it with the stream of energy flowing through the cosmos, we arrived at the conclusion

that these urges contain the potentialities of moral tendencies. The latter, consequently, are objective in nature
and not arbitrary. They can, of course, be neglected, but
this results in the destruction of the psychic and often the
physical normality of the individual. Disregard of moral
impulsions is abnormal because it works against that normality which Goldstein, in his work on the structure of
the organism,[1] defines in the statement: "An organism
which actualizes its essential peculiarities or, what really
means the same thing, meets its adequate milieu and the
tasks arising from it, is 'normal.'"

In following our desire to protect our children, to defend what we love, to actualize ourselves in serving human society, we are not simply choosing one mode of behavior that we could easily change for another. On the
contrary, we are following the demands of our own nature.
But *our* nature, as we have already asserted, is not really
ours; in a much more total sense, it is Nature itself, natural forces flowing through us without our consent or will.
We do not possess them; they possess us. If we human
beings recognize such a thing as crime and use the word
to denote a specific act, then it refers to a man's tragi-
cally successful effort to actualize one isolated potentiality in himself and to obstruct, in this way, the flow of the
full stream of nature through his personality. Crime cannot, therefore, be sufficiently described by the use of ju-
ridical categories or the categories of social ethics. Crime
is offense against law or society only because it is first of
all offense against the constructive powers of life.

Here is to be found the deeper meaning of the religious
concept of "sin against God." For it would be mere an-

[1] Goldstein, K., *The Organism.* American Book Company, 1939. Page 427.

thropomorphism to believe that God could be "offended" by an offense against ourself or a fellow man unless He were thought of as the essence and the symbol of the productive energies of the universe and of man, who, as a part of it, bears a share of responsibility for the whole and sins in neglecting this responsibility. When St. Paul, to choose a particular example, says in the letter to the Romans that those who commit sin and "do not obey the truth, but obey unrighteousness, indignation, and wrath" will suffer "tribulation and anguish," there is behind these words a more universal concept than his specifically Christian one. Those who offend against a truth and law immanent in the cosmos exclude themselves from participation in the whole and must consequently suffer and cause others to suffer "anguish and tribulation."

It may seem strange that through the interpretation of such religious concepts we learn to understand the truth in pragmatism better than through its own self-explanation. Is it not clear that our ethical decisions, when in harmony with the constructive forces of the cosmos, prove most "useful" to us? But this usefulness is more than subjective usefulness—"for me," as James says in the Lowell Lectures, for this or that group, or within a given span of time. It is productivity in a cosmic and objective sense that cannot be covered by narrow personal categories and considerations. On the contrary, "for me" crime and sin may be "useful" in the sense of an immediate gain. But they are, nevertheless, sinful or, to use a less religious term, destructive, in that they offend against laws of nature working in the universe and in humanity as part of nature and the universe. It is in this way that we must understand the cruelly impersonal pronouncement of the Old Testament that the sins of the fathers shall be visited upon the children even to the third or fourth generation. Are not the "sins of the fathers" during the World War and the succeeding peace now visited upon their children and grandchildren?

Generally speaking, all human individuality has a tragical quality, since it means separation from the whole of nature. Whether the whole is tragic we do not know; we have, according to William James, the right to believe the opposite. But since all individuality means isolation, struggle with the environment, competition, restriction, and death, the individual and what he considers useful for his limited and isolated existence can never completely harmonize with the whole. There is a necessary conflict. But the greater, the wiser, and the more ethical an individual, the more he endeavors, through the use of reason and a wise balance of his natural gifts, to harmonize his individual interests with the universe. The question "how it works" no longer applies exclusively to him or even to his group, but, rather, it asks to what extent he and his actions are in harmony with the greater forces he voluntarily acknowledges. This does not lead to asceticism and self-sacrifice, which have, on the contrary, often been the outgrowth of a hysterical self-concern and self-isolation. But, on the other hand, in certain situations an individual may prefer self-sacrifice to continued life, not because this decision has a "cash value," such as fame—this would be the hysterical solution—but because an individual feels himself bound so deeply to universal laws that he adheres to them in spite of all external menace, as religious and scientific martyrs have done.

We also find here the deeper explanation of the problem of happiness. As long as we are physically and mentally healthy, we all want to be happy. But in spite of this profound desire in man, "hedonism," which puts happiness before all other goods, is wrong in theory and practice. It involves isolation of one life trend from the totality. The attempt to become happy by focusing our whole existence on this goal is just as erroneous as the attempt to satisfy a lust for power, which is also a deeply rooted desire in man. Happiness can only be achieved by living a full life, a life that challenges our forces to the utmost, thus enabling us to actualize ourselves through experiencing and realizing as many of the creative potentialities of the universe as our individual natures allow. If we live in such an intensified reality, an overtone of happiness may accompany even the most somber accords of our life's music.[1]

Having shown that many of our ethical tendencies are not merely relative but emerge from our natural motivating urges, we can pass to the consideration of another aspect of human behavior, the concept of freedom, which we have discussed in the preceding chapter. We explained that human freedom, which we may revere as the loft-

[1] In his book *Colonel Lawrence of Arabia* (Dodd, Mead, sixth printing, 1937, p. 353) Liddell Hart says about Colonel Lawrence:

"He certainly diffuses an atmosphere of contentment such as I have rarely felt in meeting men of active intelligence, and never among those who are actively pursuing the bubbles of what the world calls success. That feeling has grown stronger at recent meetings with him, and it led me not long ago to challenge him with the direct question—'Are you really happy?' After a moment's reflection, he replied, 'At times. No one who thinks can be really happy.' He went on to say that he had learnt very early the truth that happiness lies within, not in externals, but had also learnt later that those who did not think could be happy, the kind he lived among now. With himself, he found that happiness was intermittent—it came in 'absorption.'"

iest of human qualities or may try to deny, exists because there is, in the human being, a certain amount of elasticity in the gearing of urges or propensities to abilities, giving these urges the possibility of self-realization in a variety of activities. A man who has lost this quality is not normal; a man who denies it theoretically denies natural and observable facts; and a man who would refuse it in his own life, if he could, would degrade himself to the level of an imbecile.

The realistic and empirical foundation for freedom prevents us from advocating either determinism or the concept of perfect freedom defended by the radical idealists. The latter assert that man is free in an absolute sense and point to spiritual powers that enable the soul on rare occasions to break through the walls of its bodily prison. Some selected men—selected not by educators but by their own depth and power of inspiration—can have this sublime experience. Perhaps many have had the experience in some unforgettable moment. But even the most spiritual persons, we must remember, have clear vision only through the help of their physical organs, however much these may have been tuned to the exaltation of spirit. These organs, furthermore, can respond only because of their specific nervous structure, which is a product of inherited and acquired qualities. In persons of unusual mental intensity this structure often deviates considerably from normal health. The life and self-revelations of Blaise Pascal and of many other heroes in the realm of spirit are sufficient witness to this deviation. Therefore, though we do not deny the power of freedom and the reality of mystical exaltation, we see that even the most unusual experiences are bound to nature. What we have to admire is not what is called "the victory of mind over matter," but the realm of freedom and elasticity which nature allows to all of us and perhaps in particular to certain men. It is not necessary to elevate the spiritual at the expense of the natural or to degrade spirit in favor of a materialistic interpretation of nature. The two are indivisible in life, and we must learn to respect them in their unity.

Let us proceed one step further in our consideration of the ethical problem, continuing to parallel our earlier discussion of the psychological structure of man. After describing the psychological "raw material" of the human being, we asserted that the latter cannot be fully understood without taking into account his relation to values.

Now, we have already shown the embeddedness of values in the unreflective sphere of human nature. But we are not permitted to rest content with this reference of moral behavior to vital urges, because with the development of individuality and the development of the race a conscious and sublimated group of values raises itself above the more organic level where, for example, the parental instinct rests. While the unreflective values are, in consequence of their connection with vital urges, more motivational in character, the conscious values growing with the history of civilization assume, though not entirely unconnected with the first group, more the character of "ideals" and of "directions." Therefore, in the context of this chapter on the ethics of education the problem of values described in our psychological chapter may be reformulated in the following question. Are the consciousness of values and our reflections about them, whether concerned with moral or with intellectual ideals, merely arbitrary and fluctuating in character, or is there some underlying certainty and permanence to be found in them? Are we, in other words, entitled to believe in a relation between subjective values and an objective background which gives them more than a merely transient validity?

It seems to us that the skeptical and relativistic schools of philosophy, in denying to values any other meaning than the merely tangible outcomes of action, attempt to be empirical even at the expense of sound empiricism. Through trying to avoid any "intuitionalism" and unprovable assumption, they fall into the unconscious mysticism of reducing the richness of human existence exclusively to such problems as the changing forms of competition, welfare, and survival. They are, as we have said, explicable as protest against assumptive idealistic dogmatism, but neither science nor mankind can live always upon protest. However inaccessible ultimate truth may be, it would be wrong to deny that there is among normal people a certain agreement about both thinking and acting, not only from the point of view of effect, but also from the point of view of truth and rightness.

Though relativists emphasize the differences in our thinking, it must not be forgotten that the logical category of differing presupposes the category of agreeing and that, when we observe the whole process of life, it is seen to be more solidly based on the latter than on the former. There exists, in spite of all differences of opinion, a relatively great store of commonly recognized knowledge and common understanding. We not only understand each other, but we plan together, practically and scientifically; we master our environment with a certain steadiness and success; and our knowledge, in spite of all failures, covers increasingly wider fields. But we speak more of the exceptional than of the normal and habitual. The daily newspapers, for example, report the abnormal activities of criminals more frequently and in more detail than the usual activities of people following constructive behavior. Yet we would not place much value on a description of the life of a nation based upon such news.

We observe also some degree of coincidence between our thought and the world of appearances. The work of Copernicus, Kepler, Galileo, and Newton gave to the period of the Enlightenment a feeling of the identity of the human mind with the immanent laws of the universe. There is a fine, fresh enthusiasm for the newly discovered power of reason in the works of such men as Newton, Voltaire, Condorcet, Franklin, and Herder.

Nothing [as one of the younger writers [1] in this great period said] so much exalts the mind as this contemplation of the grand structure of the universe; and never, perhaps, did human thought attempt so bold a flight, and in part with such success, as when in Copernicus, Kepler, Newton, Huygens, and Kant, it conceived and confirmed the simple, eternal and perfect laws of the formation and motion of the planets. . . . When I open the great book of the universe, and see before me that immense palace, which the Deity alone can fill in every part; I reason as closely as I can from the whole to its parts, and from its parts to the whole. . . . When I perceive that the place

[1] J. G. Herder, *Outlines of a Philosophy of the History of Man.* Translated by T. Churchill. 1800. Book I, Chapter I.

occupied by our earth in this temple of suns, the path described by it in its course, its magnitude, its mass, and everything thereon depending, are determined by laws, that act through infinity: I must not only be satisfied with the place allotted me, and rejoice that I am so enabled to perform my part in the harmonious choir of beings innumerable, unless I would madly revolt against omnipotence; but it will be my noblest occupation, to inquire what in this allotted place I ought to be, and what in all probability I can be in it alone.

Certainly, in their enthusiasm the thinkers of this period sometimes forgot the limits of human reason and the dark abysses of human life. On the other hand, their self-confidence was more than illusion. However little we may apprehend the absolute energy, the *Ding an sich*, or the Noumenon, we are nevertheless able to describe the apparent effects of certain laws working behind and within the phenomena.

But there still remains the fact that a comparison of different individuals, races, and historical periods shows an incontestable variety of opinions about the good and the bad, the true and the false, about what ought to be and what ought not to be. There are polygamous and monogamous nations, peaceful and warlike peoples, and there are periods when the peaceful and warlike spirits are to be found even among the same people. Are these facts not sufficient to show that only change and relativity persist?

But the relativity even of these data decreases if we ask for its reason. Often the apparent contradiction is not a real one, for we are likely to think that judgments are irreconcilable if they are simply differing assertions about one and the same object. But a real disagreement of opinion exists only when the same quality of the object or the same relationship of the object to another is referred to. Taking this into account, we see that many differences between individuals and nations are but the result of unlike environmental or intellectual conditions. To what extent moral judgments differ in essence could be discovered only if one could bring the persons in consideration into an identical physical environment and onto the same level of intellectual maturity. It is generally not regarded as a sign of the relativity of moral values that a child's judgment of them should differ from the judgment of those with more and profounder experience. Are the differences between times and peoples not often similar in nature?

Nevertheless, these and other logical considerations do not completely erase the existing differences in moral values.

There is, however, one undeniable, persistent factor operative within and in spite of all differences of ethical behavior and opinion; namely, the desire of mankind to create values, to believe in them, and to use them as directing principles of action. The constant change of value contents is, in a sense, possible only on the background of a continually self-renewing ethical awareness and disposition, or whatever one wants to call this ceaseless creative power which, as we have already supposed, is connected with the motivational urges at the basis of personality. This continually self-renewing ethical awareness and disposition is identical with human consciousness. In other words, conscience exists as a permanent factor in spite of the ever-changing external aspects of history and their re-percussions on the human being.

No period and no nation really know the ultimate con-tent of this awareness, and, nevertheless, they evaluate actions and ideas according to their nearness to the ideal implicit in it.

Now, is it too bold to venture the assertion that this ceaseless creation of ethical and intellectual values that we observe in the flow of history shows some progress? Some-times we may not think so, and good reasons for such a view can be given, particularly with respect to the po-litical conditions of the twentieth century. But as we believe that the Ptolemaic world system has been im-proved by the Copernican, so we may believe that in spite of all relapses into barbarism our conscience has been some-what refined. The very conception of "falling back into barbarism" indicates that this statement is true. In earlier times slavery was morally acceptable; Stoic philos-ophy, Christianity, or modern humanism has not suc-ceeded in completely abolishing slavery or enslaving in-stitutions. But we know now that we ought to be rid of them, while the Greeks, in spite of their great culture, did not have our bad conscience. Many of us are still too much inclined to attach to political opinions we disagree with the character of moral inferiority and to ask for persecution before the point is proved. We still attempt to settle in-ternational differences by means of war. But we hope in the depths of our souls for a time when these political bar-barities will be as outmoded as the settling of private dis-putes by violence.

It is also possible to observe, in spite of all the differ-ences of ethical opinion between different periods, a common store of values with respect to immediate conduct. To betray a friend in danger, to lie for one's own interest against that of others, to destroy other people's happiness for no other reason than envy and jealousy have never been considered good.

Would it really be unscientific to believe that these attitudes express something more than merely accidental and haphazard feelings, that they symbolize certain inner principles of life?

Would it be unscientific to suppose also that there is a certain similarity between our ethical and our theoretical reasoning and that both not only *are* something—a gesture, a habit, a reaction, let us say—but that they also *mean* something of a persistent nature?

Here an objection is often raised by the critical naturalists, whose opinions we mentioned in the first chapter in the discussion of the causes of culture and education. They say that both our ethics and our thinking are nothing but means for self-preservation and, therefore, there is no true morality, but only interests. Here a fundamental question emerges. Is a moral action degraded in any way by being useful for an individual or a group? Is it not more natural to think that between the interests of mankind and its morality there is a harmonious relation? Strangely enough, both Kant, with his ethical rigorism, and his naturalistic opponents, with their materialistic dogma, start from the same fallacious either-or concept, an absolute dualism between mind and matter, morals and interests, ideals and usefulness. But what compels us to think that there cannot be an identity between what is true and good and the forces that preserve and foster life? Since we are a part of the cosmos, why should we erect a false dualism that separates our will to live from our will to think and act correctly, as if they represented qualities entirely unrelated to the concrete reality of the world? If our theory of the integral character of the vital urges has any truth in it, then it must also support our antidualistic conception.

With such an ethical philosophy in mind we can also do justice to the idea that the development of culture, ethics, and education is a process of "adjustment," as some modern pragmatists and realists have pointed out. If the idea of adjustment has any significance, then it cannot be simply a passive adaptation to an ever-changing environment unless our optimism is so great as to lead us to suppose that our environment and the universe are changing steadily for the better and that we have only to follow the most recent currents of the time in order to co-operate in that betterment. As the idea of growth, in order to be meaningful for the educator, implies faith in the power of man to find ultimately constructive elements within the apparent conflicts of the universe, so also the concept of adjustment is meaningful only if it relies on a similar faith and tries, on this basis, to develop a militant and realistic ethical philosophy. The process of adjustment, then, requires ceaseless activity and the constant use of criteria by which to judge of the compatibility of the diverse factors of our environment with the interests of the whole man, who is both a physical and an ethical creature and doomed to degenerate if his totality is not sufficiently respected.

How man became able to reach beneath the surface of ever-changing appearances into the "deeper dimension of being" where these criteria are discoverable is probably his greatest secret. There is only one hypothesis possible, already suggested in the psychological chapter: that man is able to reflect upon nature and upon himself as part of nature and in doing so reaches with his mind into the vital sources of all existence.

Mystical though this hypothesis sounds, the world and the role of man within this world become still more inexplicable if we do not resort to such a metaphysical assumption. We saw that even the thought of James and Dewey, who are strongly opposed to premature metaphysical assumptions, leads inevitably along this way. Their "directionalism" contains, and where it does not contain the weight of its inherent logic implies, a metaphysical hypothesis of the sort we have expounded. Even the philosophy of the exact sciences has arrived at similar conclusions during the past few decades. And, however much one may differ in other points from Sir John Adams's work on *The Evolution of Educational Theory* [1] and from the kind of idealism he defends, some of his basic assumptions are nevertheless cogent for any consistent thinking.

Underlying all this is the great assumption on which Idealism is based [he says]. It is assumed that the universe is rational, that is that things act upon each other in a consistent way, that there are certain invariable laws, and that these all work so as to secure the systematic order of the universe. All this is practically assumed not only by the idealist but by everybody who thinks. Ultimately it has to be recognised as more than an assumption; it may not unfairly be claimed as a postulate, even as an axiom: it is involved in the very act of thinking of any object. The reference to the mind of the thinker himself

[1] Macmillan, 1912. Page 291.

destroys pluralism, as it destroys every other form of scepticism. The negative of the sceptic, as always, implies a positive and the affirmation of irrationality is really a negative. . . . We cannot trust our own intelligence without assuming the rationality of its object.

This assumption does not lead to the re-establishment of an idealism that believes it possesses the philosophical instruments for a complete anatomy of the innermost nature of the universe. We have become too modest for such an enterprise. Our philosophy may be called idealism in the broadest sense of the term provided that that term is also applied to the philosophy of James and Dewey. We are again in complete harmony with the "directional" aspects of pragmatic philosophy in emphasizing the fact that we have not thought deductively from preconceived logical or ethical generalizations. Rather, we have been led to our conclusions by carrying experiences inductively to their own implications. In order to make clear this "directional" attitude we would give the philosophy just elaborated the name of "self-transcendent empiricism." When we started on our exploration we had in mind no fixed goal toward which to chart our way; but we allowed the most antagonistic views, from relativistic utilitarianism to extreme idealism, to work upon our thought. Our only purpose was to ask these philosophies, and our own experiences as well, whether we have to accept the antagonism of all possible opinions, or whether their analysis would discover some criteria for thought and action. There remained, at the end, two self-exclusive conclusions: either all existence, including that of human beings, must be considered a medley of accidents and any desire to order it, such as culture and education imply, is a self-contradiction; or, by the method of self-transcendent empiricism, we arrive at the assumption of a deeper dimension of being. The ultimate nature of this being, we had to confess, is beyond our grasp; but we were able to affirm the right to believe in a logos actualizing itself, not only in the laws of the universe, but also in ourselves the moment we are willing to see ourselves as parts of a great and permanent, though constantly evolving, order.

The means by which to arrive at such a belief is, as we saw, not reasoning as an isolated process, but responsible and self-conscious action. Reason alone, as the history of philosophy shows, leads us from one potentiality to another. We can arrive at clearness about ourselves and at criteria of action only through action, or, in other words, through actualizing ourselves as individuals within a community of other individuals. In this process experience shows us that we can come to the best of ourselves only in serving those powers which we find to be constructive, and even the danger that we may err in critical situations does not detract from the value of this experience. We differ from Kant's conception of a morality that begins when man acts against himself; we think, perhaps not so much in contradiction to Kant as it may appear at first glance, that self-realization and morality are inseparable. But we agree with him in one important point: it is not the critique of *pure* reason or the intellect, but the critique of *practical* reason or action, by means of which men can come to guiding criteria.

Chapter IV

THE STRUGGLE OF THE EDUCATOR
WITH THE PROBLEM OF VALUES
(EDUCATIONAL POLICY)

A. THE MAJOR FACTORS INFLUENCING
EDUCATION

1. THE DEPENDENCE OF EDUCATION UPON THE GENERAL
CHARACTER OF A PERIOD

The discussion of ethical criteria remains a futile intellectual exercise unless it springs from the desire to map out ways of individual and social conduct. Productive ethics arises from actual life and ends in actual life, as rain, drawn from the moisture of the earth, falls back upon it and waters its dry fields. Ethics reflects what people think they ought to do, what they wish to do, and what they actually do; it is, therefore, the philosophic science most related to practical life and to education. Long before teachers thought about psychology and the methods of their work, they meditated upon its relationship to the moral standards of society. Necessarily, if these standards are no longer certain, insecurity in education follows. The latter, in turn, has its repercussions upon practical activities and the morality of a nation, and so we

153

find ourselves here in one of the many vicious circles to which complex civilizations are so abundantly subject.

This interconnectedness of all the trends of civilization explains also the consonance of the rhythm of a nation's social and political life and the rhythm of its education. Periods of general expansion are accompanied by vitality and harmony in the rearing of youth, those of retardation by educational conventionalism, and those of crisis and fermentation by unrest and contrasting experiments.

But even the most fortunate periods in the history of a nation are never in a state of complete balance. A certain amount of conflict is essential for cultural progress; only statesmen and educators who mistake external conformity for basic health and security believe that all differences should be suppressed. And in that belief they find support from reactionaries and dogmatists and from those citizens who are convinced that no generation was ever condemned to live in a period of such utter unrest and decay as their own. These people might perhaps take comfort by reading so ancient a thinker as Aristotle, who wrote in his *Politics* [1] as follows:

> That education should be regulated by law and should be an affair of state is not to be denied, but what should be the character of this public education, and how young persons should be educated, are questions which remain to be considered. As things are there is disagreement about the subjects. For mankind are by no means agreed about the things to be taught, whether we look to virtue or the best life. Neither is it clear whether education is more con-

[1] 1337a 11–1338b 4. English translation from *Selections*, edited by W. D. Ross. Scribner. Page 319.

cerned with intellectual or with moral virtue. The
existing practice is perplexing; no one knows on what
principle we should proceed—should the useful in life,
or should virtue, or should high knowledge, be the
aim of our training; all three opinions have been en-
tertained. Again, about the means there is no agreement; for different persons, starting with different
ideas about the nature of virtue, naturally disagree
about the practice of it.

If one looks for the causes of the present unrest in education, he will surely discover that one of them is the problem
of pragmatism versus idealism transferred into the realm
of practical education. Conscientious parents and teachers
want to educate children for the future; they want them
open-minded, adaptable, able to live without dogmas and
prejudice. But not only is the environment at present dis-
organized and chaotic but parents and teachers themselves
are troubled by disagreement and conflicting views. They
must decide upon what their children shall be adapted to.
If they are to be free from prejudices, what are the prejudices to be abandoned, and what creeds can be accepted or
preserved? If they are to be open-minded, to which of the
conflicting trends should they open their minds, since to be
open to them all would mean chaos or at least a life as
changeable as that of a weathercock. And to be closed to
all of the present trends would mean either extreme skepticism or indifference and isolation. We can master life
only if open-mindedness and adaptability are given a compass with which to steer a course through the "boundless
sea" of life and to defend us "against the wreckful siege
of battering days."

But where is the compass? Or let us formulate the question more concretely. How can we explain the fact that even those who agree philosophically about the general aims of culture as elaborated in the preceding chapter do not know what action to take in the face of the bewildering variety of educational possibilities?

In order to answer this question, let us first investigate the causes of the confusing situation that gives rise to it and devote some time to a consideration of the causes of the disintegration of those working philosophies of education which in previous times gave parents and teachers a feeling of certainty and a clear conscience about what they were doing. We shall deal, first, with the disintegration of the religious philosophy of education; second, with the disintegration of the humanistic ideal; and, third, with the effects of relativism. Thereafter we shall pass from the field of ideas to an analysis of environmental factors and discuss, at that point, the disintegration of the social and economic basis of modern civilization.

After having described in this order the spiritual and social background of education, we shall show how the main trends of this background and their disintegration have been reflected in educational theory itself; we shall deal briefly with the ideas of the Moravian educator John Amos Comenius, one of the greatest representatives of the religious interpretation of education; with Pestalozzi, who led the religious ideas of the Reformation into more rational and humanistic forms of thought; then with Herbart, as the advocate of humanism; and finally with the modern period of eclecticism, pragmatism, and nationalism in education.

After this we hope to sketch, in a chapter on the tasks of

modern education, a working philosophy for educational practice.

2. THE DISINTEGRATION OF RELIGION

Earlier Christianity gave to its adherents not only a body of religious ideas but also a code of conduct, though there was never complete conformity among the members of the Church either as to creed or as to practical life. Dissenters are as old as the dogma, and rebels as old as the Commandments. In addition, the cruelty of the economic struggle and the political interests of nations prevented Christianity from permeating mankind with a lasting spirit of brotherhood. The existence of a separate diplomatic and military code, indifferent not only to religious ideals but to the most primitive feelings of individual honesty, is still the scourge of man. But in spite of all these limitations, Christianity predominated Western civilization at least to such an extent that it called itself Christian and acknowledged divine criteria for the judgment of human actions. The conscience of man relied upon a revelation and commandment of the righteous God, Him who had appeared to his people "in the morning, that there were thunders and lightnings, and a thick cloud upon the mount, and the voice of the trumpet exceeding loud; so that all the people that was in the camp trembled."

This belief in a Lawgiver who had descended in fire upon Mount Sinai was destroyed by the rationalists of the eighteenth century. Most of them, however, retained a fundamental belief in the immanent spiritual nature of the world and substituted philosophic deism for the earlier belief in a personal God. To what extent this creed of the Enlightenment really touched the common man it is difficult to say, but it can be asserted that the extremes of skepticism—for example, radical materialism—were confined to small groups.

A widespread radical secularization of ethical concepts resulting in significant social movements is not to be found, except in prerevolutionary and revolutionary France, before the first decades of the nineteenth century. Critical and comparative theology, the great discoveries in the natural sciences—particularly Darwinism, anthropology, and historical research gave the modern man another kind of life-consciousness. The beginning of these disciplines and the methods they applied can be traced back to the Renaissance and even further. Philosophies issuing from these attitudes played a great part among the leaders of the American Revolution. But that they began to mold common opinion so decisively as they did in the nineteenth century is due to several circumstances: first, to their own powerful development; then, to modern universal education; and, finally, to the spread of knowledge by the modern printing press, which enabled even the simplest workman to buy and read a newspaper or a book. This latter development, in turn, made possible the propagation of the thought and politics of modern liberal movements. The leaders of the lower middle classes and of the working classes discovered how much the older conservatives had profited from linking their political interests to the authority of the Church. Authority for the new political doctrines was found in the work of the so-called unprejudiced thinkers—the scientists, the sociologists, the philosophers —who soon proved to be more powerful than the man in the pulpit.

Only ignorance or blind reaction can deny the values inherent in this development. No one who reads the documents of the witch trials, of crude religious superstition and religious wars, of bondage and exploitation by government in the hands of the privileged few, can help being appalled by the sinister mixture of obscurantism, fear, and brutality against which the bearers of modern enlightenment had to fight. The degree of confusion which even modern historians can achieve is shown when one of them, James Joseph Walsh,[1] can call the thirteenth century the greatest and the eighteenth the lowest of all centuries. Although modern historical research has achieved a more just appreciation of the thirteenth century, we are not by that compelled to deny the contributions of later centuries to the advance of culture. Nothing worse could happen even to the most orthodox Christian Church than a reversion to the narrow limits of thought and social activity to which they were confined before the century which Walsh calls the lowest. What is, after all, the value of historical categories such as "greatest" and "lowest"?

However, the accomplishments of the rationalists and empiricists must not be overrated and will not be when we consider the alarming discrepancy between our great theoretical and technical knowledge and our capacity of using it for the good of man. Our modern civilization is still in the sorry position of the *nouveau riche* who used a part of the millions made from his revolver factory to build an estate in imitation of one of the finest Renaissance castles in the south of France. The best kinds of wood, metal, and stone were selected; wood carvers were brought from Italy to copy the old patterns; and the finest porcelain was

[1] *The Thirteenth, Greatest of Centuries.* Georgetown University edition. Catholic Summer School Press, 1910. Pages 482 ff.

chosen to welcome the guests of the house as splendidly as possible. But there was one room in the building which the architects had not succeeded in giving daylight or comfort—the typical cold, dark corner to be found in all old castles—and this was the old gentleman's favorite room. His soul had not grown with his fortune, and the new luxury, instead of making him free and happy, bewildered him.

The result of this bewilderment in the world at large is that many modern nations are spending between fifty and eighty per cent of their tax income, not for the preservation and advancement of culture, but for machines of destruction; preparation for war has become more important than peace and dignified living, and we are sometimes inclined to doubt whether science is not a curse rather than a blessing.

In the course of these last few centuries religions and philosophies which formerly determined the aims of schooling have been losing their influence. They have not been completely extinguished, because goals and values which have once profoundly molded man's actions and ideals never entirely die out. But today, though they continue, they no longer retain their power to absorb and integrate new knowledge and experience and are continually forced into unsatisfactory compromises. The older concept of religious education survives in our denominational schools, but only with a shadow of its strength. No longer radiating into the consciousness of people in general, it has become a sectarianism rather than the concern of our whole civilization. In those countries where the churches had so far been dominant, as in Russia up to 1918 or until recently in Mexico, or where, as in Germany and Austria, their influence on the school was considerable, they were not only helpless against the rising tide of an antireligious nationalism but fostered it unconsciously by their backwardness. In Italy, where public education still retains its religious forms, it is difficult to believe that a true Christian spirit pervades the schools when the leader of the country proclaims, in such obvious contradiction to the principles of Christianity, that "war alone brings up to its highest tension all human energy and puts a stamp of nobility upon the peoples who have the courage to meet it."[1]

Seen from the vantage point of a historian, the frankness with which anti-Christian philosophies of government are expressed in our day may have its good side. It clears the atmosphere. Up to this time governments have disguised their policies, at least to the mass of people, behind the conventional ideology of "Christian government," with such phrases as the "offended honor of the nation" and the "ultimate interests of humanity," although their actual policy has not been much different from Mussolini's. The issue has become increasingly evident: either man must succeed at no matter what sacrifice in harmonizing national policy with the needs and just claims of foreign nations or the citizen will become the serf of a military class instead of its master. Then Western civilization will break down under economic burdens and the cruelty of wars whose only result is to necessitate still other wars. Governments must have power and must use it. But is it to be used hesitatingly as a dangerous instrument for the adjustment of internal and external affairs, or will it become for those who wield it an end in itself? So long as

[1] Hans Kohn, *Force and Reason.* 1937. Page 25.

no attachment is felt to an idea of transcendental value, the latter course will always be chosen. For only such an attachment can save man from the temptation of the immediately seizable advantages and the exploitation of his supremacy over others. Victory quite clearly lies not in the holding of power but in the use that is made of it. And by this test all governments have so far failed. They are still far from an active realization of the essential interdependence of their people's interests and the laws of civilization. The churches also have not yet attained to the freedom from their environment that would enable them to represent the mutual responsibilities of classes, states, and races. Instead of representing the Christian conscience independent of economic and political influences, the clergy has constantly admitted the most degrading contradictions of their own principles. The result is that it is more and more difficult for the common man to order his confused feelings by resorting to Christian faith and education.

3. THE DISINTEGRATION OF THE HUMANISTIC IDEAL

The predicaments of religious education are paralleled by the plight of the humanistic ideal, which played so great a role in our secondary and tertiary schools up to the end of the nineteenth century. Humanism originated in the period of the Renaissance, and attempts to reconcile it with the Christian tradition were made by such men as Erasmus of Rotterdam, on the Catholic side, and Philipp Melanchthon, on the Protestant side. Other humanists felt less concern about Christianity and gave it mere lip service. Their ideal of the *uomo universale*, of the all-round educated and well-bred man, owed more to the ancient pagan heritage than to the Sermon on the Mount. Yet they were externally loyal to the Church, and their ideal suited the interests of the upper classes, whose sons had always been brought up in the realistic Roman tradition rather than that of the Christian prophets; for so long as the concept of ruling undergoes no fundamental changes, "realism" is necessary. The humanistic ideal, therefore, became the refined successor of the ideals of medieval chivalry; it was largely influential in shaping the ideal "gentleman" and the curriculum of the English public schools, and it similarly influenced the development of the German Gymnasium and French classical training. But today the humanistic philosophy of education is on the decline, partly because it has repeatedly shown its tendency to degenerate into mere instruction in ancient languages, partly because of changes in our social structure, partly because the widening of our scientific horizon shows the narrowness of an exclusive attention to the humanities, and finally because the increased competition in modern economic life requires a more practical education for the wealthy groups.

This shift from the humanistic to a more technical education has not been entirely advantageous, since there has resulted no well-rounded and organic training of the modern man. Even he cannot live by bread alone nor by the sciences, though both are essential for living. They are the means but not the end, as they have tended to become. An introduction to the methods of experimentation, to the materials of technical procedures, and to vocational life is needed on every level of a modern educational system. On the other hand, unless we are to become slaves of a technical civilization which for lack of human freedom ceases to be a civilization, we must master it through the capacity to subordinate our labor to a meaning which satisfies human existence in its totality.

4. Relativism

The disintegration of our older educational philosophies is due not only to the as yet unresolved antagonisms between religious and political, humanistic and vocational standards but also to another factor, which we may call the factor of relativism in education.

An important branch of modern thought has been the comparative study of such subjects as history, anthropology, government, and religion. Such comparison destroys prejudices and narrow-mindedness and is responsible for many of the virtues of the best type of modern man: his intellectual honesty, open-mindedness, and tolerance. But, as Dante wrote, any virtue carried to the extreme may turn into its contrary. So it is that comparison has not seldom led us to forget that civilization depends not only upon freedom and diversity but also upon common and persisting ideas. There is a complex dialectical interrelationship between obligations and liberty. A nation lacking organic human interests and standards (in other words, a nation acting without restrictions upon its liberty, if liberty is taken to mean unlimited choice of action) would no longer foster its own welfare or the welfare of general human culture. In the same way a person with an absolutely unbounded intellectual and emotional life would be rootless and unconstructive. We have rightly become suspicious of the sophisticated and unattached intellectual. His mind might seem to be closest to the ideal of thinking—to complete freedom from subjective limitations—yet it would, nevertheless, not be objective. Being open to all potentialities, it would end in impotence. It would be the opposite of a similarly negative extreme, that of a will directed toward so special a goal that, though for a short time astonishing achievements may be made, it is finally defeated by its disregard for the richness of reality. What we need—and again we are faced by the problem of growth and directedness—is a synthesis of flow and form, of freedom and purpose. Unfortunately, this need is most difficult of fulfillment, for it defies logical categories and recipes. Such a synthesis requires a science and logic informed by intuition and wisdom. But these latter qualities being so rare, what we have are, on the one hand, democracies facing increasing difficulties in integrating their diverging forces and, on the other hand, dictatorships. And as our national and international politics are disrupted by this time-honored antagonism, so our educational theory and practice have oscillated between the two poles of exaggerated freedom and absolute authority. But the wise educator, like the wise statesman, knows that a balance of the two is needed.

5. The Disintegration of the Social and Economic Foundations of Civilization

SOCIAL

The present lack of satisfactory patterns for social living is due not only to unresolved conflicts in the spheres of religion, science, and education but to social and economic factors as well. Modern society, under all regimes, is characterized by the dissolution of the old barriers between different social levels. These distinctions between classes and groups had a natural foundation so long as the medieval social structure with its feudal hierarchy, its guilds and corporations, was the expression of the needs and functions of the people. When, in consequence of economic and political changes, this system broke down and was replaced by absolutism, the new governments were still too much entangled in the previous social order to construct a really new social pattern. They eliminated the rivalry of the feudal lords, they crushed the power of the old corporations, and they brought the independent cities under central control. But many of the social codes and the external forms of medieval society remained and were to some degree necessary in order to reconcile the old feudal elements with the new centralized state machinery. But since the medieval class distinctions had lost their natural function, they persisted as artificial residues that were largely negative in character, the medieval hierarchy of obligations becoming a hierarchy of forms and privileges. As is always the case under such conditions, those who profited by the old forms were intensely interested in their perpetuation. England's educational system suffered under the restraints of these anachronistic forms, in spite of her democratic political life, up to the nineteenth century; France shook them off in the Revolution; Germany, the former Austria, and Hungary still suffer under them.

The country where belonging to the privileged or the unprivileged first ceased to be a kind of inescapable destiny was the United States. Her population consisted to a large extent of men and women who had left the old continent to escape persecution, or of the offspring of such people; the floating population of newcomers did not allow much fixity of forms, nor did the tasks facing them in the new continent favor the older structure of European society.

Ten days before his death, in 1826, Thomas Jefferson wrote a letter to Roger C. Weightman which is significant of the democratic spirit of the United States: [1]

> May it be to the world, what I believe it will be (to some parts sooner, to others later, but finally to all), the signal of arousing men to burst the chains under which monkish ignorance and superstition had persuaded them to bind themselves, and to assume the blessings and security of self-government. That form which we have substituted restores the free right to the unbounded exercise of reason and freedom of opinion. All eyes are opened, or opening, to the rights of man. The general spread of the light of science has already laid open to every view the palpable truth, that the mass of mankind has not been born with saddles on their backs, nor a favored few booted and spurred, ready to ride them legitimately, by the grace of God.

When Jefferson expressed these ideas, he was living in a society which, compared with ours, was rather homogeneous and stable. He himself was a highly educated man, the master of several ancient and modern languages, a lover of science who believed in the power of education, an admirer of thoroughbred horses and of agriculture and gardens, and an enemy of the accumulation of people in industrial centers.

[1] *Alexander Hamilton and Thomas Jefferson*, edited by F. C. Prescott. American Bo᷒k Company, 1934. Page 403.

In the meantime many of the cultural foundations for his democratic optimism have disappeared. Most of the governors of our modern countries in their leisure time, if they have any, probably no longer take refuge in the wisdom of Horace or Theocritus, as Jefferson did. Most of the people who go to the polls today have a better education than Jefferson's farmers. But, on the other hand, they do not have the tradition and faith that the majority of these farmers had; they have no grounds of their own, no gardens, no animals, no fixed markets, and not very much security. Those who determine the social standards of today probably possess more knowledge than the average squire of previous times; but one would have difficulty in finding, even among the most cultured, a father who would take the time to write such letters as the Earl of Chesterfield wrote in 1746 to his son,[1] who was on a grand tour of the Continent.

> Dear Boy [he said]: Your distress in your journey from Heidelberg to Schaffhausen, your lying upon straw, your black bread, and broken *berline*, are proper seasonings for the greater fatigues and distresses which you must expect in the course of your travels; and, if one had a mind to moralize, one might call them the samples of the accidents, rubs, and difficulties, which every man meets with in his journey through life. In this journey, the understanding is the *voiture* that must carry you through; and in proportion as that is stronger or weaker, more or less in repair, your journey will be better or worse; though at best you

[1] "On the Fine Art of Becoming a Man of the World and a Gentleman," in *Letters to His Son. By the Earl of Chesterfield*, edited by O. L. Leigh. Page 1.

will now and then find some bad roads, and some bad inns. Take care, therefore, to keep that necessary *voiture* in perfect good repair; examine, improve and strengthen it every day: it is in the power, and ought to be the care, of every man to do it; he that neglects it, deserves to feel, and certainly will feel, the fatal effects of that negligence.

Certainly it was wealth and power and not merit alone that made men the object of emulation in those days and formed the standards of society. And if external eminence proves to be lacking in ethical qualities, the process of social patterning becomes infected and the body politic shows signs of disease. But every sound nation needs its aristocracy; democracies need it even more than fixed forms of society, where a solid framework of discipline protects the whole from breaking asunder. Thomas Jefferson wrote in 1813 to John Adams as follows:

. . . I agree with you that there is a natural aristocracy among men. The grounds of this are virtue and talents. Formerly, bodily power gave place among the aristocracy; but since the invention of gunpowder has armed the weak as well as the strong with missile death, bodily strength, like beauty, good humor, politeness, and other accomplishments, has become but an auxiliary ground of distinction. There is also an artificial aristocracy, founded on wealth and birth, without either virtue or talents; for with these it would belong to the first class. The natural aristocracy I consider as the most precious gift of nature, for the instruction, the trusts, and government of society.

The formation of a natural aristocracy has always been one of the most difficult conditions of self-preservation for great nations to fulfill. All the important revolutions resulted from flaws in the intercourse of the various social strata and from the failure of the ruling classes to use their power in the interest of the whole nation. Many of our present social disturbances spring from the same evils. We have not replaced the "artificial aristocracy, founded on wealth and birth," of which Jefferson speaks, with a real aristocracy, but have often substituted for an aristocracy of birth a class that rules by money and power. Our public life, with its contradictory interests and movements, its propaganda, its misleading strategy in political affairs, increasingly frustrates the rise of a "natural aristocracy," and still more the public acknowledgment of its role "as the most precious gift of nature, for the instruction, the trusts, and government of society." Our education reflects this situation. It lacks the ability to choose the best from all classes and to direct them in the finest fulfillment of their inherent potentialities; and, lacking this ability, all educational endeavors are bound to be theoretical and unenduring.

ECONOMIC

The confusion of the modern man has been increased by a series of economic crises radiating unrest from the financial centers to almost every corner of the inhabited world. The theories of economics that the man of forty learned twenty years ago in college have been outmoded by completely unforeseen financial and industrial happenings beyond the control of even the most highly competent nations.

There still exists, perhaps more than in former times, the reciprocal interdependence of all great nations. But in spite of improvements in communication and production, or perhaps because these improvements are still too new and surprising, modern nations attempt to isolate themselves from one another. In addition, they are divided into democratic, fascistic, and bolshevistic systems and show all the characteristics of an inharmonious family the members of which are as much united by their hatred as by their relationship. Even citizens of the same nation are divided about the course that business and industry ought to take. As a consequence of these developments, modern occupational life no longer offers a chance for every industrious citizen successfully to apply his natural abilities, support his family, and gain the degree of public commendation necessary for his own self-esteem. This means that for many of us the basic and secure source of growing maturity, of continued education during adulthood, has been lost.

B. THE OPERATION OF THE MAJOR FACTORS IN THE THEORY OF EDUCATION

All the factors, both constructive and destructive, that we have observed operating in public life are mirrored in the theory of education proper.

1. COMENIUS

At the time of the Thirty Years' War, the last Moravian bishop, John Amos Comenius, wrote his *Didactica Magna* (*The Great Didactic*). It was by no means the first book dealing with educational problems. But it was unique in its systematic comprehensiveness, and it initiated modern education in that it demanded psychological observation, thoughtful didactical procedures, and a systematically organized school structure. If one compares the unrest of Comenius's life with the philosophy of his writings, one cannot but wonder at his certainty about the meaning and the ends of life. His homeland had been destroyed by the House of Hapsburg, his Moravian fellow men dispersed by the Counter Reformation, his books and manuscripts burned by invading armies; he himself had been forced to migrate from one country to another, dependent upon the help of friends in a time of the utmost cruelty and destruction. But in spite of all his sorrows he possessed a wonderful tranquillity arising from his unshaken faith in a divine order and man's participation in it. A single quotation [1] will illustrate this quality:

All our actions and affections in this life show that we do not attain our ultimate end here, but that everything connected with us, as well as we ourselves, has another destination. For whatever we are, do, think, speak, contrive, acquire or possess, contains a principle of gradation, and though we mount perpetually and attain higher grades, we still continue to advance and never reach the highest. . . . It is evident, then, that the ultimate end of man is eternal happiness with God.

2. Pestalozzi

More than a century after the Moravian bishop wrote his *Didactica Magna* as a fugitive, another great educator,

[1] John Amos Comenius, *The Great Didactic*, translated by M. W. Keatinge. London, A. & C. Black, 1896. Pages 180 and 188.

the Swiss Johann Heinrich Pestalozzi, faced financial ruin and the failure of his first educational enterprise. In a night of disillusion and despair he felt the need of composing himself through jotting down an account of his educational ideas. In its aphoristic form this essay, "The Evening Hours of a Hermit," gives immediately the impression of a humanistic theory of education with a strong emotional accent. The process of breeding and schooling, and the whole process of human culture, cannot succeed unless it follows the "path of nature"; that is, the natural growth of the psychophysical organism of man. Good education needs, first of all, a sound soul in a sound environment.

What man is, what his needs are, what elevates and what degrades him, what invigorates and what weakens him, that is what is necessary for the highest and for the humblest to know.

Men feel the need of this everywhere. Everywhere man is toiling and straining and struggling upward. Because of lack of this knowledge successive generations wither away with their lives unfulfilled and at the end of life the majority of mankind cry aloud that the completion of their course has not satisfied them. Their end is not the ripening of the perfect fruit which, having completed the predestined course of development, sinks to the rest of the winter.

Why does man grope after the truth without system or purpose? Why does he not try to discover the fundamental needs of his nature in order that he may base upon this the enjoyment and the blessedness of his life? Why does he not seek truth, which is peace and the enjoyment of life, truth which satisfies his innermost cravings, which develops his powers, gladdens his days and endows his life with happiness?

Man under the compulsion of his needs finds the road to this truth in his innermost being.

The infant, its hunger satisfied, learns in this way what his mother is to him. She calls forth love, the essence of gratitude, in him before he can utter the words "duty" or "gratitude." The son who eats his father's bread and warms himself at his hearth finds by this path of nature his happiness in the duties of the child. . . .

Pure human wisdom rests upon the firm basis of the knowledge of one's immediate relationships and of a capacity for management that has been trained in the handling of one's most intimate affairs.

The man who hovers around and lightly tastes of every branch of knowledge and fails to develop strength through the quiet steady application of knowledge, he also deviates from the path of nature, he loses that steady, clear, attentive glance, that calm, quiet feeling for truth receptive to real happiness.

Faltering and uncertain will be the course of those men who in the multiplicity of their knowledge find much occasion for talk, but who have sacrificed to it the quiet sense of pure human wisdom. Notwithstanding their noisy pride, their immediate surroundings are to them barren and obscure while those of the truly wise are lighted up by the light of intelligent understanding.[1]

[1] Pestalozzi, *Selections*, "The Evening Hours of a Hermit," edited by L. F. Anderson. McGraw-Hill, 1931. Page 12.

Pestalozzi shows the empirical and psychological trend, initiated in the period of the Renaissance, which gives to the work of Comenius also, in spite of its strongly religious background, its concern for method. But Pestalozzi's concept of "nature," like Rousseau's, is completely different from "naturalism." Nature for him is the unity of both spirit and matter. And so also he conceives of man not as a separated and self-sufficient individual but as embedded in the spiritual and material universe. Therefore, it cannot be surprising, though at first it sounds so, that he continues his description of the natural and immediate relationships necessary for the growth of man in the following words: "But the most important of the immediate relationships of man is his relation to God."

Of course, the separation of education from a superhuman sphere, or, in other words, the declaration of the autonomy of human civilization, gained ground at the very time that Pestalozzi lived. Against his own will almost, he gave education a naturalistic bias through his scientific "method" intended to serve the educator as a tool as reliable as the physical formulas of the engineer. There is some truth in the reproach of a contemporary, the French councilor Glayre: "*Vous voulez méchaniser l'éducation.*" [1] It does injustice to Pestalozzi's personal intentions, but it anticipates a danger. Education, like any other work organized on a large scale, needs elaborate methods and good craftsmanship. But nowhere does the danger of all craftsmanship—namely, degeneration into routine—cause more harm than in this field, which needs constant renewal of spirit. Those who praise the "born

---

[1] Pestalozzi, *How Gertrude Teaches Her Children*, translated by Holland and Turner. Page 56.

teacher" and despise all methods apparently do not know how miserable elementary education was in general in all countries before Pestalozzi's ideas could gain a firm footing. On the other hand, the discipline of didactics and methods of teaching, when placed in the wrong hands, has deprived many students of education of their enthusiasm and brought the training of teachers into disrepute.

But methods can turn into ends in themselves rather than means only if an activity lacks in general buoyancy and inspiration. What Pestalozzi himself and his disciples contributed to education through their sense of social responsibility and their intrinsically religious belief in the mission of an improved elementary education is clearly reflected in Fichte's *Addresses to the German Nation*, where he admonished his people to restore the morality of the nation, after the defeat by Napoleon, by means of education in the spirit and according to the methods of Pestalozzi.

3. HERBART AND THE VICTORIAN ERA

The secularization of education is reflected in the popularity which the educational philosophy of Johann Friedrich Herbart acquired in many modern countries, particularly in Germany, England, and the United States. Herbart moves with the trend of the nineteenth century through his emphasis on the strictly scientific aspects of education. Equipped with a better logical intellect and with better methods of investigation than Pestalozzi, he elaborated a psychology which, though now outmoded in most respects, is, nevertheless, one of the profoundest of the early attempts in this field. He makes use of the exact sciences of mathematics and physiology, to the latter of which the Swiss physician, biologist, and poet Albrecht von Haller (1708–1777) had already contributed the terms sensibility, irritability, and vegetation to explain animal life and its individual peculiarities. Herbart is, nevertheless, far from being a materialist.

No materialistic physiology is required [he writes in his *Letters on the Application of Psychology to Education*] [1] to remind us that bodily differences must be reflected in mental expressions, and you will not be vexed if I ask you to glance even beyond physiology, at the science of medicine, so that we may see, not only the general fact of the union between soul and body (for this is not the subject of our research), but the characteristics of these bodily differences.

In his psychology itself he considers intellectual functions, which he calls representations, as the basic activities of the mind. In relation to them all other mental states, such as feeling and willing, are secondary and derivative. His psychology, though fundamentally antinaturalistic, is, nevertheless, in congruence with the contemporary trend toward scientific causality. He is eager to show the exact relationships between the different psychological functions, the process of learning and the methods of teaching. His well-known formal steps, about which we shall speak more thoroughly in the fifth chapter of this book, are not the result of mere formalism but of the attempt to find a scientific basis for teaching. He conceived of education as an art which cannot be carried on with haphazard procedures but must take into account the

[1] J. F. Herbart, *The Application of Psychology to the Science of Education*, Letter IV. Scribner. Page 28.

totality of the psychic functions of the learner in combination with the general human significance of education.

The human significance of education he finds to be morality. Though Herbart, as we have seen, lays the greatest emphasis on the reconciliation of the principles of education and human psychology, he declares with respect to the formal aim, morality, that it cannot be derived from psychology.[1] At this point he comes very close to the ethical dualism of his great predecessor in the philosophic chair of the University of Königsberg, Immanuel Kant. He says:

> The preceding remarks relating to character were a specification of psychological phenomena. But every one who thoughtfully considers the word *morality* will acknowledge it is not satisfactory merely to have *any* kind of character.
>
> It is taken for granted, then, that certain claims lie at the basis of morality as against any given character—claims which cannot be compelled to resign their rights by the opposition which in fact awaits them, although they do not possess an intrinsic power to accomplish anything. And these claims have nothing in common with the real, the natural, even with that which *is* in any sense, but come to them as something totally strange, and come in contact with them only to judge them. And a judging power does not engage in strife with the object upon which it pronounces sentence.

[1] *The Science of Education*, translated by H. and E. Felkin. Heath, 1892. Page 205.

Here are nature and the realities of life, and there is morality as the judge of them. Nevertheless, in explaining the contents of morality Herbart hesitates to transgress experience. He feels himself logically and empirically compelled to admit the transcendental character of morality and its rootedness in religion; but wherever he speaks of religion, he conceives of it not so much as self-revelation of the Absolute but induces it as far as possible from empirically found human tendencies.

It is true that in his chapter on "Synthetic Instruction" [1] he says that the idea of God "must always be placed anew at the end of Nature, as the *ultimate presupposition of every mechanism* which shall at some time develop to a given end." But it is more characteristic of him when, in the "Analytical Course of Instruction," he explains the nature and function of religion in the following way:

Sympathy with the universal dependence of men is the essential natural principle of all religion. We must direct the pupil's eyes where human beings express the feeling of their limitations, and point out to him every piece of arrogance, as a false and dangerous imagination of strength. Worship should be represented as a pure confession of humility; neglect of worship, on the other hand, as leading—which it really does—to the suspicion of a proud activity, bestowing too much care on transitory success. Continuous observation of the whole of human life and destiny, should make reflections easy on the shortness of life, the fleeting nature of pleasure, the equivocal worth of this world's goods, the relation between reward and

[1] *The Science of Education*, p. 181.

work. In contrast, should be placed the possibility of frugality, the peace of those whose needs are small, the contemplation of nature, which meets our needs, makes industry possible, and on the whole rewards, however much it forbids dependence on its single isolated results. Thence we should lead the pupil to a universal teleological search, which however must remain in the sphere of Nature, and not go astray in the chaos of human pursuits. Above all the mind must keep Sabbath in religion. It should turn to it for rest from all thoughts, desires, cares. But for its highest solemnisation, community with many, with the church, should be welcome. Only the pupil must remain sufficiently temperate while there, to·despise fantastic and mystic jugglery, as well as the affectations of mysticism, as being far beneath the dignity of religion.

Even if we admit that the rationalization of metaphysical experience is always a precarious procedure and that Herbart rightly fought against the sophisticated romanticism of his time, we cannot avoid the feeling that this mixture of moralization and speculation is wan compared with the religion of Comenius and Pestalozzi. To apply words of the latter to Herbart, we could say that God is not his nearest "relationship." It shows the blindness of the Prussian reaction after 1848 that it forbade the teaching of the doctrines of the "atheist" Pestalozzi in the normal schools, while Herbart, though he personally did not lay any value on this honor, was invited to court and his system introduced into the institutions for the training of teachers.

Herbart had to pay for the privilege of seeing his educational philosophy become the standardized system in the Prussian and later in all the German normal schools. These schools did not attract the best type of instructors; they attracted either theologians with speech impediments or secondary-school teachers with bad examinations, and, furthermore, the students were the immature sons of the lower middle classes or the poor farmers. Naturally Herbart's ideas were dragged down from their philosophic heights and degenerated into a pseudoscientific psychology and a spiritless admiration of methods from which the science of education in almost all countries has not yet recovered.

There must be some explanation for the fact that Herbart's educational philosophy spread so quickly not only over Germany but over almost all the Western countries. We see it in the general spirit of the Victorian era. This era shows certain similarities in England, the European mainland, and the United States. Herbart, though he belonged to the preceding generation, naturally appealed to it through his happy mixture of tradition and progress, of discipline and liberty, of technical exactness and taste for the liberal arts, of empiricism and faith. His theory of the many-sidedness of interests as the basis of a good general education was in congruence with the trends of the period. His ideal of harmony and of a well-balanced equilibrium of all human qualities, his suspicion of exaggerated emotions, and his individualism were all attractive to an era that indulged so intensely in a feeling of progress that even the misery of the masses in the early industrial period, child labor, the famines in India and Ireland, and the breakdown of the liberal movements in central Europe could not deeply disturb the happy equilibrium of the typical bourgeois.

It was, nevertheless, a great era, just as Herbart's philosophy is a great work. Every large country during this time harbored many of its profoundest thinkers and, with rare exceptions, allowed them to speak and write freely; universal education was generally introduced; and there were as many fighters against injustice and exploitation as in any other period. What makes many of us today so inclined to severe criticism of the generation of our grandfathers is partly the consequences of their good deeds. They educated the large masses so that now they are asking for their share in the common wealth, which they cannot be given without revolutionary changes in our economic and political systems. They opened their minds to the cultural influences of the whole world and their countries to world trade, so that now we find it difficult to establish a balance between the abundance of possibilities and concentration of our efforts. They gave free rein to experiment and investigation and consequently to trial and error. The men of this period were still so mentally vigorous and resistant to the disintegrating centrifugal forces they had set free that they could believe in the final capacity of humanity to melt in the crucible of advancing culture even the most contradictory trends. Among them the burning of forbidden books and the persecution of heretic religions had almost disappeared; today both have been revived. In some countries they had, if not complete freedom of teaching in their universities, nevertheless more than in any other period. Since their era ended, broadly speaking, in the World War, we have a right to question the value of what they did. But the

Christian Middle Ages had its Hundred Years' War between France and England; the period of the Reformation and Counter Reformation ended in thirty years of destruction, and the period of Enlightenment in the French Revolution and the Napoleonic wars. And who knows toward what future events we are driving?

In addition, the nineteenth century, in spite of its individualism, was the first which took the education of the large masses of teachers seriously. And when it used Herbart as its guide, it did not make a bad choice. No modern philosopher-pedagogue has yet arisen able to comprehend and formulate the achievements and needs of our times as Herbart succeeded in doing for the post-Napoleonic period. An educational philosophy which has as its goal the determination of moral behavior by the use of reason is not the worst of choices for any period. The elementary teacher educated in the normal schools of the nineteenth century generally knew his subject much better than his predecessor in earlier centuries; he was a good schoolmaster interested in his children, a hard worker with a low salary and inadequate social prestige, intellectually awake, eager to learn and to raise the standards of his profession. Herbartian humanism was an educational movement of great success and productivity. Have we today its equal, if we take into account the difficulties with which Herbartianism had to reckon when it began its work?

4. Modern Eclecticism, Pragmatism, and Nationalism

Herbartianism has been replaced, in democratic countries, by eclecticism in regard to the aims and methods of education and by the so-called progressive-school movement; and, in authoritarian countries, by an indoctrination of the official philosophy of the political state, which can make external technical use for its own purposes of the methods of any pedagogical school—Herbartian, eclectic, or progressive—without any allegiance to their spirit.

The Fascist philosophy of education became acceptable in consequence of two factors. The first was the increasing separation of the process of education from any persistent religious or humanistic criterion. The second was the unrest and the defeatist psychology arising from the insecurity of the political and economic situation. The two factors together create a sense of fatigue and of the relativity of all formerly stable values, which, combined with a fear of the future, causes men to desire submission to a directing power. The situation that gave rise to Fascist education is similar to that which, after the collapse of the French Revolution, made possible the rise of Napoleon and his creation of the "université imperiale," the completely state-governed school system.

In democratic countries education has relied largely on empiricism and experimentation. Much of it—for example, the interest in adapting the educational process to the mental and physical growth of the child—has been a natural continuation of the work of previous periods. But in consequence of the development of psychology, physiology, and medicine, these methods could be greatly improved and intensified. Only an extreme *laudator temporis acti* could deny the improvement in the relations of teacher and child, the better hygienic conditions, and the beginnings of an effective co-operation of the educator with the physician, the dietitian, the psychologist, and the sociologist in the interest of the child,

Why, under such conditions, is not success so great as we have a right to expect? Partly because we have not yet mastered the effect of the social changes on our schools, partly because the majority of teachers are still insufficiently educated to apply modern knowledge to their work; but not least because we do not possess an inclusive philosophy and policy of education such as the nineteenth century possessed in the Herbartian system. In proportion as the opinion has spread that the end is either undefinable or negligible, in education and in any other field of life, ways and means have gained in importance and are liable to be substituted for the end. But this substitution has always proved fallacious.

So it is not only with a feeling of pride for what we have gained but with a feeling of the utmost modesty that we should read the works of Comenius, Pestalozzi, and Herbart. In modern educational theory and practice many good suggestions have been advanced for the improvement of the technique of teaching, for psychological insight, for the organization of education, and for the measurement of its results; but these specific suggestions can come to their fruition only if they are embedded in a comprehensive understanding of man, and of instruction and knowledge in the framework of civilization. And this understanding we have yet to gain.

C. EDUCATIONAL PRACTICE

1. The Necessity of Decision

The question that troubles conscientious educators and parents in our time is whether there is any possible way to be found of making the school an active source of culturally constructive values.

In attempting to answer this question theoretically and practically we must first of all dismiss any hope of finding a solution in the indoctrination of an inherited pattern of ideas, no matter what glorious tradition it may represent. Those favoring such a solution usually point to the futility of historical periods given over to rapid but undirected change. Undoubtedly such periods, even those with a high degree of freedom, were essentially futile, for freedom is a *fata morgana* unless men have a purpose for which it is worth while to be free. Late antiquity was perhaps the freest period, if freedom means absence of a common religious and ethical tradition. But eventually control of the empire fell into the hands of the dictators, and at the same time the Christian Church had to build up a rigid dogma in order to stem the tide of sectarianism within its own walls. Nothing so dispersed and dissipated the original energy of the Reformation idea of religious individualism as the centrifugal forces of the social and religious revolutions that followed it. The ideals of liberty and equality that motivated the French Revolution were denied by the absolutism of Robespierre and Napoleon, and the lack of great international political ideals during the recent postwar period explains the rise of the modern dictatorships.

Facts of this sort support the conservative who demands stability and the fixation of the present conditions. But other facts bear testimony to the contrary. There is in humankind an unceasing power of creativeness, and any attempt to thwart it deprives man of the wonderful gift of rejuvenescence. Even if one assumes that this periodic renewal does not generate anything previously unknown, just as spring does not create completely new forms of nature, still one may hold that every generation should be given a chance to have its youth. Periods that deny this birthright are those either of undeveloped primitiveness or of despair and dogmatism. If one goes deeper into the problem of the rise and decline of civilizations, he may even discover that excessive liberty and excessive reaction are twins, and that in periods of decay both are at work. For the analysis of such situations a concept can be applied which we have already used for the explanation of the problem of personality; namely, the concept of "form." Growth and form must go together in order to give living unity both to individuals and to civilizations, or vitality will run wild, the resulting fear of chaos will kill vitality, and the vicious circle is completed.

But in those epochs that retain form even sharp conflicts can be harmonized. Then contrasts too powerful for other times resolve themselves into a higher unity and are the stimulus to constructive thought and action. The twelfth and thirteenth centuries showed such power of synthesis. After a long period of untamed adolescence the western European countries suddenly matured from a prevailing feeling of passive reference to authority to an active acceptance of ancient thought. The Church first forbade the use of pagan philosophy in the lecture rooms and libraries; it felt—not quite mistakenly, as Luther's criticism was later to show—the completely alien character of the new element. But the burst of intellectual enthusiasm was too strong, the Popes had to yield to the fervor of the new learning, and the result was the foundation of the modern university and the theology of Thomas Aquinas, today still of canonic value for the Catholic Church. Youth faced maturity, adventure opposed reaction—but these contrasts worked together toward the first great renaissance of Occidental civilization. What help would it be, therefore, if we today forbade new ideas because they are frightening to those who do not want to be thrown off their accustomed course of faith and action? Our period must either find the power to synthesize movements that at first may seem hopelessly contradictory, or it must admit that it has lost its vigor and for that reason cannot be saved. We must, of course, examine, refute, and select. But nobody is more certainly doomed to failure than the hysteric who sees an affliction and the danger of chaos in every trial and thinks to save himself by escape instead of by facing the problem.

The prolongation of outworn forms of life means a slow decadence in which there is repetition without any fruit in the reaping of value. There may be high survival power. For decadence, undisturbed by originality or by external forces, is a slow process. But the values of life are slowly ebbing. There remains the show of civilization, without any of its realities.[1]

In view of these considerations, we see, then, that our question must be reformulated as follows. How can our strivings and our conflicts, no matter what novelties they may give rise to, be so molded that they will enrich and not destroy us? How can we have flow and form together? And, to move from the general problem to our specific interest, how can we educate our children so that they may face the new with courage and an open mind without losing themselves in meaningless adventure?

[1] Whitehead, *Adventures of Ideas*. Macmillan, 1933. Page 358.

In order to give an answer we must refer to our previous discussion of the moral problem. Education can discharge its obligations to modern man only if it succeeds in inculcating in him an ethical attitude that combines the spirit of experimentalism with a profound faith in a deeper meaning of life. The power to realize this meaning gives man his special dignity and enables him to elevate himself above mere chance, to be himself and to preserve himself.

The belief in a persistent ethical trend throughout the history of man does not, however, deny the existence of moral conflicts. There not only is the frequent antagonism between our temporary personal inclinations and our obligations, but conflicts arise that are genuinely tragic, making us guilty whatever solution we choose or however long we try to delay our decision. Hamlet's predicament is only a particularly cruel example created by the imaginative genius of a great dramatist.

There will always be conflicts between justice and injustice, bravery and the desire for self-preservation, egoism and sympathy, patriotism and our oneness with all humanity, truth and reverence for tradition. If it were not so, one of the greatest and most poignant stimuli to human history, its dialectical character,[1] would be lacking as an incentive to thought and action. But here we come upon the fundamental issue. Conflicts springing from the antagonism of values, even when most destructive or chaotic, are distinct from critical situations brought about by the degeneration of values. When *values* conflict, those who suffer are always involved in problems of

---

[1] We use the term "dialectical" here and in other places in a freer sense than Hegel and without his metaphysical implication.

profound significance; they become wiser and stronger even in error and retain dignity even if they perish. The tragic hero in a play of Shakespeare, Racine, or Schiller elevates the minds of men even in his distress and his death. But if struggle goes on in an individual or a society because the ethical urge is no longer felt, it means that decay is present; and the meaninglessness of the struggle is felt by both the participants and the spectators.

What are the concrete materials and the practical means by which the educator can convey to the younger generation a sense for the values previously analyzed?

2. THE SCHOOL AS SOCIAL ENVIRONMENT

One of the most essential answers has been given by Pestalozzi. In "The Evening Hours of a Hermit," which we have already quoted, he speaks of the importance of "next relations." The child's immediate environmental experience, the atmosphere that he breathes, is of primary importance, because it appeals constantly to the totality of his being and not to any special capacity such as his intelligence. The child lives in, and is nourished by, the concrete; and though his world is small, it is, nevertheless, as intense and inclusive as any. In earlier times the child's world was usually sounder than it is today: consider how natural and simple were the village, the father's and mother's work, the farm, the fields and the animals, the neighbors and relatives, compared with the modern industrial city. Hence, the old schoolmaster was perhaps more entitled to content himself with the teaching of subject matter than the modern educator can be. But there were, of course, extremely dark pictures in those earlier times. The village was not always idyllic, as we see the moment

we examine the life of our forefathers in different countries without historical sentimentality, or read such a book
as Pestalozzi's socioeducational novel, *Leonard and Gertrude*. Here, as in his "Evening Hours," the author lays
emphasis on healthy surroundings and not on formal
schooling. The latter cannot achieve much unless it grows
out of a supporting spirit in the homes and in the village
life. Therefore, Pestalozzi gives the prime role in his fic-
tional reform of a desolate Swiss village to a simple woman,
Gertrude, the wife of the mason Leonard. She has turned
her home, in spite of all difficulties, into an ideal educational microcosmos from which radiates an influence that
affects the whole community. Not until her influence has
prepared the ground can the patriarchal governor of the
district go to work and an inspired philanthropist, who
has observed Gertrude's efforts, hopefully found his school.
His school is not founded upon the thought of philosophers
and statesmen but upon Gertrude's practical intuition.

Though the external situation has changed so greatly,
the modern school, even in the large city, can still profit
from the ideas of the mason's wife into whose mouth the
Swiss educator puts his own wisdom. As a matter of fact,
the rise of that kind of progressive education that regards
the school not as an isolated institution but as a social
agency coincides with the rediscovery of Pestalozzi. The
progressive movement has seen that the home and the
community alone cannot be relied upon to provide the atmosphere conducive to healthy growth. Hence, we must
provide by artificial means, or, better, by the use of art,
those productive "next relations" which Pestalozzi holds
to be essential for the formation of the child's character.
Only in such a way can the children not favored by good

social conditions outside the school be enabled to associate the knowledge they acquire with habits and morals conducive to its use. But even those children who enjoy helpful environment outside the school now spend half their waking hours in school and carry from it not only the results of the teacher's instruction but decisive personal experiences. Therefore, the forms of social address and contact among teachers and pupils need to be cultivated. The child must learn to be a comrade and to be respected as a comrade, to recognize the claim of an adequate and understanding authority, and he must be given the freedom to develop his own interests and individual qualities. He has also to co-operate in various forms of self-government in order to learn early the rules and responsibilities of a self-governing body. Those schools which bring the child into contact with either industrial or agricultural work and which induce him to use his hands for production, to plant flowers and vegetables, and to take care of animals have a deeper social significance than the teaching of special abilities. If managed in the right spirit, such activities reach into the unreflective, character-forming regions of the individual life; if wrongly understood, however, they may do nothing but contribute to modern restlessness, subjectivism, and lack of intellectual discipline.

In respect to the cultivation of social relationships, we can fully subscribe to some sentences in a leaflet entitled *The New Education Fellowship and the World Situation*, published by an international educational society, the New Education Fellowship:

If we set up as our ideal an organization of society that shall allow of the fullest development of every human being, we must build our educational institutions in such a manner that this ideal is directly experienced as a way of living. We must therefore strive to make the school into a functioning community in living relationship with the larger community outside. We must make cooperation a day-by-day reality, giving each individual a feeling of responsibility for the whole and a share in determining the common life of himself and his fellows. We must foster the habit of independent thought and expression of opinion and seek to establish the method of discussion and persuasion rather than of compulsion, and we must accept as a matter of course respect for the individual conscience. In such ways democracy in the profoundest sense of the term will become a part of the mentality of the children in our educational institutions. They will pass from the school into the world at large without having to readjust their basic values, and they will be fitted to take their place in the great adventure of bringing into being a society based on these values.

The idea of the school as a living community might be considered as the educational application of some essential parts of our earlier chapter on psychology. We spoke there of a large sphere of unreflective forms of behavior closely connected with vital urges working at the basis of human personality. The progressive movement in all countries has transferred to education the insight that sound growth of these unreflective elements of the person is of greatest significance for his entire psychophysical development. Since they cannot be cultivated by merely verbal approaches, the only way to influence and use them profitably is to place the child in a living environment that stimulates this more "instinctive" side through a conducive atmosphere and natural forms of activity.

Here we have also the psychological explanation of Pestalozzi's emphasis on the right "immediate relationships" in earliest youth and throughout the whole process of life. His prophetic mind had understood that education cannot get beyond the superficiality of words into the "innermost nature" of a person unless the educator is aware of his responsibility for the unreflective sphere. The latter forms our character more significantly than all influences that remain only on the level of reflection and reason.

3. The School as a Place of Instruction and Mental Discipline

The radical wing of progressivism has sometimes been inclined to emphasize the psychological conditions of individual growth at the expense of introducing the child to the objective side of civilization. Civilization is not what a number of children and teachers would like to make it, but it has weight of its own and exerts pressure upon its members. The more it advances and the more its individual members want to participate in its advancement, the more they need knowledge, broad human understanding, and trained intelligence.

The gradual change from protected childhood into the freedom of the adult, with its demand for self-discipline and responsibility, is impossible without learning. Doubtless Herbart has not sufficiently emphasized environment as a factor in education. He is, however, more realistic than many modern educators in his appreciation of the value of instruction. It is not only that later in life knowledge and reason are needed but that the right way of acquiring them, right learning, is indispensable for building a steadfast and rounded character. Mental discipline in the profoundest sense is not only something "externally imposed," though it needs a certain amount of enforcement. If carried through in the right way, it becomes an attitude or an "ethos" that regulates behavior, influences tastes and decisions, and becomes the recognizable characteristic of an educated person, whether a college graduate or not. Teachers who have neglected to give this discipline to their students are guilty of an irreparable sin of omission.

The demands of instruction may now be seen to converge with our psychological and ethical philosophy in a twofold way. First, learning means discipline and acquiring an idea of purpose that, as we saw, is requisite to the formation of an integrated human personality; second, learning deals with subject matter, in the acquisition of which a growing individual can find the necessary substance for his purposes.

Now, the contents and values of civilization have not descended from the blue but have resulted, whatever their ultimate origin may be, from the continuous struggle of the human race for its total self-realization. Therefore, it is the business of education to help the younger generation to project itself in a sympathetic way into those deeds and ideas that have contributed to the rise and richness of our Western, Christian civilization. It is not that we think this the only civilization worth being acquainted with; but it is the environment in which we live, for which our fathers in different parts of the earth have worked and fought, to which we owe our happiness or unhappiness, and for the preservation and modification of which we are responsible.

If we follow the consequences of this position, the ethical aim of the school subsumes an increasing factual content and descends from an abstract ideal to the realms of tangible reality.

4. THE HUMANITIES

As one result of this position and its implications, we are led to doubt the wisdom of the increasing tendency in education to neglect our religious and philosophic tradition and other fields of the humanities, such as history, literature, and languages. Advocates of sound traditionalism frequently hear the objection that in a time when technical inventions and the experiences and tasks issuing from them have given a greater complexity and a new content to our lives it is no longer desirable to emphasize the abstract interests and the "bookish learning" of an earlier time. The automobile, the radio, the airplane are doubtless more than objective additions to our civilization; they are also a challenge to the young mind, which adapts itself to the new situation they create with rather amazing ease. When modern children speak with easy familiarity of the latest innovation in automobiles and airplanes, it almost seems not only as if they know more than we but as if their intellectual energy has grown with the increasing demands upon it. But so optimistic a belief in the creative power of our modern technical civilization is contradicted by another consideration.

If we read the works of those thinkers on whom our civilization essentially rests, we come to the conviction that their intellectual and ethical qualities have been equaled by only a very few modern geniuses and surpassed by none—if any comparative evaluation of such achievements is possible at all. The growth and progress in culture during the past two thousand years has been possible only because humankind has constantly returned to the great creators of its spirit, to the founders of its religion and to its poets and philosophers—to Plato, Aristotle, Plotinus, Descartes, Spinoza, Goethe. The changing contents of civilization, of course, force every new generation to adapt their minds to tasks and to develop methods unforeseen by their predecessors; our mental organism becomes, perhaps, an increasingly finer receptor of outer stimuli and, perhaps, our nervous system more irritable and refined. But we have not gained equally in profundity. The field has grown larger, but the plow does not go deeper.

This consideration and the obligations of the schools we have previously discussed suggest the one-sidedness of the modern tendency to content ourselves with studying only the present. Culture grows and is continuously reshaping itself as history advances. Therefore, the study of modern times can come to full fruition in understanding only if the students simultaneously enrich themselves by going deeper and deeper into the fundamentals of our Western civilization. This requirement is, of course, not fulfilled if, in consequence of deficient organization of content and bad methods of learning, indigestible bits of historical knowledge and literature are forced down the throats of the young. The humanities become of human value only if the subject matter has been absorbed and vitalizes the mental functions as good food does the body. But as the physical organs cannot make use of the energy in our food without the physical and chemical co-operation of the total organism, so also the learning process cannot assist in the production of a personality unless the student develops from a passive receiver into an active person. This development is the central principle and common denominator of an education. In the course of time the individual must even come to rejoice in overcoming difficulties involved in the process of schooling and to recognize that with each advance a broader scope of the world's meaning is opened to him.

The development away from the humanities has often been justified by referring to the necessity of professional and vocational training. But this argument does not take into account the fact that during the last decades the time of school attendance has been extended and young people have until eighteen or later for the fully rounded education they deserve. Again, the humanities have been objected to because instruction in this field has often failed to adapt itself to the interests of the young and has lacked immediateness and vitality. This has, doubtless, been true. Progressive education itself, however, has developed improved methods of teaching that can vitalize these subjects, and one must not forget that, according to an ancient Greek saying, the gods have put the toil of sowing before the harvest. The older humanistic training, we should remember, with its emphasis on the ancient languages, was designed for a selected group of students, and it would be harmful to advocate giving it a monopolistic position in a modern American high school with a school population completely different from that of the older classical institutions. Even there many of the students were longing for the day when they could burn their grammars and textbooks; many graduated from school disappointed with the education they had received, empty and unprepared for the natural kind of life they were entering. It is easy to understand why the controversy over the value of the ancient languages should have begun so soon, not long after the rise of the vernaculars and after the Humanists of the Renaissance, scoffing at the predominant international Latin of the Middle Ages, had displaced it with their slavish imitations of the Ciceronian style.

There were, of course, the finest of men among the teachers of Greek and Latin, men so firmly rooted in an old culture that their eye for the faults in the contemporary scene and the tasks that needed to be faced was almost infallible. Many of those who studied under them, under the avowed influence of their classical breeding, became the "democrats" and the "radicals" of their times. For they had been inculcated with the power of logical thinking and with standards that did not allow them to succumb to the inducement of their governments or the fads of the time so easily as some devotees of modernism.

But a considerable number of the classicists who cried out most loudly against the loss of noble standards and the increase of vulgarity felt no obligation to transfer their convictions into actuality They were self-conceited, distrustful of any new ideas, and supporters of political and cultural reaction. The inexhaustible vigor of antiquity is best shown by its ability to survive this misuse and to remain for thousands in the Western world the part of their education they are convinced is most valuable and which they want their children to have the benefit of. It is short-sighted to allow the pressure of masses to lead to the neglect of these more subtle claims by those who would be able to fulfill them if the school system not only provided opportunity but exercised a wholesome pressure. No modern nation is strong enough to dispense with these old resources of culture and to live increasingly on substitutes without lasting harm, just as no nation is strong enough to dispense in general with the knowledge of foreign languages and thus to lose contact with the achievements and the failures of other peoples.

But the decrease in emphasis on the classics has not led, as one might expect, to an increase in learning of the modern languages. If the classical studies, for reasons which we have tried to explain, are more and more pushed aside, then at least a reading knowledge of two modern languages should be required of every student who has the ambition to prepare for a profession or to arrive at a leading position in other fields of life. Such knowledge has greatly contributed to the competitive power of those nations which have demanded it, and its neglect will lead us more and more into regionalism; lack of good international orientation in economic, political, and scientific respects; and, consequently, to dependency on secondhand sources and propaganda. Strong school standards in the preparation for intellectually creative positions impede, by the way, not at all the acknowledgment of the "self-made man," so necessary for a dynamic society. On the contrary, his chances have not gained during the past decades. The reason is that he is, on his way up, just as much hindered by the competition of masses of candidates for every desirable position as he would be by the maintenance of old class privileges.

We must be honest enough to see that much of our modern opposition to languages and to a thorough historical foundation of learning is not the result of loyalty to positively new ideas, but of a desire for comfortable self-deception. In reality, it results from the unfortunate convergence of three factors. First, many teachers and teachers of teachers do not possess the equipment necessary for a real appreciation of the value of the disinterested studies for the formation of the individual and his civilization and disguise this fact behind a merely utilitarian philosophy of education. For this reason we need a much more intensive interest of *all* faculties in our best colleges and universities in the training of teachers. Second, our schools, particularly our secondary schools and colleges, have not yet found the adequate curricula and ways of selecting and classifying students, necessitated by the growth of the school population, which will guarantee both the highest possible development of the intelligent and care for the needs of the mediocre. The solution of this particular problem is one of the most crucial needs of the American high school. Finally, we have not yet found a synthesis of the valuable insistence of modern educational psychology that we respect individual differences and the fact that there are, after all, objective purposes involved in the business of education and that a nation must "risk its boys in order to raise men." [1]

Solicitude for the mental hygiene and joyful learning of the younger generation is one part of the interests of a good educator; the other is solicitude for high quality of

[1] See *The Report of the President of Harvard University, 1937–38*; Henry W. Holmes, *Shall Teachers Be Scholars?*; and Robert Ulich, *On the Reform of Educational Research*.

the civilization which he has also to serve. If the objective standards of civilizations are emphasized at the expense of the psychic and physical welfare of the youth—as was, doubtless, the case in some older European school systems—then grave disturbances in the individual adjustment of many children and even social crises may be the result. But if the personal interests of the child are too much put into the foreground, then educational psychology glides over into a hedonistic misinterpretation of the business of education. The whole process finally ends in a lowering of the child's and the nation's efficiency and in all those conflicts which necessarily arise if the wonderful human gift of solicitude mistakes itself for overgreat softness. And then, also, psychological and social maladjustments and loss of real human happiness will come in the wake of such a misleading philosophy of life.

Even such studies as sociology, civics, and government cannot give either the teacher or the student the full amount of their inherent value until he knows the history and nature of the movements and groups that have been woven into the structure of society and that have made it what it is, with both its good and its evil.

5. The Organization of Instruction

But here a conflict arises. The intellectual world has grown too large to be viewed by one individual alone. Departmentalization and specialization work against the essential wholeness of life. Herbart tried to solve this contradiction by applying two notions, that of the many-sidedness of interests and that of moral strength of character. The development of many-sidedness of interests was considered the way to reconcile the natural limitations of the individual with the richness of culture. The purpose of instruction, said Herbart, is, therefore, to awaken the student's interest in the most important cultural components. But in order to avoid an un-co-ordinated knowledge and consequently a confused personality, education has at the same time to aim at the formation of a strong character, able to select and to tie together the different parts of knowledge. With this combination of many-sidedness and strength of character Herbart has not only described two trends that we find in every well-developed personality but has also outlined the prerequisites of any good education. For a good education shows, like respiration, a continuous rhythm of expansion and contraction. But rhythm needs a melody, a movement or an idea, running through the rhythmic expansions and contractions, so that the two elements are woven into a higher and more meaningful unity than either could possess alone. In the same way the school must not present its students with disjointed facts from the various categories of knowledge and experience. It must know that true education and character building are possible only when learning is not simply accumulative but is rather an expanding circle of understanding.

Education as organic growth has often been neglected for two reasons: first, because the schools have attempted to adapt themselves to the rapidly increasing complexity of modern civilization by a corresponding increase in the number of subjects in the curriculum and in this attempt have been overwhelmed by the very conditions they were trying to meet; second, because the modern elective system, a praiseworthy attempt to allow for individual preferences in the organization of a student's course of study, is likely to neglect the fact that the growth of individuality is the very contrary of arbitrariness in the choice of tasks or of choice on the basis of least resistance.

The result of these unfortunate developments is that we have schools where the student, without accompanying courses in the history of civilization, is allowed to begin a course in a foreign language and to drop it as soon as he feels the first difficulties, in this way cheating himself of the rewards of his labor. Or he may choose chemistry without knowledge of mathematics or physics and the study of current events without a clear idea of the past of his own country. Naturally there emerges from this training a flighty personality with flighty knowledge and methods of work. The good intentions of thinking educators have been turned into poor accomplishment, and both subject matter and the formation of character have suffered.

The difficulty of the task we must face is, of course, that, as with all relationships in education, the relation between many-sidedness and strength of character and between expansion and concentration is functional. A formula cannot be offered that will answer all questions concerning the amount of expansion and restriction, the centers from which to expand, and the rhythm of learning and instruction. The answers depend upon the sort of school, the type of training, the subject matter, the individuals involved, and many other factors. The teacher without a certain sensibility for values and an insight into the trends and needs of the student will never be a good guide to growth. Just as the physician needs, in addition to his technical knowledge, a feeling for the intangibles in the personality of his patients, so the teacher needs an insight without which he will either overdose or underdose and, as a curriculum maker, will mistake the mechanics for the essence.

Much of our modern education, in its lack of clearness and proportion, reminds us of the Victorian architecture of the late nineteenth century. In the fine arts we are beginning to acquire a new and better sense for style. It is no longer the pompous mansion of the 1890's that pleases us, but its older neighbors with their simple but well-balanced proportions or a modern house with emphasis on purposeful simplicity. Will education succeed in finding a similar mixture of good taste and sincerity?

6. NEW WAYS TOWARD EDUCATIONAL VALUES

Our demand for an organic and concentric education leads us to ask why, if the older forms of education succeeded in arranging their material around a clearly defined core of interests, we could not do the same with subjects in which the modern man is naturally more interested than in the classical studies of earlier centuries.

This problem is essentially not only that of the school but that of civilization. When the Middle Ages placed religion at the center of education and the following centuries the humanities, they were expressing more than merely pedagogical convictions; they were furthering the realization of the spirit of their own times. Our modern age, likewise, cannot truly find itself unless we find for our schools an organizing idea which will simultaneously make our youth and ourselves aware of the needs of our time and its particular mission in the history of mankind.

If we should succeed in permeating our schools with such a uniting spirit, it would be at the same time a symbol and a prophecy: a symbol of the power of this period to find in the midst of all diversity its own integrating idea, and a prophecy that American youth imbued with this idea could assume with good hope of success the task of reconstructing the Western world, a task which Europe's failure places in the hands of America.

This task will consist in carrying the great achievements of the preceding period—religious consciousness, individual liberty, and scientific freedom—into a period which will, whether or not we welcome it, be primarily concerned with superindividual planning and collectivistic enterprise. We shall have to speak later of this great problem in more detail. Here we can only emphasize that any method of concentrating human effort toward better co-operation will lead to suppression and human disaster unless it is combined with an evolutionary understanding of, and a deep faith in, the body of values which our ancestors called the "natural rights of the individual." If they are suppressed by social "engineers," whose "empirical" thinking regards only the whole and disregards its parts and is, therefore, not really empirical, the solution of our economic and political problems will not be made in harmony with the profoundest demands of human existence which we discussed in the ethical chapters of this book.

The principle of organization which we desire for modern education must not, of course, be interpreted primarily in terms of one specific and fixed body of subject matter. The Middle Ages did not limit instruction to religion nor the humanistic period to the classics; still less could we, in modern times, give a monopoly to any particular subject. Each part of a modern curriculum must be at the same time part of a unified whole and a discipline with methods of its own. Leveling and dull uniformity are the very contrary of our aim. What we want is to create in the student an attitude entailing a certain way of looking at things and of meeting the challenge of the times with courage and a living logic. Nevertheless, in instruction, as everywhere, spirit and attitude are not completely separable from actual knowledge of a certain subject matter, and, therefore, there must be a core in the modern curriculum that represents the primary source of direction and inspiration.

Two spheres of knowledge, brought to the fore by the cultural development of the last centuries, offer themselves to the modern educator as the nucleus of a new curriculum: one, the social studies; the other, the natural sciences. So far neither has achieved the degree of unity possessed by the classical schools at their best.

SOCIAL STUDIES

The social studies undoubtedly have one great advantage: they can be related to problems of the greatest and most immediate actuality. They could also form the natural center of a curriculum designed to explain the meaning of the political, social, and spiritual history of the nation and of mankind. They could reveal the genesis and development of language and literature. They would lead easily to studies of the community and to the organization of instruction with respect to the industrial and economic environment of the school. In the intelligent student they would awaken the desire to acquaint himself with the important historical sources and with the languages in which they are written. They could open avenues toward the understanding of both the spiritual and the practical basis of life. The student could learn the role of applied science and scientific technique in our modern civilization. Manual and theoretical work could easily be linked together. Even mathematics could, without difficulty, be integrated with the general field. In most classical schools of the nineteenth century mathematics was thoroughly cultivated as a method of logical training; but it was often something like the suburbs surrounding an old city, which have not yet arrived at a style of their own and have no organic connection with their center. Alongside the study of ancient and modern languages, mathematics was often a stranger; and the teacher felt himself similarly isolated. Of course, it could have been nicely woven into the spirit of the older classical school had it been taught according to the historical method, following it from its beginning in the ancient civilizations up to contemporary times. It would then have stood forth clearly in the minds of the students as one of the most ingenious of man's ways of gaining power over the external world, using for this great purpose not verbal but numerical symbols. But a school centered around the social sciences could most likely find other and better methods than the historical method in order to show the young the nature and the necessity of mathematics without in any way depriving it of its proper methods and qualities. Actually, there is nothing which could not, by gradually progressing from the immediate to the more distant activities of man, be related to the social sciences provided they understood themselves profoundly enough as the discipline dealing not only with the external relations of men but also with values and meanings behind or within these relations.

Such a system of studies would allow for unity within multiplicity, and not only with respect to subject matter but also with respect to individual differences. The more practical-minded might branch out into application; the more theoretical, into history, languages, and general thought. And even the child with a modest degree of intelligence could be led to see some sense in the great interests and activities of mankind. Some progressive schools have already been built on similar ideas and have proved successful.

So a thorough training centered in the social studies could accomplish more than the older, one-sided classical schools if only it could equal them in one respect, the accuracy of thinking which training in languages requires. A boy learning to read, and particularly to write, his own and a foreign language is working with one of the most admirable achievements of the human mind. He is forced constantly to logical thinking in analyzing grammatical and syntactical relations in order to express a thought as clearly as possible. Those modern educators who have laid so much value on the principle of learning by doing have themselves failed to realize that there is scarcely anywhere so much possibility for learning by doing—intellectual doing—as in translating from one language to another. This training has the further advantage that blunders in thinking immediately reveal themselves. There is, especially in the beginning of linguistic studies, no doubt about the correct or incorrect use of the majority of grammatical and syntactical rules. The social sciences, following the historical method, do not offer such clear criteria of accurate thinking. In order to avoid the dry memorization of chronological and statistical data which older people remember from their history course, progressive schools lay the main emphasis on developing the sense for human relations. But much of this instruction consists primarily of an exchange of personal opinions, which involves, undoubtedly, a certain type of mental gymnastics, for the complexity of social problems leaves room in many cases for the defense of different standpoints. But this, in turn, is liable to result in a relativistic attitude, in arrogance and premature skepticism, or, in other cases, in a passive acceptance of the opinions of the teacher. Many children leave the course in current events more confused than when they entered, while the language courses at least help to develop thoroughness and exactness.

NATURAL SCIENCES

The other group of disciplines which could be used in our time as the core of a concentric curriculum consists of the natural sciences. The possibilities are great. First of all, the natural sciences offer in their laboratory techniques excellent opportunities for learning by doing. They can be used to give youth an understanding of the physical nature of man; the climatic and geographical environment in which he lives; the natural conditions upon which his agriculture and his industry depend; the requisites of private and public health; and, finally, man's relation to the great laws of the cosmos, with an approach to the ultimate problems of natural and general philosophy. Yet there is a remarkable discrepancy between the role of the sciences in our practical and intellectual life and the part they now play in the education of our youth. The reason lies in the philosophic immaturity of popular teaching of the natural sciences. Most of the great leaders in science, even in the positivistic-materialistic era of the nineteenth century, were, and are today, philosophically profoundly interested in the implications of their work. But the second-rank scholars, who form the main body of our college and secondary-school teachers, and the most successful of the popular writers in the field of the natural sciences have indulged in a form of scientific self-sufficiency which can but be harmful to true culture. There arose an enmity for the mere name of philosophy, departmentalization, and the fear of any personal synthesis of scientific problems which may have had advantages for laboratory work but most certainly had the greatest of disadvantages for the educational values of the natural sciences, except training in exact and unbiased observation. The latter is important, but it is not all.

Many representatives of the natural sciences are vivid examples of the thesis which we have so often stated in the context of our considerations; namely, the modern tendency to confuse ends and means. Since the natural sciences, in their methodical procedures, have, though only hypothetically, to conceive of nature as a mechanically working system of cause and effect, their adherents often transfer their methodical presuppositions into a mechanical and deterministic interpretation of the meaning and the ends of life.

The most recent developments in the natural sciences themselves show, as will any deeper and more complete philosophic thinking, the scientific illegality of the generalizations resulting from the transfer of the principle of scientific method to the interpretation of the essence of life. Nevertheless, these generalizations, usurping the impressive title of the only exact interpretation of life, have paved the way for merely "biological" interpretations of history and politics, in which machines, race, and power are elevated above mind and human culture. Certainly the elements of nature that we have so far discovered can be seen to play a part in history and politics, but we must use our knowledge to arrive at a complete understanding of life and not as an instrument of power. If knowledge is so misunderstood and misused, ruthless forms of competition and imperialism must inevitably arise and shake the national and international structure of society almost to the point of complete breakdown. Even an avowed democrat cannot constantly indoctrinate naturalistic and deterministic ideas without the risk that people will take them seriously and give up their faith in political freedom and democracy, which cannot be forced into a covenant with philosophic naturalism. Democratic institutions alone cannot automatically create a better society by the mechanical operation of the rule of cause and effect. They need a supporting spirit that believes in the human principles underlying democracy, or the egoism of power groups will destroy them.

The philosophical narrowness of the popular teaching of the natural sciences is, however, only historically conditioned and will, if the signs do not deceive us, be overcome before long. But there is another essential factor to be taken into account in examining the relationship between the natural sciences and education. This has been given classical expression in the statement of Thomas Hobbes that the main concern of man is man. This is particularly true at the age when the young are being introduced into the spirit of human society. Therefore, even our firm belief in a change in the philosophic attitude of the sciences cannot remove our doubt that they will ever become, or ought ever to become, the organizing center of the curriculum. Yet one must wish that their great values for education could be more fully realized than is the case today. For this reason it would probably be best to include them much more organically than has so far been done in either the traditional or the social-science curriculum. As we have already intimated, this could be done in the first curriculum by using the historical approach and showing the rise of science as part of the development of civilization.[1] How easily it could be done in conjunction with the social sciences has already been shown. In such conjunction the problems of nature are protected against isolation from the immediate problems of man. Instead of isolation there will be cross-fertilization between the methods and the contents of the scientific and the humanistic disciplines.

THE MODERN ORGANIC CURRICULUM

Once the social studies and the study of nature are harmonized, we shall arrive at a curriculum which, as Pestalozzi desired, will start with the "nearest relationships" of man as the center of the circle of social sciences, which will include man's relation to nature. This inner circle would cover the years of elementary training.

Around it swings another, expanding to meet the demands of secondary education. According to their interests the students are led either into the humanities or into the study of man's relationships to nature. In so far as both spheres of interest are seen as part of the social studies, they form a unity. They are not mutually exclusive in that the student specializing in one field is allowed to

---

[1] With regard to the science of medicine the historical approach has been most effectively used by H. E. Sigerist in his book *Man and Medicine*. 1932.

omit the other completely, for it is impossible to understand history and human culture without mathematics and natural philosophy or the relationship of man to nature without knowledge of his culture. The difference is one of degree and emphasis. The old and, for any sound secondary education, still important idea of the fundamental unity of culture must be preserved in order to allow the majority of the community to partake, as a cultural community, of the efforts and achievements of humanity. The two great spheres of business and technics, on the one hand, and the humanities, on the other, are already dangerously divided, and this increases the divisions from which our modern life is already suffering in consequence of its economic conflicts.

There ought to be, in addition, one uniting educational and national element in all forms of schooling, so important that it is hardly necessary to speak of it; namely, the cultivation of the vernacular, respect for its clarity and its euphony, and love of its literature.

Many boys and girls at the secondary-school level want a predominantly vocational training; and in this they should be encouraged, since our economic structure is already oversupplied with a white-collar proletariat. The connection of vocational training with a curriculum centered in the social sciences offers an excellent opportunity for giving vocational education more cultural breadth than it generally has today and for relieving the vocational departments of the reputation of narrow utilitarianism.

Equipped with such an elementary and secondary-school education, those entering college and professional schools would be able to combine the theory and specialization unavoidable at this level of learning with the necessary understanding of the real conditions and responsibilities of society. Those who after secondary school immediately begin to build their own lives would be prepared to do so with a certain insight into both the realities and the general values of culture, and those forced to leave school even earlier might be expected to be, at least, more at home in the world of their activities than they are at present.

For the educational success of the social sciences one prerequisite is a staff of teachers who understand the conditions and the functioning of society better than most educators do. Beneath the surface of the external relations lies the totality of the human being and the great problems of humanity. Society consists of more than the surface relations between men and between groups; it reaches beyond the surface into energies of a spiritual nature that only a philosophic mind can make conspicuous. But once the understanding or the recognition of these deeper forces is included, the social sciences can embrace all the fields so isolated in our customary curriculum. We might then hope to revive in the "New Humanities" the best spirit of the older, the great leaders of which were never mere historians and philologists, but men interested in man. In addition, this teaching will not be restricted to a selected group; rooted in universal elementary training, it will branch out organically from that into the more abstract and more difficult fields of knowledge reserved for the intellectual elite.

Chapter V

POSTULATES OF TEACHING

We have now arrived at a stage in the development of our ideas when it may be worth while to consider a topic of apparently more technical character; namely, methods of teaching.

With the progress of civilization a large variety of ways of conveying knowledge to the younger generation has been elaborated. Especially in recent times the problem of educational methodology has occupied the attention of teachers and parents to such an extent that it has threatened to overshadow the equally or even more significant problems of the substance and aims of instruction. The question now before us is: Are we able to discover behind all the different didactical devices worthy of our regard certain principles that may serve as criteria for distinguishing the sound and thorough from merely segmental approaches to the art of teaching? What are the philosophical postulates of method in teaching?

At the start we may briefly mention a commonplace in the theory of teaching. Good teaching is not identical with mechanical cramming of diverse subjects into the heads of children. Though this wisdom is as old as methodical thought on education itself—it is, for example, the leitmotiv permeating all pertinent chapters in Plato's *Repub-*

lic or *Laws*—it must, nevertheless, be constantly revived, lest the most insidious enemy of professional teaching, routine, creep into its marrow. But after dismissing this merely negative point, we find that a positive answer to the question as to what constitutes good teaching is not so quickly delivered. First we encounter one general difficulty; namely, an antinomy resulting from the contrast between the desire to make all methods universally applicable and the unique character of each individual educand. This antinomy renders educational method very different from the procedure of the exact scientist or from the medical treatment of one relatively isolable physical organ. In serious cases, however, both physician and educator have to do with the total individual, and there is no total individual completely similar to any other.

In respect to teaching and learning, which are but a part of the whole educational process, the contrast between the universalism of method and the uniqueness of the individual decreases to some degree, because the mental development of men, particularly within similar civilizations, runs along at least some foreseeable common trends.[1] Nevertheless, the antinomy remains true in so far as these common trends, like light reflected in mirrors of diverse polish, work and appear differently in different individuals. Inherited qualities and the influences of various environments produce an infinite number of different reactions. The process of maturation and finding one's self is easier in a naturally equipoised than in an irascible adolescent, or quicker in a boy whose interests and external opportunities converge than in a boy who has to struggle with inadequate conditions.

[1] Compare Chapter II.

It was in the hope of fitting teaching to the common traits of men that Comenius, Pestalozzi, and Herbart tried to elaborate a general methodology. It was due to the individual differences of human persons that the thought of these men failed to avoid the danger of over-simplification, particularly after it had passed over into the minds of mechanical imitators.

Still another factor ought to caution us against the claim of methods to general applicability; namely, that even the profoundest ideas on educational theory and practice display to some degree the individuality of their authors. The mixture of the divine and the realist of the seventeenth century shows itself in Comenius's *Didactica Magna;* the mixture of the idealistic humanist and the eighteenth century's rationalist in Pestalozzi's *How Gertrude Teaches Her Children;* the mixture of the mathematician and the philosopher in Herbart's *Science of Education*, and the mixture of the speculative disciple of Schelling and the social reformer in Froebel's *Education of Man.*

On the other hand, it would be erroneous to see in the dependence of systems of method on individual and historical factors nothing but limitations. These systems have deepened our thought and improved our practice of education, just because they originated in men of unique qualities of mind and character. Only through the very intensity and radicalness of their individual effort and through their power of introspection have these authors succeeded in acquiring generally significant insights into human personality. Without being profoundly at home in himself, one cannot be at home in the objective world of being; and no one who was not more deeply in possession of himself than is the average citizen has ever created

a work of universal value. This is also one of the great
paradoxes of life.

But as this paradox exists, we can never prescribe the
same patterns of method and technique to all teachers,
for all children, even if such patterns are traditionally
sacred or worthy of national emulation because of their
progressiveness. Nevertheless, certain fundamental postulates emerge if we try to pierce through the mere foreground
of techniques into the essential qualities of efficient instruction. Eight of these postulates must be considered
in this discussion.

A. THE POSTULATE OF INDIVIDUALISM OF METHOD

If teaching, not as routine, but as an art, is inseparable from the total qualities of the persons concerned with
it, then the following factors have to be taken into account before we decide to prefer one method over another.

There is, first, the personality of the teacher. A relatively intellectual and logical teacher will do his best with
a method of instruction different from that most suitable
for one whose strength lies on the emotional side; abstract
and practical minds will organize and convey even the same
subject in different ways. For the same reason different
types of students will be differently attracted by different
teachers. In addition, many environmental influences and
questions related to the goals of instruction and the aims
of the pupils enter into the situation. In a rural or in a
city school, in an industrial or in an academic institution, not only the spirit of the system and the curriculum,
but also the methods of teaching, will differ. This fact
does not indicate that each teacher ought to be allowed

to indulge exclusively in his personal predilections. Nobody is such an ingenious teacher or so strong an individual that he may not learn from other people's experiences. Furthermore, the necessary respect for the various individualities of his students and for the particular character of his subject matter compel a conscientious educator to combine awareness of his individual talents and limitations with attentiveness to the whole range of methods that may help him to extend the scope of his personality. But a good school principal will find out the inner qualities and potentialities of his staff and student body. Through wise individualization he will, as much as the circumstances allow, stimulate the varieties of human personality and develop the potential wealth of methods inherent in his profession, instead of vitiating education through dull uniformity.

B. THE POSTULATE OF TOTALITY

It is a paradox, but true, that the principle of individuality leads logically to a principle of totality. The "individual" is the total "indivisible" person. Good teaching, therefore, must address the total personality of the student in both his intellectual and his emotional aspects. In the latter we count also the function of will, though, in order to avoid the attacks of suspicious critics, we may again affirm that we do not adhere to the older faculty psychology. But in face of the tendency to neglect in our schools the training of what is commonly called the "faculty of will," we must make it clear that will is an important human quality, no matter what theory concerning the possible classifications of psychic life we may hold. Not only feelings, sentiments, or logical skill, but also the power of endurance must be cultivated in the early years of schooling if we are to help the young meet the test of life.

Under the principle of totality we do not want to insinuate that at every moment of his work the teacher can appeal to all possible parts of the human soul. Even the most interesting occupation, if thoroughly pursued, cannot uninterruptedly exude the incense of fascination. The best teacher, particularly with his more mature students, will sometimes be obliged to lead the way through dull stretches without an inspiring intellectual landscape, until a hill is reached from which again the eyes of the young travelers can take delight in the beauty of cultural creations. But as we like those journeys best where hours of strain alternate with hours of happy excitement, and hours of solitude with hours in good company, so also the journey through school should leave the student with recollections representing all the possible richness of educational experience. For if on the one hand we learn in order to master life, on the other we also learn in order to grow richer.

The postulate of totality refers not only to different mental and emotional activities, but also to the relation of body and soul. The Greek philosophers have expressed convictions about psychophysical harmony [1] through the combination of physical and musical education to which not even the most progressive schools of today have begun to live up. Only Goethe, in the Pedagogical Province, [2] comes close to the Greek ideal of the complete

---

[1] Compare especially Plato, *The Republic* and *The Laws*.

[2] Goethe, *Wilhelm Meister's Apprenticeship and Travels*, translated by Carlyle. Chapter X of *The Travels*. A new edition, revised, Boston, 1860. Vol. II, pp. 306 ff.

formation of man. But while Plato and most of the Renaissance educators, who tried to revive the ancient ideals, were caught in the prejudices of the Athenian or feudal-class society and detested the most natural form of physical exercise—namely, useful manual work—as debasing the gentleman, in more modern times manual work has been advocated as a requisite of all-sided human development, necessary not only for the worker, but also for the professional and businessman.

C. THE POSTULATE OF ADEQUATENESS

If teaching is intended to approach the total personality of the student, it must be adequate to his nature.

In observing ourselves and other people we discover that the effectiveness of learning depends very much on the inclination to learn. Inclination can spring from two sources, which under normal conditions will converge. The first is self-motivation; we like to read this book or to carry out this plan because we feel that to do so is in our own interest. The other source is motivation from outside. Somebody convinces us that our personal advantage lies in the acquisition of some special portion of knowledge, or he makes us interested in it through skillful stimulation of our perceptive background. The good teacher is, in this respect, not at all different from the good novelist or dramatic writer. But whatever the source of our voluntary attention and readiness for co-operation, whether self-motivation or motivation from outside, in either case interest and aim have become one and the same. We do not feel it a burden or an imposition to learn but, in consequence of the fusion of our will with our activity, we identify ourselves with our endeavor. Consequently, we feel it as a process of transcending and simultaneously finding ourselves. In other words, we are happy, because we are voluntarily engaged in the pursuit of something meaningful. Even the hindrances we meet on the way do not discourage us; instead, they work as a challenge for intensified use of our strength. This is the ideal pedagogical situation and, in vocational and professional life, the greatest fortune and grace a human being can be given. It offers an explanation for the fact that unusually hard workers of relatively tender health, if voluntarily absorbed by their vocation, can live a long and healthy life, while others, engaged in meaningless work, sometimes break down exactly at the moment when success is in sight. In the latter case an artificial outward stimulation has been taken away, and there remains nothing but an overworked creature. It also explains why exaggerated ambition is often to be found in individuals whose careers are inherently unsatisfying. In such cases the external success of money, power, honor, or decoration is the only way to enjoyment. Nowhere are decorations more needed for stimulation than in wars which do not fully grow out of the convictions and the self-decision of a nation.

But the principle of adequateness of learning involves considerations which go beyond the customary concepts of motivation. It is possible, and not infrequent, that either through our own initiative or through outside influence we acquire interests supposedly our own, but in reality alien to us. An impressive or dominating teacher may inadvertently direct the work of a sensitive student along lines which are not best for the student. The adolescent, often rather uncertain about his immanent nature, is susceptible to personal magnetism, particularly if unconscious or conscious erotic elements play their part in the pupil-teacher relation.

Real and highly educative interests grow out of and develop those capacities and trends in a person which help him to extend and, at the same time, to find himself. Again we must refer to the second chapter of this book, where we spoke of the harmony of all the diverse qualities and activities of a person which finally gives him the certainty of being united within himself.

Even if we avoid classifying the variety of human personalities into strictly separated types, we may suppose that every normal person possesses a certain structure of dispositions and character trends partly inherited and partly acquired. In this structure some qualities dominate and others recede, with the result that after a certain time even very common skills have almost receded and other skills have been trained to an unusual degree. The director of a great firm would no longer be a good office boy even if he had begun as such. To find the right methods and subjects for different types of personality and to construct school systems so that they help foster this endeavor instead of hindering it are among the most urgent issues in modern education. Our selective systems, with their differentiated curricula, are not only the results of the differentiation of modern vocational life; they also result from our modern insight into the principle of adequateness.

D. THE POSTULATE OF DIVERSITY OF SUBJECT MATTER

In theories of education several factors, sometimes even factors that are contradictory, have to be considered. Just as we set the postulate of totality alongside the principle of individuality, so now the principle of adequateness needs its complement. Excessive leniency to the changing whims of a young learner often leads to an exaggerated individualism in education and violates two important principles in the total process of education, one of them of psychological, and the other of objective, cultural character.

The psychological principle lies in the inherent necessity that everybody shall find for himself the immanent limits of his growth through constant trial and error of his powers. Modern teachers who forget, in their one-sided recognition of individual differences, to exert a wholesome pressure on the child to know himself by many-sided efforts fail to see the essence of good training. They err at least as much as did the older admirers of an encyclopedic form of education. The modern error ignores the difficulty of leading a mature person to the voluntary recognition of the necessity of perpetual effort and experimentation with himself when he has not learned these virtues in his youth.

The objective, cultural principle lies in the necessity, always present in a highly developed civilization, of having as many participants as possible who, in consequence of a rather comprehensive training, envision the complexity of modern private and public life and the responsibilities arising from it. An engineer who thinks only of engines, a statesman who concerns himself only with political machinery, a scholar who has never looked beyond the fences of his own field—all may be highly efficient in some respects, but nevertheless dangerous, particularly if they operate in mass and determine the ways and standards of civilization. We can fairly venture the paradox that specialization, which has built up our modern civilization, has also brought it close to ruin. We suffer not only from industrial or professional overspecialization, but also from political philosophies, economic discussions, and the amazing number of modern substitute religions which show the overwhelming influence of persons unable to see the totality of the social, cultural, and spiritual relations of man.

E. THE POSTULATE OF MENTAL ORDER

Why is it that we have a common-school system, roughly divided into an elementary, a secondary, and a tertiary level, with certain steadily developing and commonly applied methods of teaching? The answer must be —first, because we live in a civilized society that needs organization for the perpetuation and increase of its experience, and, second, because human beings display, in spite of all individual differences, a common rhythm in their psychophysical growth and a mental structure activated by certain common rules of thinking. Without accepting these premises not only would systematic education and a science of logic be impossible, but science generally, as well as civilization and culture, would not exist. As, consequently, all lasting progress depends on the increasing realization of the laws of reason in human life, so education is bound to build its own system as firmly as possible on rational elements and, in addition, to help each new generation toward their realization. On the other hand, the uncertain achievements of all our sciences and of human civilization show that we have not yet gone very far in the process of rationalization and that reason is only one of the many factors of human existence.

In spite of all difficulties which life sets up against our

attempts at classification and rationalization, we rightly speak of mental periods of infancy, childhood, adolescence, and adulthood. Though these distinctions were recognized by early educators, systematic scientific research into their specific character, their interrelationship, and their physiological background is of astonishingly short history. In this field the psychologist and educator will have to work in close connection with the physiologist in order to gain more reliable data.

Much older, however, than scientific theories about periods of mental growth are relatively detailed theories about the functions of reasoning and learning. There are the theories of Aristotle and the Scholastics of the Middle Ages. Unfortunately, though the writings of Thomas Aquinas contain much educational wisdom, they all failed to apply their excellent logical material to the theory and practice of teaching. The respectable number of post-medieval educational philosophers, beginning with Ludovico Vives and Amos Comenius, all start from the opinion not only that thought has an abstract, immanent logic, in which the Scholastic philosophers had been so intensely interested, but that thinking, and consequently also learning, must have a psychophysiological equivalent in the nature of man. Therefore, the enthusiastic demand of Comenius, Locke, Rousseau, and Pestalozzi: "Educators, observe and follow the laws of nature." But even Pestalozzi's conclusion,[1] based on the idea that the elements of learning are sound, number, and form, was still mere guesswork and in quality much below his intuitive grasp of the essential premises of education. Not before Herbart was

[1] Pestalozzi, *How Gertrude Teaches Her Children*, translated by L. E. Holland and F. C. Turner. 1898. Pages 134 ff.

it possible to build up a consistent and somewhat comprehensive hypothesis of the psychology of mental processes on which to base a system of teaching. Modern research has shown that Herbart's ideas were also based on a doubtful concept of the human mind. They are, nevertheless, much more profound and dynamic than those present educators are inclined to believe who know nothing more of his thought than the so-called five formal steps of preparation, presentation, association, generalization, and application. (These cannot be found in Herbart's own writings but were elaborated by his disciple Tuiskon Ziller.) One who goes to the original source—namely, the second book of Herbart's *Science of Education* [1]—is amazed at the richness and functional character of his ideas on teaching. It is a complete distortion of Herbart's thought that even in the more informed literature on Herbartianism so one-sided emphasis is laid on his exposition of "clearness, association, system, and method" (*Klarheit, Association, System, Methode* [2]) as essentials of instruction. It ought not to be forgotten that Herbart lays just as much stress on "interest" (*Interesse*) and "desire" (*Begehrung*), on the functions of "attention,[3] expectation, demand, and action" (*Merken, Erwarten, Fordern, Handeln*)·; that accord-

---

[1] Herbart, *The Science of Education*, translated by Henry M. and Emmie Felkin. 1892. Page 122, and especially Chapter IV, "Instruction." Herbart, *Outlines of Educational Doctrine*, translated by A. F. Lange. 1901. Chapter VII, "The Process of Instruction," pp. 105 ff.

[2] As much confusion in Herbartianism and anti-Herbartianism is due to the difficulty of translating Herbart's rather abstract terminology into English, we add the original German terms to the English version. They can be found on pages 47–77 of Herbart's *Allgemeine Pädagogik, aus dem Zweck der Erziehung abgeleitet* (1806), in Vol. X of Herbart's *Sämmtliche Werke*, edited by G. Hartenstein. Leipzig, 1851. Where our English translations deviate from the edition of Felkin, Felkin's translation is given in a footnote.

[3] Felkin (p. 130) says "observation."

ing to him learning and teaching ought to follow the rhythmic succession of concentration on "outside objects" (*Vertiefung*) and assimilation through "reflection" (*Besinnung*).[1] Herbart differentiates between the "presentative, analytical, and synthetical stages of instruction" (*bloss darstellender, analytischer und synthetischer Unterricht*). Most important of all, he is fully aware that instruction has to be conceived of as a necessary and enriching process complementary to experience and social intercourse, and that knowledge and instruction cannot pass over into constructive and moral behavior unless they are driven to do so by an emotion, affecting the whole personality. He calls this emotion "sympathy" or the "desire for active participation" (*Teilnahme* [2]).

Therefore, the four more intellectual phases of instruction which Herbart designates as "pointing out, connecting, instructing,[3] and philosophizing" (*zeigen, verknüpfen, lehren, philosophieren*) have to be supported by four more emotional-ethical phases which Herbart calls "illustrating,[4] continuous, elevating, and leading over into the sphere of reality."[5] And as Herbart, in spite of an aristocratic individualism, does not forget the social side of the educative process, so, in spite of his intellectualism, he sees the superlogical character of the intellect and speaks of "scientific imagination or intuition"[6] (*wissenschaftliche Phantasie*) as a prerequisite for productive thinking.

[1] Felkin uses the terms "concentration" and "reflection."

[2] *Teilnahme*, in German, can mean both "sympathy" and "participation." Felkin (pp. 132 ff.) uses exclusively the words "sympathy" or "demand for sympathy." This conveys at some places a false meaning to the reader, particularly at the end of the chapter on "Steps in Instruction," p. 146.

[3] Felkin (p. 147) "teach."

[4] Felkin (p. 147) "observing."   [5] *Ibid.*, "active in the sphere of reality."

[6] Felkin (p. 157) uses only the term "scientific imagination."

In spite of all changes in detail and the general distrust of modern educators against Herbart, his scheme of partly successive, partly concurrent stages of mental procedure is still essentially maintained. John Dewey, to take one example, in *How We Think* differentiates "five phases, or aspects of reflective thought"; namely, suggestion, intellectualization, hypothesis, reasoning (in the narrower sense), and testing the hypothesis by action. Like Herbart, he emphasizes that the sequence of the five phases is not fixed.[1]

The reason for this similarity is that both Herbart and Dewey point at essential processes in the nature of thinking and learning. In order to understand and to assimilate something, our minds must proceed from the known to the unknown, from the near to the remote, and from the less to the more difficult. And in order to provoke thought the customary flow of our ideas must hit a snag and our curiosity must be aroused. Having singled out the object of our attention, then we try our strength on it by means of associating, comparing, and experimenting; and finally we incorporate the newly won insight into the general set of our ideas or, if the circumstances are of more practical character, we try to put it into action. If, through exercise, a teacher acquaints a child with these mental processes, he is likely to lead him through a procedure similar to that which Herbart brought to light.[2]

---

[1] *How We Think. A Restatement of the Relation of Reflective Thinking to the Educative Process.* D. C. Heath, 1933. Pages 106 ff. In the first edition of *How We Think* (1910) Dewey enumerates (p. 72) "five distinct steps in reflection"; namely, a felt difficulty, its location and definition, suggestion of possible solution, development by reasoning of the bearings of the suggestion, and "observation and experiment lending to its acceptance or rejection; that is, the conclusion of belief or disbelief."

[2] Compare Comenius, *The Great Didactic*, translated by Keatinge. Chapter XVII, "Principles of Facility in Teaching and in Learning." The modern dis-

In referring so often to older systems of educational method, we do not intend to become *laudatores temporis acti* and to belittle our present achievements. Where are the achievements to be found? They are not in the discovery of completely new educational ideas. It would not be difficult for an experienced historian to show that the great educational ideas and ideals for the realization of which modern teachers are still striving are, at least in their germs, contained in the writings of Comenius, Rousseau, and Pestalozzi. But these men had to face conditions in society, in public education, and in the training of teachers which made the realization of their ideas impracticable. Furthermore, their ability to transfer their largely intuitive grasps into reality was not yet sufficiently developed, and they were unaware of their own deficiencies. Apparently this ability matures only in relation with the refinement of the tools necessary for such transfer and with constant experimentation. It is, for example, astounding to see how Comenius in his textbooks on languages, with one exception—the *Orbis Pictus*—grossly neglects the rules of teaching and learning which he himself had set up in his *Didactica Magna*. And even the *Orbis Pictus* offers the linguistic concepts to be conveyed to the pupil ready made, instead of inviting him to find them through his own activity.

In the face of these facts it is difficult to resist meditations about the nature of human progress. Most of our

cussion on "Laws of Learning," etc., is reviewed in books such as: William H. Burton, *The Nature and Direction of Learning* (1930); Boyd H. Bode, *Modern Education Theories* (1927); Henry C. Morrison, *The Practice of Teaching in the Secondary School* (1939); Walter S. Monroe, *Directing Learning in the High School* (1927); and Paul Klapper, *Contemporary Education, Its Principles and Practices* (1929).

great ideals are more than two thousand years old and yet insufficiently, or not at all, realized. There is an immense difference between man's intuition and his power to materialize his insights. Even those men who first visualize the ways often do not know how to follow them. Is it not the same with society today? Our technical knowledge is sufficiently advanced to procure a healthy environment for our children, to decentralize our cities, and to abandon slum districts. We even know [1] that economically such achievements would be feasible and certainly much less expensive than preparing the nations for attacking one another. Nevertheless, much water will run down the rivers and perhaps much blood, too, before our ethical will, or our "sympathy," as Herbart would say, will be sufficiently advanced to follow reason. The discrepancy between insight and practice makes it imperative for total progress that intellectual training does not get bogged down in lip service—Pestalozzi called this the deadly corruption and hypocrisy of modern civilization—but goes hand in hand with education toward active responsibility. As long as our civilization suffers from the gigantic dualism between knowledge and application, it does not fully deserve its name.

But these considerations have led us away from the answer to the question of where the achievements of modern education are to be found. Achievements lie in this very refinement of our sensitivity to the transfer of ideas into reality, which has just been described as essential to progress. In diminishing the number of pupils in our classes, in divorcing higher education from class pre-

[1] Compare Lewis Mumford, *Technics and Civilization* (1934) and *The Culture of Cities* (1938).

rogative, in raising the professional level of the teacher, and in trying to occupy the total personality of the child in the process of learning through organization of instruction according to the principle of self-activity, we have taken the ideas of the great educational pioneers more seriously than they themselves would imagine.

The desirability of combining thought and action can be proved with reference to some of our modern educational experiments. Practical educators have too often been inclined to consider a new method as the solution of all problems, not only because of the natural joy we all have in discovery and pioneer work, but because of their frequent lack of acquaintance with the total problem of education. And it was particularly the postulate of mental order that the progressivists in all countries were inclined to forget, partly because they saw too clearly the shortcomings of the traditional intellectual and formal education, and partly because the principle of mental order has something sober and rather antienthusiastic about it and can too easily be overlooked by those who are charmed by the glamour of new techniques. Nevertheless, even the most modern method, with almost complete withdrawal of the teacher, cannot succeed unless it leads the pupil along a certain orderly path.

F. THE POSTULATE OF CORRELATION OF SUBJECT MATTER

The principle of mental order has, as its corollary, another postulate of teaching, that of correlation of subject matter. If somebody asked the large number of intellectually interested city dwellers how many of the numerous lectures attended have made a forming impression on their minds, they would confess that it was very few. And if somebody started an inquiry about the educational effect of our daily perusal of magazines, digests, and pamphlets, again the answer would be amazingly negative. Lasting impressions generally result only if one premise has been fulfilled: we must have been sufficiently prepared not only psychologically, through interest, but also materially, through some knowledge of the subject or at least of related fields. Herbart's postulate that each new object of teaching must meet an "apperceptive mass" in the student's mind is based on similar considerations.

Naturally such considerations ought to have much bearing on the curriculum. We have seen in previous chapters that a curriculum cannot fulfill its socioethical purpose within civilization unless it is united by, and draws on, a centralizing idea. Now we have to complement this statement with respect to the imminent requirements of teaching and learning. As it is difficult for an adult to digest atomistically scattered informations, particularly if they spread over a very wide range, so it is a pedagogical mistake to impose on the child a curriculum without inner coherence.

The reply could be made that, in consequence of the increasing complexity of our civilization, it is impossible to merge all the roads on which the pupil has to be led to the understanding of this civilization. No doubt we meet here one of the central difficulties in education, the antinomy between the diversity of modern life and the inner harmony of the individual. Nevertheless, much can be done to relieve the pains of this conflict. It was, for example, one of the central ideas of Froebel to let the children start from a symbolic apprehension of the essential unity of the cosmos. This unity was for him, the disciple of Schelling, a metaphysical a priori extending into all spheres of nature and culture. Many of us may not share Froebel's transcendental faith in the unity of the universe and especially in the sometimes strange methods of education he derived from it. But we have to respect the psychological demand for unity of the empirical individual with his empirical environment. Therefore, we must attempt to show children the cross-relations between all important human activities, in order to avoid having human existence appear to them more as a heap of accidents than as a steady struggle for inner form.[1]

G. THE POSTULATE OF SELF–ACTIVITY

The seventh postulate of education, about which people have been speaking for centuries without sufficiently applying it and which we have already mentioned in connection with Herbart's thought, is the principle of self-activity. All good teaching consists in changing passivity into activity; the demand of learning by doing or by experiment, the idea of *Arbeitsschule* or of the *école active*, are derived from the same consideration.

The newly discovered activity principle was too quickly identified by some educators with manual training, especially by those under the spell of proletarian class ideologies. They forgot that thorough thinking and learning are also a doing. Even from the economic point of view the mastery of theoretical concepts is necessary as a short cut of thought and a vehicle of progress. It helps us to profit from other people's experiences and saves every

[1] Compare Chapter II. Also, as an excellent illustration of an organic curriculum, compare B. B. Bogoslovsky, *The Ideal School*, especially p. 412.

new generation from the constant repetition of the history of mankind. But in spite of limitations in its application the activity or experimental movement is one of the few international forces in the field of education which have, through associations like the New Education Fellowship, stirred up traditional routine. It may change even more vitally the aspect of our modern school systems.

After the World War the idea of self-activity aroused widespread interest, because it was held to foster democratic attitudes. Europe of 1914, proud of its cultural maturity, had seen one nation after the other subjected to war psychosis and fail to mobilize its intelligence against the disaster. Surely—so people thought—the schools must have had something to do with this tragedy. Had they bred nothing but obedient subjects who easily fell victims to political propaganda?

The hopes concerning the democratization of our modern public and international life were not fulfilled. The educational enthusiasm of the first postwar decade forgot that education is not an autonomous area of life but, as we have tried to show in other chapters of this book, is dependent on many political and economic factors. These factors, as the crisis of modern government shows, were certainly not conducive to the ethical ideals of true democracy, to a large extent in consequence of the mistakes of the great democracies themselves.

But there was still another reason for the discrepancy between the enormous efforts of modern methodology of teaching and its final result. We arrive here again at conclusions of general philosophic character. Our modern teaching has to carry its share of the general disease of present education and civilization; they suffer from the lack of unifying ethical convictions. Consequently, all our accumulated energy does not know what to do with itself.

H. THE POSTULATE OF ETHICAL DIRECTION

Goethe says: "The secret of teaching consists in reducing problems to postulates." In other words, if teaching is intended to activate toward productive purposes, it needs ethical direction. This direction must not only point toward an immediate practical aim; as, for example, education toward "citizenship" or "character education," though both aims are essential for civilization and have so famous an advocate as Plato. But Socrates and Plato knew that there is still a question behind these aims; namely, why and under what conditions ought one to be a good citizen, and what is a good character? From the point of view of self-transcendent empiricism the answer would be that teaching is insufficient if it is only instruction; it is also insufficient if it is merely a conditioning of the character toward one particular, socially desirable trend of behavior. Important though these aims are, they receive their full strength only if teaching, in addition to all its immediate and tangible purposes, leads the student to the realization of essential values. These values, though they are not outside the sphere of constant application, are not to be derived from practical necessities alone. They serve as the motives and criteria of action. If we want to be good citizens, it is because we are desirous of a good state in which human virtues, human dignity, and human happiness can freely develop. But for the very sake of such deeper loyalties we ought not even intend to be loyal citizens if a government which offends these essential values of good life demands obedience from us. For under the guise of "good citizenship" it would try to force us into attitudes and actions contradictory to ethical principles to which the state itself must be subject. The fact that the state is the greatest organization of power that the human race so far has produced does not free it from allegiance to ethical principles, but increases its responsibility for them. It is significant to notice that the founders of the two greatest spiritual movements on which our Western civilization has lived were sentenced to death because of their being bad citizens: Socrates, the founder of ethical idealism, and Christ. In other words, good citizenship either can mean readiness to co-operate in a state for the increasing realization of essential and regulating principles of life or can become a disguised formula for degrading and enslaving mankind. The result depends on the ethical convictions of the nation.

After these considerations it is unnecessary to point out, also, that the process of character education is either a way of relating the younger generation to the ethical sources and resources of humanity or a mere process of adapting the younger generation to the ephemeral needs of society. But has not experience sufficiently proved that moral education does not work? If teachers who do not possess the confidence of their disciples insert some unctuous phrases into an otherwise dull or prevalently critical instruction, if all the other experiences which the students receive from their daily environment impede the growth of positive convictions, then moralizing does not work. On the other hand, does the fact that the traditional practice of moral education has produced many young rascals prove that it has not also produced many good men? Do we not know of many of them who confess that a book read, or a word heard at the right moment, changed their way of life? Or, to bring a very obvious analogy, does the fact that in spite of laws, courts, and police we still have criminals offer any proof that we would fare better without institutions for order and justice?

But to come to the main point. It is not verbal admonition at all for which we argue in defending the principle of ethical direction. There is no such simple exorcism of the devil in humankind. If teaching, according to its immanent purpose, promotes in the young the right kind of learning, then the discovery of values lies to a large extent in the process of learning itself. It involves more than contact with subjects through which the child acquires insight into the thoughts and struggles of the race and the working of nature. Regardless of the material knowledge dealt with, intensive learning itself awakens the sense for thoroughness, truth, justice in judgment, and love of inquiry which end not only in desire for new knowledge but also in respect for the great unexplored mysteries of life.

We need not deal here with the subtle problems of transfer—sometimes handled in a very unsubtle way by modern "exact" experimentalists. So much at least has been shown[1]—and this is neither more nor less than what great educators have always asserted—that the effects of intelligent mental training in one field tend to be transferred to other similar activities. We may, consequently, fairly suppose that learning pervaded by an immanent ethical direction can form the ethical behavior of a personality.

Under this aspect the old controversy of liberal versus vocational education receives new light. If it is, on the one

---

[1] *Secondary Education*. With special reference to Grammar Schools, etc. London, His Majesty's Stationery Office, 1939. Appendix V, "On the Cognitive Aspects of Transfer," pp. 439 ff., with important bibliographical notes.

hand, evident that we can no longer maintain the old separation of the theoretical studies which mold the "educated
man" and the applied studies which provide the necessary
mechanical drill for the inevitable contingencies of the daily
life, then it is, on the other hand, an urgent concern of humankind not to be drowned in a philosophy and practice of
education which has not a large liberalizing element in itself. But what does it ultimately mean if we speak of a liberalizing principle which ought to permeate both applied
and theoretical teaching? In order to explain this we may
quote very freely a fable of the old Chinese philosopher
Dschuang Dsi, which has, also, the advantage of being one
of the profoundest artistic expressions of self-transcendent
empiricism. If education, in whatever branch of knowledge, has led both the teacher and the student beyond mere
intellectual or manual skill to a vivid understanding of
Dschuang Dsi's fable, or, to use another point of reference,
if it has led them into those "deeper dimensions of being" of which William James speaks, then education has
been liberal in the most ethical sense of the word. It has
enlarged the mind through relating it to values of general
and fundamental character.

Teaching and learning which reach into these dimensions give us, at the same time, the only productive attitude toward the problem of methods itself. The liberal
mind knows that false methods make a slave of man; good
methods, like silent and invisible friends, help him to
understand the inner laws of his work through obeying
the immanent laws of the universe, and in this way they
free him from the bonds of his environment. Or, as
Dschuang Dsi says, they help us to "identify ourselves
with our art" and, in this way, to "find the right tree."

THE WOOD CARVER

A wood carver made a post to hang bells on. When the post was finished, all people admired it as a miraculous work of art.

Also the Prince of Lu looked at it and asked the master: "What is your secret?"

The master answered: "I am a simple artisan and do not know of secrets. There is only one thing to be considered. When I was about to make the post, I was on my guard not to allow my energy to be diverted by any other idea. I fasted in order to bring my mind to balance. When I had fasted for three days, I did not dare any longer to think of reward and honor; after five days I did no longer dare to think of praise or blame; after seven days I had forgotten my body and my limbs. At this time I did not even think of His Majesty's court. In this way I identified myself completely with my art, and all temptations of the outer world had vanished. After that I went into the forest and looked at the natural shape and growth of the trees. When I happened to see the right tree, the post for the bells stood ready before my eyes, and I could go to work. Otherwise I would have failed. And the people hold my work divine because my innermost nature became merged with the nature of the material."

This is the meaning which, in spite of all differences of philosophic aspect, we learn from the great philosophers of education from Plato up to Froebel or from the American who philosophically was so close to them, Ralph Waldo Emerson.

Chapter VI

EDUCATION AND SOCIETY

A. CONTRAST AND INTERACTION OF SOCIAL COMPONENTS

As we have already pointed out on several occasions, education is dependent upon the ever-larger circles of society in which it operates. Now, society has never been and will never be in a state of complete equilibrium. We may even doubt that an educator would be interested in such a state, if it were attainable, since education profits from a certain degree of friction as much as society itself. The question can only be what proportions of harmony and discord are most conducive to the healthy advancement of the social body and, consequently, of the school. Nations and civilizations advance always along a narrow line between too much tension and too little, between restlessness and stagnation. In the terminology of Hegel, the issue is whether the constant struggle between thesis and antithesis, characteristic of any changing civilization, is allowed to become so violent that society will break down or is so controlled and directed that conflicts are resolved into a higher and more adequate synthesis. If the synthesis is achieved, if change grows into form, then society will convey this form to education. If no form takes shape and society disintegrates, the school may resist for a while, since there is rarely a period when men despair so greatly that they cease to care for their children. But, in all eras, without a genuine and concentrated cultural vigor education likewise fails in drive and productivity. It perpetuates itself but loses the power of rejuvenescence.

Nevertheless, it is impossible to label historical periods like bottles of wine. They all reveal many contradictions. Those with great weaknesses in some respects have displayed high productive powers in others. And nations that lack internal equilibrium are also not always unproductive. Civilization is too manifold to be reduced to a common denominator. Therefore we must not consider spiritual, political, or economic forces separately as the ultimate energies of culture. It is impossible for the rower of a boat to follow all the movements of the waves surrounding him, and similarly it is impossible to discern exactly the rules of history. The moment the first and most natural instincts are satisfied, civilization produces an infinite variety of energies. Everyone is at the same time driven by and trying to direct a stream of manifold interests. Isolations and abstractions are mostly the mind's retrospective attempts at clarification. In actual life the businessman, the scholar, and the politician are concerned each with his own affairs, and yet altogether contribute to their common history.

It is of the greatest import for a true understanding of a modern, and especially a democratic, society to notice that the life of a nation never depends upon one factor alone, but upon the interaction of diverse components. From one point of view they may appear to be incompatible; from another, as a reciprocity of complementary elements. They form that inextricable mixture of biological, social, and mental forces which we encounter in ourselves and everywhere in our environment. The nation is made up of the large mass of the people with equalitarian standards and a smaller group with more aristocratic ideals; freedom is restrained by authority, and yet the two are indispensable to each other; individualism tends to protest against collectivism, and independence against leadership. For each of these and many other factors, or components, a normal and healthy national life provides the opportunity to contribute to the whole. All normal periods are normal because they combine a high diversifying and creative power with an equally strong shaping and controlling power.

Completely normal periods, as we have already shown, do not, of course, exist, as there exist no completely normal nations or completely normal individuals. But we are perhaps justified in saying—in the year of our Lord 1939— that the English nation has achieved a relatively high degree of form and balance; that the Germans, with their extremely different qualities, are still a nation struggling for form; and that the same is true of the Russians and was true of the Jews throughout their whole history as a united nation. The French nation reconciles its internal tensions by a strong patriotic and cultural unity; but with this nation, when the tension becomes too great, a stream of pent-up emotions is released, as is often the case also with individuals who are accustomed to discipline themselves with a style that is not entirely their own. This might explain the great contrast between the French Revolution and other outbreaks of Gallic fury and their customary emphasis on Descartian clarity and order. While the integration of a nation's life generally takes a long time, some unforeseen furies may undermine its stability in a few months.

How significant for an integrated national life is the sound co-operation of the various components of society and how little schools and all formal education can achieve without their support may be illustrated in the following way. During the eighteenth century and the first half of the nineteenth England had the most lamentable schools of any of the great European peoples, and Germany had probably the best. But England steadily instilled into the population the one national educational ideal that today still embraces the educated and the uneducated within a nation. This was the gentleman ideal. The understandability and the essential soundness of this ideal are proved also by the fact that other nations have added this concept to their vocabulary, though they apply it in practical life with varying success. England has also developed a form of democracy that embraces both a certain amount of equality and a sense for the necessity of an elite. Germany, on the contrary, in spite of her older and superior popular education, is still without a balanced educational ideal, and she has not succeeded in her attempts at democracy. The spirit of Weimar and the spirit of Potsdam have not arrived at a higher synthesis; one lives always at the expense of the other.

But today those countries which ten or twenty years ago imagined they were at least on the way toward a certain steadiness in their social and political life are again in a critical situation. At the end of the World War the democratic nations believed that the world had become safe for democracy and for themselves. Yet new conflicts arise everywhere, and only the future can decide to what extent they are ultimately destructive or constructive. Along the very frontiers of the democratic countries, and even within them, we hear the clamor of diverging political theories, and doctrines hostile to the older concept of liberal democracy can no longer be silenced by mockery or disdain.

It would be arrogant and amateurish to attempt to give the reason for this condition or to describe even the majority of all the contributory causes. But one of the causes that lie at the very root of our troubles in modern society is the mistake of thinking that equilibrium, integration, and co-operation within the nation and humanity as a whole can be achieved by a minimum of eight years of education and the operation of a miraculously self-regulating social mechanism. Even in the very heyday of liberalism the so-called *laissez-faire, laissez-aller* doctrine misunderstood the energies and motive powers of its own time. The theory—never really advocated by the leading theorists of liberalism—that it was only necessary to free society from all fetters in order to arrive at the greatest welfare for the greatest number could become popular in a period that was in understandable revolt against the restraints of political and economic absolutism. Actually, the admirable results of the liberal era were largely due to the fact that it could draw upon, and still continue to produce, cultural values which partly balanced its one-sided emphasis on techniques and material production. It was able to draw upon old religious resources that still maintained vitality. Its research was grounded in an embracing philosophic conception of truth which balanced the growing dangers of specialized analysis and of the natural sciences with a concern for the problems of man. There still existed, in other words, the co-operation, necessary for a healthy cultural life, between offsetting components—between tradition and change, concentration and diversification.

There were other complementary components of a sociological and economic nature that helped the early industrial period to grow strong in the shelter of the older structure of values. Craftsmanship and its system of apprenticeship still continued and helped to cultivate a respect for work of quality and substance. The large agricultural districts served as reservoirs from which large numbers of willing and law-abiding workmen could be drawn into the factories. The whole world was made available as a source for raw materials and a market for the finished products. In the United States the open frontier allowed for expansion westward, and in 1849 the adventurous sons of the East were called to the natural abundance of the Pacific coast. So far as the treatment of the underdog is concerned, the period of early capitalism could compete in cruelty with any others and surpass them in many respects. But the socially suppressed were neither powerful nor educated enough to upset by riots the relative equilibrium of the more privileged groups.

Nevertheless, the ravages of the early industrial revolution incited social critics from both the right and the left wing to protest against the results of economic individualism, the consequences of which such men as Marx, Engels, and Carlyle foretold with a most astonishing combination of analysis and prophecy. They drew a picture of a society which, fascinated by the accumulation of wealth, failed to see that it was creating the same social unbalance that had led to a crisis in the eighteenth century. The history of some of the greatest European countries has proved the correctness of their prophecies.

We have often mistaken formal and institutionalized education for the whole process by which a society educates itself. But it is only a part of it. Whether the various components of national life are working together successfully is evident, first, in apparently trivial situations. It comes to light when a child or an adult speaks to a policeman on the street—it is done very differently in different countries: in some, the policeman is to the law-abiding citizens a symbol of a self-regulating society; in others, he is rather a symbol of the power of armed authority. It comes to light when the income-tax office is crowded with people during the last days before the returns are due, in the immigration and naturalization offices, or when a young clerk in a drugstore or a young worker in a factory makes his first mistake. It is evident in the story a workman who had recently come to this country from Europe told to some friends about his experiences during the first difficult years. He said that he had learned nothing about technical and business matters that could not be found or easily developed in his own country. What had struck him most was the treatment accorded him on his first job as a metal turner when he broke an important gear. He had to pay for the damage, but the foreman, in reporting the accident to the engineer, said, "This gentleman has made a mistake." Though treatment of this sort, he had learned, was not typical everywhere in America, it was more generally so than in his own country. The fact that he was not humiliated but was treated as an honest and responsible man seemed to him to explain why things are more likely

to work out satisfactorily in this country than in others
that are, perhaps, equally industrious and intelligent.

Thus, in the social sphere we meet the same factors
already mentioned in connection with our emphasis on
the school as an educational environment and which we
related systematically to our psychology. A person is
unhappy if the physical, emotional, and intellectual elements run counter to one another instead of in harmony.
Even the most highly endowed intellect is frustrated unless it rests on a secure groundwork where the less conscious factors of personality co-operate without too much
friction. Similarly, the life of a nation from its most humble to its most sublime creations depends not only upon
its material or its mental richness but upon the interaction of all the parts that make up the whole.

B. THE GROUNDWORK OF SOCIAL LIFE

Although this groundwork is so deeply embedded in
individuals and in society, we must not make the mistake
of believing that it consists merely of formal and habitual
behavior patterns. As we have already seen, we have not
done with the matter when we have called it habit; for
social habits consist largely of ways of behavior ingrained
in the younger generation because the older regard them
as expressions of values. The fact that these values are
not always accorded high-sounding ethical terms does not
detract anything from their importance. On the contrary,
it only shows that they have been turned from brain processes into spontaneous action. Hegel, who even by his
most fervent enemies cannot be accused of lack of intellectualism, attributed to this domain of almost instinctive
reactions an enormous importance. According to him the

spirit of history in its still natural and unreflective form expresses itself in this groundwork of life. Through it, even the simple man who knows nothing about theories of ethics and society is unconsciously bound to the highest aims of mankind. On the other hand, the disintegration of this groundwork not only is evidence of a maladjustment of men and things upon the surface of society but is primary evidence of a deeper illness. The ideas that men have about each other and about the meaning of human life are always at stake, and these meanings are just as important as environment and external conditions.

As this groundwork is so essential for the regulation of our life and the development of "common sense," it must not be allowed to crystallize. But this is the very danger of all customs, folkways, and unwritten laws of conduct. They preserve what has proved wholesome, they discourage harmful violations of normal codes of conduct, but for this very reason they are also opposed to the unusual which is not inferior but superior to the normal. Doubtless many of those ideas which at first seem disturbing and revolutionary are gradually absorbed, but in the process they are diluted and soon come to form the dogma that later will be used to ostracize the bearers of the next great and unusual thought. Christ could be killed because the Pharisees were supported by Jewish folklore; when His teachings had permeated the civilization called after Him, many men who were closer to Him in spirit than their judges were burned and outlawed in His name. Whenever a political or ecclesiastical dictator or a blind mob has desired the destruction of a new leader or prophet, the clever appeal to sacrosanct "traditions" or the creation of the fear of change has usually done the trick.

This experience has led many thinkers to see in the more

embedded mass of opinions and attitudes nothing but prejudices and a barrier to progress that an enlightened era must exert itself to remove. But this is one-sided. Relatively few people live exclusively according to their own thinking. Perhaps nobody does. Even the most original genius is acting in large spheres of his existence on premises which he approves because they are common. It is precisely the society that contains a large number of advanced individuals that stands most in need of a cohesiveness to offset the centrifugal forces of social separatism. This cohesiveness is provided by the very customs and attitudes which are the cause of chagrin to the free minds.

Here again we meet one of the qualities of group life which defy all logical analysis. We can never know exactly when the social equilibrium is safely stable. In order to be creative, it must always have a slight displacement caused by the antagonism of minorities and majorities; it must always maintain a rather precarious intensity due to opposing forces. Only a little too much displacement in relation to the movement and weight of the social body and the unbalance may go so far as to overthrow states and civilizations. Nobody can foretell the future exactly. We do not yet have a science of social mechanics, though a thorough elaboration of the ideas just expressed could teach us much about sound national and international policy. But this book is not the place for that.

C. THE "UNCONSCIOUS" AND THE "CONSCIOUS" IN SOCIAL LIFE

We must not, however, give too much weight to the unconscious factors in social life. The social body needs for its inspiration and guidance conscious ideas and ideals sufficiently powerful to hold the limelight of public attention. A nation's production of such leading ideas depends upon many circumstances, upon political and cultural configurations from which a great purpose emerges into consciousness. It depends also upon the existence of leaders able to translate the vague emotions of the people into clear and challenging concepts. But here it must be observed that it is not theories and abstract ethical concepts that vitalize a community. The aims which are to become common property must be embodied in palpable realities; they must be aims observable in action.

The need for aims capable of such embodiment, together with the importance of the less reflective spheres of life, explains the fact that inferior ideas often have a greater effect upon the minds of the people than the results of profound and deliberate thought. This disappointing reality has often been explained by reference to what is called mass psychology. Doubtless the fact that men in masses do not rationalize but feel and are moved by simple concepts rather than by subtleties partly explains the greater power of the vulgar in effecting group integration. But the interpretations of mass psychology alone, though nowadays very much in vogue, can make us too pessimistic about the relation between culture and society.

Although its impression is not immediately apparent, the work of the scholar and thinker exerts influence even upon the more embedded reactions of the people. Through a thousand channels it seeps down into the broader regions of society and in the course of decades modifies common thought and attitudes. It would be an interesting study, though difficult, to investigate how much time it takes and what circumstances it requires for ideas originally confined to a few to be widely disseminated. It is an error to suppose, we can be sure, that new ideas can be reserved for the few. Even so wise a man as Voltaire committed this mistake in thinking that one could disillusion the intellectuals and at the same time preserve the illusions of the people. With our modern forms of popularization the transfer is greatly accelerated. This, doubtless, has the advantage of increasing the proximity between the different layers of people. It has the disadvantage that the shortening of the span of time between the conception of ideas and their transference to the people eliminates one of the most efficient selective agencies. This more rapid transfer and the machinery of modern organized propaganda explain the fact that the spread of education coincides with the success of demagogues whose ideas and intentions are often barbarically vulgar. This degeneration is to be seen in religion as well as in politics.

The foregoing analysis of factors working on the various levels of our social life shows that the totality of man and his education is much greater than we generally conceive. Our usual educational theory and policy have remained in a stage of development comparable to the psychology that considered the psychic life of man to consist only of his individual and conscious mental property. In reality, it consists also of a large subconscious or semiconscious sphere out of which a continuous stream of influence flows into his conscious sphere of thought and action. Education, therefore, is not independent and self-sufficient; neither education nor any other social institution can subsist solely on its own energies. If it attempts to do so, it may, as the result of its one-sided concentration, intensify its energies, but it is certain to defeat its own ends.

D. THE EDUCATOR AND THE OPPOSING
DEMANDS OF SOCIETY

It is evident that our discussion of general social and cultural problems has bearing also on the responsibilities of the educator. The course of history does not, certainly, yield to the schoolmaster's command as do the pupils in his classroom. Historical actualities hover like gigantic powers over education, causing us all to doubt sometimes whether we can influence forces shaping society in ways that often appear more like the working of impersonal laws than human achievements in the realm of moral freedom. Our description of the forces operating in the groundwork of society ought to make it clear that they are beyond the will of a single individual or a comparatively small group of educators, and that we must appeal to something like the common will of a nation or even of a whole civilization if we want to direct these forces. Since they result from partly unconscious collective attitudes, only collective effort can give them new meaning and direction. But one thing must be asserted. Even if history advances according to irresistible laws of which we have not yet found the formula, we should still have a large margin of freedom in reacting to the operation of these laws.

There are great differences in the behavior of individuals. One despairs and another finds means to survive; one submits to mass feelings and to the appeal to destructive instincts, another preserves his humanity in spite of inhuman conditions. And how the individual responds, adequately or inadequately, depends to a large extent upon the education and the teachers he has had. Therefore, if educators co-operate in the recognition of their common responsibility for the social and moral framework of the nation, they can direct the growth of the people as they direct the growth of individuals. And what is most important of all, attitudes and forms of behavior do not appear and disappear without radiating influence into their environment; they create both new moods and new conditions. Even under strict historical determinism there would be room and necessity for education.

Here we are at the center of the relations between education and society. Both condition each other, and the degree to which they co-operate determines to a large extent those powerful components of group life to which we have referred and which are requisite to a healthy national life. Whether a nation, even in times of crisis, will love its freedom and understand how to accept the necessary amount of control without allowing it to destroy self-responsibility, whether it can undergo the strain of internal and external conflicts without consuming its strength and intelligence in hatred—all this is due to the way in which we condition our conditions; in other words, how we educate ourselves. The theory of conditioning is right in asserting that we are constantly conditioned by our social environment, but the orthodox representatives of this theory forget that, as we have said, we ourselves possess a certain amount of freedom to change our conditions. Consequently, determinism needs to be blended with indeterminism just as the old idealistic philosophy of freedom needs to be strengthened by some of the naturalism of the conditionalists.

However small the prestige of the individual teacher, because of the relation between education and society that we have just described the profession as a whole has received much attention ever since the art of printing made public schooling on a large scale possible and the state began to take interest in influencing the masses.

To understand the political importance of the teacher at the present time, we must refer to our description, at the beginning of this chapter, of the various contrasting components to be found in society. Education now finds itself pressed by the opposing demands of individualism and collectivism and of change and preservation.

The relative importance of the first two contrasting components seemed to be fairly well established up to the World War. The individualist movements were on the progressive side and seemed to be favored by the advancing tides of history. They strove for the independence and autonomy of the individual against the imposition of any ideas with which he could not identify himself after conscientious self-examination. They fostered democracy and parliamentary government in the political field; and in education they humanized the treatment of children, introduced better methods of teaching and the interpretation of childhood as a stage of development with rights of its own.

Since the World War, individualism and liberalism, against all expectations, have been put on the defensive, collectivistic tendencies have asserted themselves in both government and economics, and education, not only in fascistic and communistic countries but even in democracies, seems to have tired of individualism. This reversal would not have been possible if the liberal era had remembered that freedom is just one component of which co-operation is the necessary complement, as the critical prophets of the nineteenth century whom we have already mentioned clearly saw. This, again, is one of the more important reasons why modern education should lay stress upon the school as social agency and environment. Only the educator's awareness of his obligation to introduce the pupil into his role in a social framework as well as to develop his individuality can help us to synthesize our liberal tradition with increasing social responsibility. This is the synthesis for which we are all longing and which alone can save Western Christian civilization.

The second pair of components between which education is now caught is change versus preservation, another inevitable conflict in human society. Whether a person prefers change or preservation depends generally upon two factors. If satisfied, he tends to retain the circumstances responsible for this satisfaction; if dissatisfied, he wants to alter the circumstances. But temperament also has something to do with the attitude toward change: one person is placid and inert, another has a surplus of energy that must find release in useful activity, a third is perhaps a restless adventurer. Whether the tendency toward change or preservation in entire nations is due more to circumstances than to something that might be called national temperament is a question that will always be open to controversy. In observing the large masses in different countries one comes to the conclusion that if undisturbed and not hungry they tend toward conservatism, even if belonging to an opposition party. A European revolutionary has spoken angrily of "the damned self-contentment of the masses." It would seem, then, that the uneasiness at the bottom of the social order signifies that our technical era has not yet succeeded in guaranteeing the common man's mental and material welfare. Education is in the precarious position of being pressed by both sides, the satisfied and the discontented, the haves and the have-nots, to exert its influence either for preservation or for change. And it is not easy for the conscientious educator to find a way through these competing claims. He may see that the so-called "upper classes" are not simply robbers and hypocrites; many of them, he may observe, contribute their share to society and use the relative steadiness of their position for the cultivation of values without which a civilization is doomed, though not everyone may be able to enjoy them.

Another teacher, whose school is situated in a slum district, finds his work constantly frustrated by poor external conditions, by dirt, hunger, and criminality, while a few streets away money is wasted for unnecessary pleasures. What is more natural than for him to become a fighter for the reform of a society that tolerates these conditions? The teacher is, in this respect, entangled in the same network of responsibilities as the minister. The younger generation of ministers sees the application of the principles of Christianity constantly thwarted by economic and political powers. Instead of delivering sermons about the brotherhood of man, why not fight for it positively and throw the spiritual power of the Church into the struggle? It has, in past centuries, so often used its influence for the sake of the powerful; why should it not, now that our social consciousness has become refined, use it for the sake of the poor?

We arrive, at the end of this chapter on the role of education in society, at a group of problems which has generally been included during the last few decades in the term "indoctrination." In the discussion of the role of education in social conflict experienced men have pointed to the danger arising from the school's active participation in the quarrels of the parties. Whoever enters the political arena must accept its dust and noise; it is difficult to preserve integrity in the medley of propaganda and counterpropaganda, and in case of defeat the political schoolmaster cannot expect to be treated any differently from others. Particularly for education, which needs steadiness and the respect of all citizens, the political ups and downs would be disastrous.

To these considerations the inspired reformer may rightly answer that, since other professions have their perils, why should the minister and the teacher live in the doubtful heaven of unchallenged security? Danger cannot be frightening to those willing and ordained to pursue a just cause. And, furthermore, who knows that the fight is not worth the risk and that more justice, more general welfare, and more respect for the teacher and minister will not be the result of their courage? It is perhaps more dangerous for these two professions and for civilization itself if they stay aloof while others carry on the struggle.

These objections cannot be so easily rejected. The whole controversy must remain open unless we find a more definite criterion than merely tactical considerations. Such a criterion can be found only in the essential and fundamental conditions of education itself.

Both the minister and the teacher address the community and the individual in their totality and not alone in some of their special attributes. The teacher does it by introducing the young into the driving ideas of the race and by taking them so far in their development that as adults they can freely participate, each according to his personal qualities and interests, in the formation of opinions and the future policy of his group. And since a modern nation can thrive in the long run only as it maintains diversity within its unity, the teacher must introduce his students into the diversities of the cultural landscape to foster their capacity for individual decision as well as for communal action. These dialectically related components, the forces making for unity and diversity, must work together in the processes by which a nation renews itself. Only if this interaction of two apparent contrasts is guaranteed can both the competitive and the co-operative character of an advancing society be achieved. This implies that the exclusive imposition of one pattern of thought, by killing the natural differences that arise within a society, would achieve not a functional unity but its opposite, a dull or degrading uniformity. The differences of outlook within a nation should be considered as national riches so long as they contribute to the general culture and are not used as ideologies to divide the people against themselves or to advance egoistic interests to the detriment of the general welfare.

Hence, whenever a teacher or education as a whole singles out one particular solution of an open issue within the nation and indoctrinates this to the exclusion of others, the growth of the pupil or of the nation is stifled. For then the young are not being allowed contact with the totality of civilization, the necessity of the free assimilation of cultural material according to mental types is being disregarded, and freedom of the personality and of the people is being violated. In addition, the pupil who comes from an environment with opinions differing from those taught in the school is set in conflict with either his parents or his teachers.

For these and other reasons indoctrination has never really paid. It may, for a while, make for artificial unity and concentrated effort, just as political dictatorships do. But sooner or later people will take revenge for being cheated of their freedom.

Two questions can be raised in regard to the foregoing considerations. It is sometimes said that the schools are never free of indoctrination and that power groups in the state have always used them for imposing opinions conducive to the preservation of the existing state of affairs. Consequently, the teaching profession ought to assume responsibility for the social ethics of education, since it is not interested in the welfare of any particular class but only in the welfare of the whole. Since the latter, so the argument continues, is best guaranteed by a socialistic order, the teacher and public education in general ought to be the pioneers of the "new society" and to indoctrinate its principles into the minds of the young.

This point of view, honest as it is and tempting as it sounds to those who are longing for a better world, is, nevertheless, extremely dubious.

Its first fallacy lies in the ambiguous use of the word "indoctrination." In any society, as we have already seen, it is necessary to introduce the younger generation into the national inheritance. This necessitates the conveying of ideas, ideals, and tendencies developed in the history of a particular group. Anyone who wants to call this constant rejuvenation of the national tradition indoctrination is philologically entitled to do so, since the term originally signifies nothing more than the neutral idea of "instruction." But if he does so, he must not simultaneously use it to identify the process of instilling into youth certain controversial ideas to the exclusion of others which can also be honestly defended.

It may be objected that many of the ideas that are now commonly accepted as part of the national tradition were originally also controversial. This is certainly true. The Christian, humanistic, and liberal ideas which we now consider fundamental to our civilization were controversial at one time; the ideas behind the American Revolution and the abolition movement were all highly controversial. But the difference between these ideas and those which are emerging for the direction of the political and cultural future of the nation is that the first are achievements already incorporated in the history and the common philosophy of the nation, while the second are still to be decided. The first being solutions found for problems in the past, it does not matter that they were originally objected to by many; the second are questions about the solution of which not only selfishly interested parties but many detached and serious men still differ.

The second fallacy in the demand for social indoctrination is the supposition that educators are a unified social group able to decide and to agree about the ways in which social justice, the object of any honest man, ought to be achieved. Teachers, even within the same type of school, are not a unit with identical political opinions. And if they were, we might still ask why they, rather than the members of other groups, should be more capable of discovering the ways toward social and economic justice.

The third fallacy is the idea that the school is solely the

affair of the teacher. Certainly he is not, or at least ought not to be, in the position of the employee of a private entrepreneur who runs his business for profit and judges the work of his subordinates according to this principle. Though schools have economic responsibilities, they have a purpose of another sort than private business. But this does not give the teacher the right to consider the school his own enterprise, the policy of which he can independently determine. In time, we hope, even the private entrepreneur will come to consider himself responsible to the whole community. The teacher is already, or should be, the trustee not of groups of parents who consent to or share his political opinions but of the whole nation.

We must not, however, make the mistake of considering the teacher the humble servant of the commonwealth. Such an opinion of the teacher's function reveals no serious concern with either education or the nation in its totality; it is usually the opinion of pressure groups pursuing their own advantages behind an educational ideology. For in a cultural community education can never be interpreted solely as a means. It serves certain practical purposes, as everything does to some extent. But education, as well as religion, science, art, and finally man himself, transcends itself toward a sphere of essential and permanent values which are not only for the use of man but which address him in their own right. Only if this dignity of education is guaranteed can it do its best to develop standards in the younger generation which will help them to resist the appeals of demagogues from whatever side they may come.

Therefore education, understood in this way, has the right to do even more than educate youth toward the rec-

ognition and the realization of those values essential for
the development of mankind. Provided the student is
sufficiently mature, education must also have the right to
criticize human institutions when they fail to co-operate
in the common task of improving the physical and mental conditions of humanity. Whether political parties,
pressure groups, donors, or mass organizations like it or
not, the ideas of justice, sympathy, and honesty, of religion and truth, cannot be conveyed by admonitions in a
spiritual vacuum or by references to the past which do
not commit anyone. They have to be shown as obligations which are discharged in reality and which that reality in many ways impedes. It is a futile attempt to dodge
the true problems of our time when the young are artificially restrained from discussing issues about which they
talk constantly among themselves and read in the daily
newspaper. Most of these young men and women would
already have been earning their livings in earlier times;
now that school attendance is so prolonged, they must be
treated as beings with whom it is worth while to reason.

The political control of education is particularly harmful at the higher levels. A society which cannot permit a
scientifically interested youth to discuss social and political problems on a scientific platform admits that its policies cannot be submitted to reason. Consequently, it
must expect someday to be overrun by both socially advanced pioneers and confused radicals. For radicalism
never grows so strong as in minds without opportunities
for impartial discussion. Then accidental private relations, public assemblies, or the radio, where the prop-
agandist is generally more effective than the truth seeker,
become the only agencies for the political education of the

youth. Again and again societies have tried to preserve their status by preventing the honest discussion of important issues. The result has always been a failure to assimilate the new to the old in time to avoid either rebellion or devitalization.

E. RESPONSIBILITY AND FREEDOM IN EDUCATION

What, then, is the difference between our demand that the school, at the upper age levels, must be allowed to conscientiously criticize dangerous existing conditions and the demand, which we have rejected, for the indoctrination of particular solutions to controversial issues? Is not any criticism of existing institutions, rights, and social tendencies, which some like and others dislike, a kind of partiality and favoritism? No, unless we are to call a judge partial because in administering justice he decides for or against one party. We do not do so, because the judge derives his opinion neither from personal bias for one or the other of the legal opponents nor from the desire to propagandize his own beliefs, but from a suprapersonal idea, the idea of justice, of which, in his capacity as judge, he is representative. This idea, though only imperfectly interpreted by a human being with all his limitations and deficiencies, nevertheless evokes our respect as a general value.

The analogy of the judge is, however, somewhat misleading. Though in relation to his students the teacher is often in the position of a judge, society has not appointed him to act as judge of social conflicts. There are, of course, clearly antisocial acts of which the teacher, as well as everyone else, may judge; but serious social and cultural conflicts in a complex society are on a level completely different from that of right and wrong in moral and legal matters. If they were not, we should be able to settle them more easily.

Therefore, the discussion of controversial subjects must be limited to clarifying the issues without arriving at any final decisions. If this restriction is accepted by both the teacher and the student, an attitude of respect and humility will be developed which will teach the student to understand that the great problems of mankind cannot be cited in the courts to be judged like criminals or companies involved in a lawsuit. Rather, they will come to appear as ever-new attempts to restore equilibrium in the social body and to actualize ideas which previous centuries may have ridiculed as the dreams of fools. That these attempts have often been accompanied by great errors, cruelties, and disappointments must also be said in order to show the character of the human race and its weaknesses. Perhaps, in the course of time, we may be able to do away with many of the weaknesses if, instead of cherishing our prejudices, we try to understand.

This point of view involves a certain, though not at all uncritical, conservatism in the attitude of the school. It is also the only attitude compatible with education's responsibility for the younger generation growing up in the shelter of the commonwealth. Therefore, revolutionary parties which place themselves outside of the traditions of the nation cannot expect to be supported by public education. In their initial stage they always represent a minority, and they propose a scheme that may contain good but also will certainly lead to new errors and injustices. All that a nation can hope for from education is that it will open the minds of the young so widely to all productive ideas that as mature men and women they will be able to examine quietly all new proposals, learn from them, and adopt whatever is good in them in such a way that the danger of revolution will be turned into the promise of constant evolution.

With such a policy the school will suffer least from a revolution brought about by the failure of society in general. The new leaders will expect education to adapt itself to the new ideas and, as they have been acknowledged by the will of the nation, education will do so. But the difficulties necessarily involved in such a change will not be insuperable if education enjoys the position of an agency of understanding and not of partisanship.

As with all complex functions in a changing society, the role and responsibility of the teacher is not strictly definable. Whether in precarious situations the educator will find the right way between the responsibilities he feels as an active citizen and his responsibilities in the classroom depends largely on his personal tact and his sensitiveness to the situation. It is true in this, as in so many cases, that when two persons do what seems to be the same thing it is, nevertheless, not the same. The teacher with a conciliatory personality and an inclusive view of life can go very far in the analysis of debated subjects, and his effect on the students will be one of greater clearness, modesty, and responsibility. Another teacher may have the contrary effect.

But much as the intangibles of personality contribute to the success of the teacher, they alone do not suffice. More than ever the school is in want of teachers who have not only learned their subject matter but who can project themselves into the driving forces of the life of their nation. The teacher must have a feeling for the play of those factors which we have called the components of modern society. He must be rooted in the basic elements of group life, and he must be able to follow humanity from its more instinctive and embedded functions up to its complex and conscious creations. He must not move simply on the surface of history or be caught in one specific doctrine, but he must have a feeling for the essentials and the totality of human life. These qualities alone distinguish the broad and profound personality from the narrow-minded Philistine or the fanatic, neither of whom belongs in education.

If these are the qualities we want in our teachers, every modern nation must ask itself whether it is doing all it can do to educate the educator fitted for his task and whether it encourages personalities of experience and ability to join the teaching profession so that youth may be helped to understand the society in which it has to live.

Chapter VII

EDUCATION AND THE STATE

A. THE IMPORTANCE OF THE STATE

With the increasing complexity of modern society one of its institutions, the state, has assumed supreme importance. In the course of Western history it has developed from a convenient expedient for mutual protection and attack to the most powerful creation of the co-operative spirit of man. There is hardly any important sphere of our social and cultural life which is not in some way or other related to the state.

Naturally, the influence of the state upon the totality of human life has been an important issue ever since men first became aware of the increasing power of the new Leviathan. In earlier times Marsilius of Padua led the controversy between Church and State, and Hobbes and Machiavelli elaborated the theories of the absolutistic state. Today we are again compelled to reorientate ourselves toward a more harmonious combination of the essential interests of humanity and the necessities of government. After the experiences of the last decade one may even go so far as to say that the future of Western civilization, if not of all civilization, depends upon the success or failure of this reorientation.

B. THE ROLE OF GUIDE WORDS IN HISTORY

One of the main issues arising from this problem is the relation of the growing authority of government to human freedom. How much initiative, responsibility, and personality will we retain as our own and how much will we have to give to the state? As the relation between authority and freedom is also a central issue in the philosophy and practical policy of education, we have to examine at least some of its implications.

First of all, we have to ask what the concept of freedom means.

Throughout its history humanity has periodically created new popular concepts which have served as guides for the desires and achievements characteristic of particular eras. For the Protestant Reformation it was the "Word" as opposed to ecclesiasticism. When Luther wrote, in one of his chorals, *"Das Wort sie sollen lassen stahn,"* [1] he, and those inspired by the hymn, meant a whole complex of values: the words of the Bible, but even more the divine revelation which man himself can experience without any mediator except Christ and which renews the total existence of those able and chosen to feel the miracle of grace and faith. In the eighteenth century the terms "liberty" and "freedom" grew out of the endeavor of men to establish their autonomy not only in religious matters but also in political and economic matters. This involved in the sphere of spirit the demand for freedom of thought and in the social sphere the demand for a democratic organization of society.

All such concepts are not merely products of historical

[1] Translated by H. J. Buckoll: "Our foes must let the word stand sure."

movements but themselves help to create the forms taken by those movements. They help people in the clarification of their thoughts, their ideals and desires, which before the appearance of the appropriate conceptual terms are in a state of confusion and semiconsciousness. If this process of clarification, which is part of the period's endeavor to find itself, is successful, these guide words serve as means of communication and mutual inspiration. They move down from the smaller to the wider circles of society and, as integrating cultural symbols, shape the opinions and the behavior of the masses.

In order to fulfill their purpose these concepts must appeal simultaneously to two sides of the human being, the ideal and the material. Here the same condition applies that we have found in our general analysis of the genesis of values: until these concepts embrace man in his psychophysical totality, they remain abstract and do not motivate and permeate his action.

But exactly in consequence of their relation to the vast totality of human existence these guiding concepts may easily deteriorate into dangerous sources of misunderstanding and abuse. Confusion and destruction, then, join or even displace the constructive values of a guide word. So in the French Revolution the ideas of liberty, equality, and fraternity, originally intended to free and harmonize the nation, later led to the execution of many of their best exponents. But in spite of the abuse of the concept of liberty during the hectic years of the Revolution, its history illustrates the difference between a true historical guide word and a merely temporary slogan expressive of superficial sentiments. While the latter disappears the moment the situation changes, the first reaches beyond the foreground of life and nourishes the central energies of man. It outlives its period of inception and becomes part of the permanent values of civilization.

But at this stage a new danger arises. In the period of its emergence a great guiding ideal is considered by its adherents as absolute and permanent, not simply as a new challenge and a new source of energy. Because they have fought for it, they want it preserved and with it the set of comparatively fixed conditions with which it has come to be associated. The descendants of these pioneers, especially those who have profited most by the changes brought about in society, abstract the ideal still further from reality, enshrining it and demanding worship instead of dynamic understanding of its spirit. Inevitably those guide words which once called men to action are crystallized and become a stumbling block to later generations asking for a rejuvenation of the tradition.

Hence, even if we believe, or, rather, exactly because we do believe, in mankind's capacity to acquire permanent values, we are obliged to examine continually the great guiding concepts of history and to ask ourselves whether under the present prevailing conditions we are still able to grasp and materialize their essential meaning. If the attempt to reinterpret and renew them fails, then one of two conclusions is necessary. Either a value once considered permanent has not stood the test of time, or society has so degenerated that values essential for its welfare cannot be revived. It may have lost the capacity to realize their significance because it has possessed them too long and got them too easily to know what their loss implies.

Although the continuous revaluation of values may lead

to errors, a much greater danger results from refusing to permit the free discussion and examination of our cultural heritage. This repression of the energies resulting from dissatisfaction with existing conditions creates the extremes of dogmatism on the conservative side and of radicalism on the progressive side.

What we have said about guiding ideals in general will be seen to apply to the concept of liberty. We need now to discover whether this concept is one of those that have done their work and no longer have significance for us or whether it is one of the great and permanent values of mankind.

C. THE HISTORY OF THE CONCEPT OF FREEDOM

About the psychophysical basis and limits of human freedom we have already spoken in our anthropological chapter. But psychophysical potentialities can be realized only in thought and action. Now, to show the progressive realization of freedom would be almost identical with writing the history of humanity. All we can do here is to point out those components of freedom which are still actively at work. If, for reasons of organization, we begin with the more spiritual aspects of freedom, we do not imply that these can be strictly isolated from the more practical aspects. Only the unity of the spiritual and the practical can produce freedom as a living value.

The genesis of spiritual freedom is to be found in man's attempt to understand himself as a being differing from animals to the extent that he identifies himself with the deeper dimension of being of which William James spoke and which the Greeks and the New Testament called the Logos. Every endeavor of man, that of a workman or a philosopher or a statesman, to transcend the immediate situation, to acquire perspective and to understand it in terms of a more universal interpretation of existence contributes to human freedom.

It is the philosophy of the Greeks and, particularly, the Stoic branch of Platonism which, through innumerable channels, have instilled into Western man a consciousness of his connection with powers greater than himself. This Greek form of consciousness differs in one decisive point from more primitive relations of man to the universe in that it is no longer an expression of fear or any form of complete dependency but an expression of man's participation in a higher order of the cosmos, in the Logos. In the Stoic movement this new understanding is reflected even in its political philosophy: man, whose mind is able to project itself into the laws of the whole world, must not be subjected to political tyranny.

The Greek concept of Logos and many other ideas of the Platonic philosophic systems became, during the first centuries of the Christian era, so much a part of the great body of Jewish Christian metaphysics that later writers, in spite of their hostility to the pagans, mistook some Stoic and Neoplatonic thinkers for followers of Christ. Astonishing as this may seem in view of the essential differences between the two ways of thought, it is nevertheless explainable. When Christ taught the father-son relation between man and God and, as a result of this relation, the brotherhood of all men, he was expressing in religious form an idea not dissimilar to the more abstract Greek idea of the relation between man and Logos. In some branches of Christian philosophy Christ and the Logos came to be considered the same, partly on the authority of the gospel of St. John, where the idea of the Logos had been identified with the mystical relationship between God, Christ, and man. And when the great reconciler of the Jewish and Greek cultures, St. Paul, told his followers that he knew where the Pneuma, or Spirit, was to be found, he was identifying the Christian revelation and the pagan philosophic tradition. However much this combination may have contributed later on to the complication and distortion of the wonderful simplicity of the gospel, however much dogmatism and institutionalism may have fettered man instead of freeing humanity, there was, nevertheless, at all times in Christianity an insight into man's potentiality for a mysterious participation in the divine principle of the universe. Christianity, together with antiquity, conveys to man a metaphysical concept of humanity the necessity and profundity of which we unfortunately understand best when it is in danger of being lost. And once it is lost, freedom, too, is gone.

The Logos to which ancient and Christian thought believed man to be related was the product of spiritual intuition. It is the great merit of the sixteenth, seventeenth, and eighteenth centuries that they came to an understanding of the dignity of man in a more rationalistic and empirical way. We are too thoroughly accustomed to the results of the modern sciences to imagine, without some knowledge of the historical sources, what an impression it made on the men of the Newtonian era to discover that the mind was able to read the laws governing the movements of the planets. We have already spoken of this great awakening of modern man and have intimated that in his first enthusiasm he overestimated his capacity to discover the laws of the universe; not until the twentieth century have we acquired enough knowledge to understand how ignorant we are.

It is a tragedy of Western civilization that the churches, hardened in dogmatism and on the defensive as the result of internal and external struggles, did not share the intellectual enthusiasm which the inclusion of nature in the Logos aroused in the pioneers of modern scientific research and philosophy. As we shall see in our next chapter, the two great tributaries to modern culture, religion and science, diverged from each other, thus depriving modern thought of the united power which might have made it more adequate to the demands of our complex civilization. But, in spite of the conflicts of the religious and empirical dogmatists, there was enough power of synthesis in the thought of the eighteenth century to bring about a new concept of humanity. Like the thinkers of antiquity, the rationalists understood man as a microcosm living within the macrocosm of spirit and nature. The new philosophy, however, was deepened by the intervening experiences of Christianity and scientific empiricism.

There has rarely been a period of expanding thought without corresponding social developments. And so during the eighteenth century progressive leaders gave expression to numerous feelings of dissatisfaction with the outmoded forms of social organization that impeded the transfer of the new understanding of man into social and political action. First in the Netherlands, in England, and in the American colonies, Calvinism—in contrast to Lutheran Protestantism and Catholicism—allied itself with the idea of political freedom. When the Continental Congress declared the independence of the colonies, they became the first Western country, in this case fortunately

supported by the majority of its clergy, to decide to cast
its lot for liberty and democracy.

D. THE CRISIS OF FREEDOM

How is it to be explained that in recent times people
begin to doubt the applicability of the ideas of freedom
and democracy to modern conditions?

First of all, we must recognize that historical movements
must advance equally along all fronts if they are to continue to be successful. So long as their ethical and political ideas are supported by economic advantages, people
will move with them. During the nineteenth century advance was for the most part general, and, where it was
not, the underprivileged were not yet well enough organized to disturb for very long the feeling of progress and satisfaction in which the upper and middle classes indulged.
Then with the World War, or even before it, the balance
of social and intellectual forces was upset.

Though we are often inclined to attribute the decline of
liberalism to the errors of statesmen, governments, and political parties, there are other and deeper reasons. After
its general acceptance, liberalism often changed from a
positive and constructive principle for the advance of humanity to a merely negative license for any activity that
did not openly conflict with the law. The confusion which
this negative conception of freedom introduced into philosophy has already been pointed out in our criticism of
the educational concept of growth from which the essential conditions of form and direction were omitted. In conjunction with other such incomplete theories there developed in the intellectual spheres an uprooted individualism
and specialization. Minute scientific details were amassed,

as the development of science demands, but were not incorporated in any comprehensive generalization. Exactness, another necessary attribute of good scholarship, often became either a barrier to the interpretation of facts or an excuse for routine work that put a premium on dullness and lack of philosophical training. Science and scholarship had enjoyed their privileges without justifying them by an inner obligation to the deeper dimensions of being. The Greek Logos or the Biblical Pneuma was no longer inherent in them. And the universities of many great countries, one must confess, came to resemble more an accumulation of vocational schools than a guild of scholars and students devoted to the pursuit of truth. This explains their weakness against the attacks of dictatorships in some European countries.

As the result of this intellectual trend, merely analytical abilities overpowered the creative and synthetic; merely critical powers, the constructive.

In addition to these developments, which could partly have been avoided had there been more philosophic clarity about the larger implications of scientific attitudes for the growth of culture, there were other scientific events that impressed themselves on the mind of man with inevitable power. They lay, generally speaking, in the growing intensity of the application of the mechanical concept of cause and effect to the interpretation of man. It was but natural that the scientific generations of the nineteenth century were overwhelmed by Darwin's theory of evolution, by the long line of physical discoveries, and by the transfer of these principles to society in the social philosophies of Herbert Spencer and Auguste Comte.

In some sciences, particularly biology, sociology, and

psychology, an enormous popularization was started, and there are still today professors who cannot do enough to destroy the "legend" of the supra-animal character of man, by refuting any profounder approach to the explanation of values and by postulating determinism, with its denial of human freedom, as the only possible philosophic theory. That they themselves are working on the basis of metaphysical presuppositions of very doubtful value has escaped their attention.

Dante's profound statement that many evils are only the blind exaggerations of good purposes applies to this unfortunate intellectual trend. It is, of course, a necessity of progress that the scientist should unveil the myths and errors he discovers even though they are cherished by many. In the long run, truth is always more advantageous for mankind than error. But the scholar's mission in relation to the ideal of truth, on the one hand, and the people he serves, on the other, requires him to be constructive and not to indulge in premature criticism. His work is often one of disillusionment, but it ought not to be one of disenchantment. If it is only that, he is not freeing his fellow man but is making him more helpless.

It is true that problems must often be advanced tentatively and offered to discussion before they are solved; otherwise progress would be hindered. But in what spirit should these discussions be carried on? Should whole fields of science, as was the case during the last few decades, tend one-sidedly and systematically toward relativeness and disillusionment? And should the easiest way for a young scholar to win recognition be to tear something down rather than to build something up?

One cannot wonder that students who have gone through

such a training become either indifferent to anything which is not "empirically" proved or completely uncertain of their power of judgment and that many of them despair of the possibility of any superior measure of values and believe finally in nothing but the tangible, in their professional careers, in business, or in politics. They then belong to the human material that possesses just enough intelligence and lacks just enough principle to contribute successfully to the deterioration of our cultural and political standards.

It is not difficult to draw a parallel between what has happened in the intellectual sphere and developments in our modern economic life. The industrial revolution was contemporaneous with increasing specialization in science and education. It also resulted in strange extremes: increased productivity and accumulation, on the one hand, and disintegration and helplessness, on the other. In the economic sphere, we are just as far from the freedom and liberalism visualized by Thomas Jefferson and Adam Smith as, in the intellectual sphere, we are from the ideal of freedom of thought expressed by Fichte, Schleiermacher, and Wilhelm von Humboldt when, at the beginning of the nineteenth century, they projected the University of Berlin. All these men visualized the development of liberated thought and economy as going on within the frame of an organic and co-operative community, of which scholars and men of business would also be an organic part. But it is exactly those classes that Jefferson and Smith believed should form the basic and most solid element of society— the farmers and the industrial middle classes—that are now in danger of losing their freedom entirely under the pressure of big capital and economic collectivism. No wonder that, together with the large group of unemployed, these classes become increasingly willing to sacrifice the freedom of democracy for dictatorial systems that promise some degree of economic security and stability. It is not true, as some liberals try to explain, that they thoughtlessly or wantonly sacrifice freedom for slavery. Spiritual and political freedom must of necessity become an unreal abstraction. For man cannot be free if he is out of work or in constant danger of losing his job; the freedom to starve is not freedom.

Now, in all attempts to correct the shortcomings of a liberal society the state is appealed to as the only possible means of help. Even in democratic countries many convinced democrats take this development as natural, though at least in the beginning of the liberal era its leading thinkers thought very differently. In order to become fully aware of this difference of view, let us refer to one of the most profound of the early treatises on the problem of freedom, education, and the state, *The Sphere and Duties of Government*,[1] written in the year 1791 by the philosopher and statesman Wilhelm von Humboldt. Since it contains certain ideas which are not only examples of the finest type of early liberalism but which are decidedly pertinent to our own times, we shall quote it at some length:

The true end of Man . . . is the highest and most harmonious development of his powers to a complete and consistent whole. Freedom is the grand and indispensable condition which the possibility of such a development presupposes; but there is besides another

[1] *The Sphere and Duties of Government*, translated by Joseph Coulthard. 1854. Pages 11 ff.

essential,—intimately connected with freedom, it is
true,—a variety of situations. Even the most free and
self-reliant man is thwarted and hindered in his development by uniformity of position. . . . But a
spirit of governing predominates in every public institution; and however wise and salutary such a spirit
may be, it invariably superinduces national uniformity, and a constrained and unnatural manner of action. . . . The very variety arising from the union of
numbers of individuals is the highest good which social life can confer, and this variety is undoubtedly
merged into uniformity in proportion to the measure
of State interference. Under such a system, it is not
so much the individual members of a nation living
united in the bonds of a civil compact; but isolated
subjects living in a relation to the State, or rather to
the spirit which prevails in its government,—a relation in which the undue preponderance of the State
element tends already to fetter the free play of individual energies. . . . We must not overlook here one
particular manifestation of this generally injurious
agency, since it so closely affects human development; and this is, that the very administration of political affairs becomes in time so full of complications,
that it requires an incredible number of persons to
devote their time to its supervision, in order that it
may not fall into utter confusion. . . . Wholly new
sources of gain, moreover, are introduced and established by this necessity of despatching State affairs,
and these render the servants of the State more dependent on the governing classes of the community
than on the nation in general. Familiar as they have

become to us in experience, we need not pause to describe the numerous evils which flow from such a dependence—what looking to the State for help, what a
lack of self-reliance, what false vanity, what inaction
even, and want. . . . Hence it arises that in every
decennial period the number of the public officials and
the extent of registration increase, while the liberty
of the subject proportionately declines. . . . Whence
I conclude, that the freest development of human nature, directed as little as possible to ulterior civil relations, should always be regarded as paramount in
importance with respect to the culture of man in society. He who has been thus freely developed should
then attach himself to the State; and the State should
test and compare itself, as it were, in him. It is only
with such a contrast and conflict of relations, that I
could confidently anticipate a real improvement of
the national constitution, and banish all apprehension with regard to the injurious influence of the civil
institutions on human nature.[1] . . .

Humboldt wrote these lines because he was impressed
by his observations of the practices of absolute governments. In addition, he saw how the French Revolution
was on the way to failure in consequence of methods as
bad as, or even worse than, those of the absolute rulers.
But, in spite of his real experience, his treatise reflects the
Utopian mood characteristic of Rousseauism and the Enlightenment. It would hold true for a society of moral and
self-reliant individuals living in economic conditions that

[1] Compare John Stuart Mill, *On Liberty* (second edition, 1859, p. 127): "A
people, it appears, may be progressive for a certain length of time, and then
stop: when does it stop? When it ceases to possess individuality."

allowed for the free and productive exercise of human energies. But such a society does not, unfortunately, exist. Humboldt, living in a society that was largely agricultural, in which the problems of unemployment and overpopulation did not exist and markets were relatively free, could not foresee the complexity and the complications of our technical age.

Still, the truth and applicability to our times of much that we have quoted from Humboldt must be evident to every reader. The more centralized the control of modern society becomes, the more reason we have to confess the accuracy of his analysis of the dangers of government control. Our growing habit of calling upon the State to solve our difficulties is perhaps even more dangerous than Humboldt could have foreseen, because of our failure to develop certain human qualities upon which the pioneers of American freedom and the early European liberals counted. Whether the average modern man has less courage, industry, and love of freedom than his ancestors may rightly be doubted. Given the chance to be transplanted into modern times, the hard-working farmer and craftsman of the eighteenth century might very well have refused to face the dangers and excitements of our daily life. The reason that the present population even of liberal countries takes refuge so easily in the superimposed order of state and government is that men no longer discover an understandable relationship with one another in social and economic affairs. The plans and projects of today may be invalidated tomorrow by unforeseeable changes in unexpected places: an industry may have failed, a new invention may have been put into use, a powerful country may have withdrawn its protection from a weak one. This unsteadiness and unpredictability are in every way the contrary of real freedom and to a large extent explain why people are willing to sacrifice the liberties that remain to them for some sort of security. It is not that they prefer serfdom. But dependence upon a known and tangible master is preferable to a theoretical liberty in chaotic conditions. Freedom has been relinquished before for similar reasons, at the end of antiquity and at the end of the Middle Ages.

The important question to consider is why centralized state control and regulation almost necessarily result in the evils Humboldt described and ultimately in losses that greatly outweigh any temporary gains. The answer is that a social order cannot be imposed from above but must develop from the voluntary acceptance of values and purposes that give meaning to human relations. A sociology that does not trace human relations to the deeper dimensions of being fails to reveal the essential meaning of society. It can be only a description of surface patterns, no more valid than a theory of ethics dealing only with rules of conduct or a theory of education concerned exclusively with methods. There is no simple "political engineering" that can solve our problems; the reconstruction of society depends upon the maintenance or the reawakening of a co-operative spirit both based upon and directed toward a total and meaningful human existence.

E. THE CONDITIONS OF FREEDOM

One of the greatest tasks of modern education is to bring people to see that although a certain kind of *laissez-faire*, *laissez-aller* liberalism has run into a dead end, freedom itself, as a principle inherent in the nature of man, is not dead; rather, as the result of a long historical evolution it is man's most natural desire. But it cannot grow in a society where organic life relations and values are destroyed and where the misuse of liberty has led to unrestrained license, on the one hand, and new forms of serfdom, on the other.

In this attempt to help people to re-experience the meaning of freedom, education must detect in the history of civilization man's progressive endeavors to find the freedom necessary for his own greater self-realization. The idea of liberty existed long before anyone thought of liberating economic life from state or corporate control, and even in the eighteenth, nineteenth, and twentieth centuries loyalty to the idea of freedom has not meant acceptance of the doctrines of *laissez faire* and *laissez aller* in any sphere of life.

From such a point of view, of course, one must not look upon freedom as a merely spiritual aim of the individual conscience without any practical implications for public life. It is true that most nations have gone through periods when men were unable to transfer the demands of their conscience to the environment they lived in. The way some modern "realists" have of condemning as "escapism" all recourse to the spiritual sphere proves only their lack of historical knowledge and the limitations of their own experience. Refuge in the freedom of ideas has often been the sole, and not always an ineffectual, means of preserving dignity and faith in the midst of difficult conditions. Much of what today is thrown aside as "abstract idealism" has been the greatest comfort of men in times of distress and their guide in times of action. No period, no nation, and no men can have a full life, both vigorous and purposeful, without these resources.

There is such a thing as "escapism," however, in that people may excuse their indifference to responsible action by referring to their freedom of conscience. And there is no doubt that this attitude fosters the growth of powers—such as the older absolutism, modern dictatorships, and ruthless forms of capitalism—which are destructive of freedom. Such an attitude is the result of a complete misconception of the meaning of freedom. Freedom has never meant simply freedom *from* something, as it is likely to be understood today. In all periods and in all men with a positive appreciation of its significance it has meant freedom *for* something. The nature of freedom is only the necessary consequence of the relation we have shown between freedom, on the one hand, and purpose, form, and Logos, on the other.

From the nature of freedom it follows also that all "detachment" in a moral sense—such as that defended by the Buddhists, to a lesser extent by the Quakers, and by Aldous Huxley in *Ends and Means*—is possible only if there is "attachment" to something that we regard as greater than the things from which we wish to detach ourselves. Otherwise detachment can mean only separateness and is likely to degenerate into relativism and indifference. Only the man of faith can master reality, only self-transcendent empiricism can be empirical without being overwhelmed by a mass of undifferentiated experiences, and only a nation that knows of a deeper dimension of responsibilities can successfully withstand international competition and simultaneously preserve the dignity of its citizens.

History proves the correctness of this statement about the relation between freedom and purpose. For Greek philosophers the idea of freedom was combined with the idea of the pursuit of truth and the individual's responsibility for the community. Christianity, with all its dangers for the development of free philosophizing and political liberty, aimed at freedom for the sake of the truth in which it was interested. So it was that St. John said, "The truth shall make you free." The American Revolution was fought to establish the "natural rights of man." And even modern collectivism and dictatorships cannot take away civil freedom without offering something in its place, either a classless society or increased liberty in international competition by increasing national power which, it is claimed, will ultimately yield greater personal freedom and satisfaction.

In these modern experiments the sacrifice of personal freedom is supposed to be a sort of temporary investment that will lead to a greater return in the future. The supposition fails, however, to take into account the fact that human freedom is dangerous coin with which to speculate and that a political body that does away with it discovers, instead, a mechanical dynamic that men cannot master for long. If collective independence is achieved at the expense of personal liberty, the causes of dissatisfaction have only been shifted from one level to another, and the time must necessarily come when the lack of personal freedom will be painfully felt. This feeling can be temporarily subdued by successful imperialism. But since national power alone makes for neither freedom nor happiness, civil disturbances are bound to arise. Hence, the suppression of a people by dictators has ultimately the same effect as the military suppression of one nation by another, since both destroy human freedom and organic relations and, with them, the conditions in which men can lead productive and meaningful lives.

If education could give people an insight into the dynamics of freedom, it would be doing an enormous service to modern man. If, in addition, it could give people an active understanding of those values and mutual responsibilities which bind human beings into organic groups and communities, instead of encouraging them to think of themselves in isolation from others, it would be doing still more. But, while working in this direction, education would be reaching beyond the mere conveyance of knowledge and solicitude for the individual into the heart of all cultural life. This the educator cannot do alone; he must have the assistance of a favorable configuration of those components of social life of which we spoke in the preceding chapter: the guidance of thinkers, writers, and statesmen, and the participation of parents and all citizens in the common pursuit of democracy.

A people with such a spirit in common would already be living democratically and, as there is much historical evidence to show, would be better able to establish organizations for mutual help without resorting to state authority than peoples lacking it. Social and economic reformers who look to the Scandinavian countries for examples of democratic progress must discover for us not only the techniques of co-operatives but, first of all, the co-operative spirit that gives those techniques reality. While organizations developed in such an atmosphere must have government help, they nevertheless succeed in retaining their own genuine strength and in resisting authoritarian control. They differ from modern government-relief organizations in one significant respect: the quality of the human relations and responsibilities they represent. The difference is the same as that between a real youth movement and a militaristic youth organization, or as that between an educational movement with intrinsic momentum and the prolongation of school attendance simply because there is no other way to keep young people out of mischief.

A community with the spirit of freedom as we mean it, and only such a community, will be able to check the tendency of all centralized and collective enterprise to pass beyond its original aim and become an end in itself. Only such a community can defend the "natural rights of man" against the blindness of impersonal power. It may be that in some circumstances such a community may decide in favor of more state intervention. There is, if the social groundwork and the conscious social attitude are sound, no reason for descrying an enemy of liberty in everyone who advocates governmental action. Even Adam Smith in the fifth book of his *Inquiry into the Nature and Causes of the Wealth of Nations* [1] recognizes as one of the functions of the state the establishment and maintenance of public institutions and public works which, though advantageous to society, are not profitable for individuals or small groups. And he is fully aware of the fact that the extent to which this function must be exercised will be different at different times.

[1] "Of the Revenue of the Sovereign or Commonwealth," Part III: "Of the Expense of Public Works and Public Institutions." Also, John Stuart Mill in his *Principles of Political Economy* gives the government the right of intervention if the security and goodness of the community are at stake. Compare Book V, "On the Influence of Government" (Chapter IX, section 9): "In the matter of education, the intervention of government is justifiable, because the case is not one in which the interest and judgment of the consumer are a sufficient security for the goodness of the community."

The essential point, therefore, is not whether in times of emergency a government shall intervene more than is customary in the affairs of its citizens. Freedom—and here we have to contradict Wilhelm von Humboldt—is not necessarily endangered by every form of government regulation of business, of public welfare, or even of education. It may quite as well be saved by it. A society with the ethical resources that nourish freedom can venture to give to the government the management of activities that previously were decentralized and private concerns. The government will then be expressing the will of self-reliant citizens, and its agents will share the values of the people at large. The danger lies, rather, in the discouraging tendency of political affairs to fall into the hands of men unable to compete successfully in professional and business life and who, for this very reason, turn to politics. Men of self-respect often withdraw from party struggles because they are unable to compete with the demagogues in winning over the masses to their purposes. If nations in which these conditions exist cannot re-establish the integrity of their governments, democracy cannot survive, and it is, as the history of some great nations has already shown, futile to discuss the desirability of government regulation. For then the government, or a dictator if the government is unable or unwilling to act, will intervene whether the people want it or not. If the natural creativeness and vitality which are the prerequisites of both freedom and order have died out, then either freedom will degenerate to anarchy or an artificially imposed discipline will replace the natural, free order. If the latter exists, a natural process of selection will bring the best men to the top of the political order and they will neither try nor be allowed to use their power to the disadvantage of civil freedom. They will consider themselves the trustees of the nation's total resources rather than their exploiters.

These considerations cover the fundamental points of the relation of education to the state. Although education, in modern times, has become increasingly dependent upon the authority of the state, wise governments have resisted the temptation to make the teacher merely an instrument of state policy and have, instead, encouraged him to be a responsible exponent of human culture. In spite of the increased centralization of school administration, smaller units have been encouraged to concern themselves with education. Even where education rests upon the authority of the state, a fine system of instruction and research may develop, provided the government itself is liberal in spirit. With Humboldt as Prussian Secretary of Education, the University of Berlin could be created. But the history of education in Prussia and all of Germany and in France during the nineteenth century shows the dangers arising when centralized systems are not based upon Humboldt's convictions. And, generally, they are not.

Education, as we have frequently emphasized, is not a solitary enterprise. Therefore, its future and its freedom will not depend upon its own achievements alone. It will depend upon the solution of the question central in our foregoing discussion and of the greatest significance for our whole civilization; namely, whether we shall be able to combine state regulation, which will probably increase, with freedom of action in the sphere of culture. Some European countries have tried and failed. Whether the democracies will stand the test will be decided during the next decades.

Chapter VIII

EDUCATION AND RELIGION

A. THE ANTAGONISM BETWEEN RELIGION AND REASON

With so little attention being paid to the religious side of education, one may doubt that much interest will be taken in a rather lengthy discussion of the subject. Not only has the Bible ceased to be a powerful influence in family circles but there are now many who display an active hostility to our religious tradition, believing that it has done us more harm than good.

One of the causes of this disregard of our religious tradition is the conviction of many liberal-minded people that the churches have always favored social reaction and have given little resistance to such trends as imperialism and nationalistic fanaticism so long as their special interests have not suffered. A second cause is the emergence of a modern man who has grown up in an environment totally different from that in which religion developed and flourished. The modern city dweller, cut off from direct contact with nature, feels himself dependent upon a mechanized social system and upon political and economic groups, the products of merely human energies and ingenuity, rather than upon mysterious or supernatural forces.

It is by this time quite clear that the two modern developments most responsible for the process of secularization which has displaced religion—namely, science and the state—have not advanced man as far toward perfection as the enlightened thinkers of the eighteenth century hoped for. Progress in many fields has been offset by retrogression in others. There is no need to repeat the historical details that prove this statement. Nor is it necessary to dwell long on the assertion that disappointment in the results of modern civilization, the generally felt lack of criteria for human thought and conduct, the growing self-criticism of the sciences themselves are beginning to open the minds of men to the values of religion. But much of this new interest in religion is outside the traditional representation of Christendom. The Christian minister and the churches, very often, are neither wanted nor needed.

This estrangement of the modern man from the Church has its cause not only in the conditions we have already mentioned but also and more significantly in the apparent contradiction between his rational and scientific conscience and the traditional religious interpretation of human life. Since this point is of fundamental importance both for the future of Christian civilization and for Christian education it may be worth while to examine it thoroughly.

The contradiction between the Christian religion and the quest for rational truth rests upon two essentially different but closely related factors. One is the difficulty the modern man finds in combining the experimental attitude with the disposition of mind that creates and permits religious faith. The other arises from the fact that the average citizen who is philosophically inexperienced identifies religion and the Church with the dogma of the different denominations, observes their permanent differences, and feels the contrast between his humanistic attitude and their dogmatic pretensions. His dissatisfaction with these inconsistencies has its basis in one of the sturdiest and most valuable qualities of man: his refusal to believe in anything that he cannot regard as real and reasonable. Socrates has said very correctly that nobody errs of his own free will. When he mistakes absurdities for the truth, it is usually because he has not yet discovered the divergence between his belief and the reality, or because external forces, political pressure, and unconscious prejudices prevent him from following his natural curiosity.

In man's desire for truth a moral instinct and the instinct to preserve himself both find their highest expression. We have here another example of that integral character of fundamental vital urges and ethical trends of which we spoke in an earlier chapter. To believe consciously and deliberately in opinions demonstrably false is to expose oneself to self-alienation and to the danger of destruction. Therefore, a vague idea of what we call "truth" has surely been present as long as we have felt ourselves to be human and have thinkingly struggled for our existence.

In primitive periods the capacity of searching for truth was little developed. It was limited to the realm of sensory experiences, and the untrained mind was susceptible to magic interpretations the moment it went beyond the bounds of immediate tangible experience into any deeper interpretations of it. But even the magic beliefs of earlier times were not in contrast to the will to truth; they were the subjective truths of untrained thinking and were abandoned when they proved to be insufficient. When in the course of history better tools for the testing of opinions became available, the sense for truth also became increasingly refined and the volume and importance of magic explanations decreased, until with a certain degree of maturity of the mind its conflict with ecclesiastical dogma was unavoidable. The French social philosopher Saint-Simon has described this constantly widening breach between faith and truth in the Christian world in the following sentences:

> The Roman clergy was orthodox (in the original sense of coincidence between faith and truth) only till the enthronement of Leo X (1512), since until then it was superior to the laymen in all branches of sciences the progress of which had helped the poorest classes. Since then it has fallen into heresy, because it has cultivated nothing but theology, and has allowed itself to be surpassed by the laymen in art, natural philosophy and industry.[1]

Furthermore, the intolerance and the wars of the denominations offended increasingly the educated as well as the simple man. Up to about the eighteenth century, however, the intellectual conflict between religion and science was limited to a relatively small number of learned and courageous leaders. But today public education and all the modern means of enlightenment have widened critical awareness of the conflict. The effect of this is all the greater because, to return to a previous statement, simultaneously with the rise of the modern consciousness of

[1] My translation of a quotation from Eugen Rosenstock, *Soziologie.* 1925. Vol. I, p. 45.

truth the general capacity for faith has decreased. More than was probably the case in earlier times, we have a feeling of uncertainty and uneasiness if we go beyond the realm of experimentally and scientifically provable ideas into the realm of the supernatural.

The conflict between the intellect and institutionalized religion lies, unfortunately, at the very root of our Christian era. Critical thought had already advanced far when Christianity invaded the Graeco-Roman civilization. The magic character of the early Church, as well as the social inferiority of its followers, caused the upper social strata and the educated men among the pagans to despise the new movement. The early Christians came from a group of people who, according to an ancient writer, "shunned the light of day"; certainly it cannot be said that after their rise to power they were eager to foster either independent thought or political freedom, two values on which, in spite of cultural disintegration, even the latest of the serious ancient philosophers laid much emphasis. The contrast between the doctrines of early Christianity and the scientific consciousness of the time is very obvious in the writings of the Church Fathers; one has only to refer to Augustine's defense of the possibility of eternal fire in the *City of God*.[1]

What, then, shall I tell the unbelievers to convince them that human bodies, animate and living, may endure undissolved both against death and the tortures of eternal fire? They will not allow us to ascribe this to the power of the Omnipotent, but urge us to con-

[1] S. Aurelii Augustini, *De Civitate Dei contra Paganos*, edited by J. E. C. Welldon. 1924. Vol. II, Liber XXI, caput ii, p. 522.

vince them by some example. We could answer that
there are animals that are indeed corruptible, because
mortal, and yet do live untouched in the midst of fire.
And likewise we could answer that there are certain
worms to be found alive in spring water the heat of
which nobody can touch with impunity, and yet those
worms do not only live there without any harm, they
even cannot live without this environment. But the
unbelievers either will not believe it unless they see it,
or, if we can show or affirm it by reliable witnesses,
then, in their incredulity, they will call it an insufficient
proof of the question. They will argue that these animals are not eternal and live in this heat without
pain, since these conditions suit their nature; therefore, they are not tortured by these elements. As if
it were not more incredible to live comfortably under
such circumstances than to be tortured by them! It
is miraculous for anything to be tormented by fire and
yet to live, but it is still more miraculous to live in
the fire and not to feel pain. If, then, this latter be
credible, why not the first also?

It is due to the weakness of Christianity in matters of
secular knowledge that the early Church had to leave instruction in scientific subjects to the pagan schools—a fact
which explains the strange mixture of the seven *artes liberales* and Christian theology in the medieval university
and the pagan heritage transmitted to secondary and
higher education at their foundation and still present in
them. And as the early characteristics of a movement
often—one may perhaps say always—remain inherent in it
up to the height of its development, so Christianity has

been subject to the conflict of religion and reason from the theologians of the ancient Church up to the present. This conflict was latent only during the relatively short period in Western history between the disappearance of the spirit of antiquity and the rediscovery of the works of Aristotle by the maturing medieval man. Neither Augustine nor the thinkers in the period of Scholasticism were undisturbed by the contrast between dogma and reason. Augustine was constantly irritated by the presence of pagan elements in his own mind, as were Abelard and his Scholastic disciples. Only between Gregory I (c. 600) and Gregory VII (c. 1075) did such men as Alcuin and Hrabanus Maurus feel themselves perfectly able to harmonize truth and dogma. At the very beginning of Scholasticism the papal bulls against heterodoxy began to appear; the fundamental contrast showed itself clearly in the Renaissance, and since that time we have observed the continuous struggle of the churches against almost all great and revolutionary ideas in philosophy and science. One might say, with very little exaggeration, that the history of science is not only the history of its progressive achievements but simultaneously the history of its conflicts with the official theologies.

This antagonism in the realm of spirit was accompanied by social conflicts between the Church and society. The gulf between Church and State widened during the seventeenth and eighteenth centuries, until in the nineteenth century the conflict came to its climax with the entrance of the working classes into public life. Up to the eighteenth century, in spite of the political liaison between the churches and the aristocracy, freethinking was common in cultural circles, but it was considered a privilege not to be extended to the larger masses. During the nineteenth century a strange reversal was going to take place. The common man, because of his lack of education, had generally been a pious believer in Christian dogma; but, as we mentioned in an earlier chapter, at the end of the eighteenth and during the nineteenth century he became critical both of social and religious institutions. On the other hand, after the French Revolution and the first great social upheavals of the capitalistic era, the hereditary aristocracy and the rich, previously the bearers of critical thought, shifted to the religious side, partly under the spiritual influence of Romanticism and partly because they feared that more enlightenment would destroy their privileged position. Becoming increasingly defensive, they held it their duty and interest to support the conservative social attitude of the churches. To show the contrast: Frederick the Great, living before the French Revolution, was the friend of Voltaire; his successor before and during the World War defended religion as the bulwark of the kind of society which he was interested in maintaining. The alliance of the churches with deliberate backwardness, which has continued up to the present time in some countries, has not fostered the reverence of the masses for religion. In the last decade the alienation of some peoples from Christianity has again assumed cruelly expressive forms.

So we see at the end of this short analysis that the widespread distrust of churches and clergymen is due not only to spiritually and morally negative tendencies in modern times but also to a refined conscience in matters of truth and social progress. Even persons who are critical of shallow forms of enlightenment and strongly aware of the limits of science may avoid the churches because, in their opinion, they offend against intellectual integrity.

The degree of their estrangement has often led both the large masses and the intellectuals to mistake completely the role of true religion in individual and public life; they overlook the great contributions of the churches to education and even, in earlier times, to the development of science; they fail to understand that many of the victims of ecclesiastical as well as of political reaction have drawn their revolutionary ideas and their power of resistance from religious sources. A further fallacy worth mentioning in this context is the tendency to lay all superstition and cultural backwardness to the account of religion. Both, however, are part of a general human characteristic which flourishes outside of religion as well as within it and which, particularly by Christianity, has often been offset by religious concepts conducive to reason and humanity.

B. PRESENT FORMS OF RELIGIOUS EXPERIENCE

We have described the situation with which all who are concerned with the conveyance of religious values are faced. But we cannot content ourselves with a historical analysis. If we want to investigate the relation between religion and culture, we must also examine the actual forms in which religion at present is experienced and transmitted to the younger generation. In doing so we can discern four characteristic types of religious attitudes.

1. THE FUNDAMENTALIST POINT OF VIEW

The fundamentalist, or orthodox, point of view believes in the personal existence of God, the deity of Christ, the Holy Spirit, and the literal inspiration of the Bible. Faith should not be made dependent upon individual reasoning, since in contrast to the truth of the revelation all other truths are of secondary value.[1]

The fundamentalist point of view is the result either of an uncritical aloofness from all scientific thinking or of inner experiences which lead a man to an absolute doubt in the competence of reason. Whatever the origin of fundamentalism may be, it offers its adherents certainty amidst the confusion of changing beliefs and perplexing social and moral problems. On the other hand, it may lead to the denial of the creative centers of life and thought and, consequently, may impede the development of a rounded and evolving personality.

2. THE RELIGIOUS PHILOSOPHY OF IDENTITY (HUMANISM)

In contrast to fundamentalism there has developed an interpretation of religion that may be called the "religious philosophy of identity." It is an attempt to reconcile faith and reason. Since it is connected with the humanistic thought of the Renaissance and the idealism of the eighteenth and nineteenth centuries, it might also be called the humanistic or idealistic version of Christianity. But both "humanistic" and "idealistic" suggest so many cultural tendencies that their meaning is rather vague. The same is true of the term "liberal." Doubtless the religious philosophy of identity defends a liberal interpretation of religious tradition; during the nineteenth century it was supported by the so-called "liberal school of theology," which fostered critical philological and historical re-

[1] Corinthians ii. 10–16.

search into the origin of the Church and the Bible. But this term leads people to connect religion with political and economic liberalism, an association which can be defended on good grounds but which is likely, in our age of political uncertainty, to prevent an unbiased judgment of the spiritual force of the religious philosophy of identity. For the sake of brevity we shall sometimes use the term "humanism" or "humanistic." The essential feature of the movement we are considering, however, is the attempt at a synthesis of religion and reason which starts, consciously or unconsciously, from the idea of a pre-established identity of the Divine, the immanent laws of the cosmos, and human reason. We have the beginnings of this sort of religion as early as Scholasticism, then more distinctly in the works of Master Eckhardt and Nicolaus Cusanus, whose philosophy reflects the influence of the philosophy of Plotinus on Western civilization. The line of development then goes through Giordano Bruno, Jacob Böhme, Leibnitz, Berkeley, Hegel, Schleiermacher to the liberal school of the nineteenth century.

For such a view of the world the coming of Christ may be something unique and revolutionary, the greatest of all revelations; but the whole history of man and nature and all contact of the mind with the Absolute, in the form of mystic experiences, scientific discoveries, and great deeds, are also revelations. The identity supposed to exist between the Absolute, the objective world, and the human mind must itself be interpreted as the result of a first and fundamental event in the universe which gives to all later evolutionary developments the character of an unfolding of its mystical inner unity. To make this clear, one has only to refer to Hegel's philosophy of religion and the whole structure of his system, which exercised a great influence on the theology of the nineteenth century until Kierkegaard's interpretation of religion became its rival. This mysticism, however, underlies to a certain extent all of our sciences in that they suppose that the operations of the human mind, when they follow correct principles, signify corresponding events in the objective world.[1]

The religious philosophy of identity, accordingly, visualizes the human intellect, in spite of its weaknesses, as permeated with the Divine and simultaneously raises the human being from religious fear to religious self-confidence. St. Augustine wanted to hate and debase himself in order to be able to love God and attain to grace; in contrast to him, the Renaissance educator Maffeo Vegio wrote in his *Education of Children* (*De Educatione Liberorum*): "One must have the highest reverence for oneself" ("*Apud seipsum summam habendum reverentiam*"). God is not above or against, but in the world; and this idea of the immanence of the Spirit in the world became the greatest impulse toward belief in progress and toward political freedom and freedom of thought.

From the orthodox point of view the religious philosophy of identity does not understand either the hereditary sinfulness of man or the Christian revelation as testimony of the rationally incomprehensible grace of God. But it is not necessary to be a fundamentalist to see in the philosophy of identity the danger of a fallacious optimism and autonomism. In its less profound forms it sees too easily the God in man and overlooks man's utter helplessness, his distance and alienation from the Divine, and the despair of his situation in the universe. While Scholasticism

[1] Compare Chapter III.

tried to find the measure of reason in faith, the theology of identity is often inclined to see the measure of faith in human reason. Both have succumbed to the temptation of fallaciously relating the rational and the irrational. Luther, a fundamentalist, is opposed to either side. According to him, any co-ordination of faith and reason is a fundamental misconception of Christianity. Even Scholasticism, according to Luther, with its predilection for Aristotle, bears the signs of pagan self-complacency and hinders man from grasping the essential meaning of Christianity; that is, the experience of God through deepest despair, contrition, and the joy of His grace. The problem of the relation of faith and reason is still one of the most intricate in religious philosophy.

Another objection to the religious philosophy of identity is that in practice it has led to inconsistent compromises between Christian dogma and tradition, on the one hand, and free reasoning, on the other. Adherence to reason and logic makes unavoidable the elimination of large parts of the Biblical tradition and dogma. But liberal ministers and religious teachers have usually evaded the problem. They treat the Christian miracles with a mixture of awe and uneasiness, not daring to do away with them although their presence imposes a considerable burden upon their rational conscience. Even in one of the best books of the liberal religious movement—Adolf Harnack's *What Is Christianity?*—the problem has not been solved. Though the reader has been given knowledge and understanding, he is left with questions still unanswered: Who is Christ, the Son of God or a man? What is man, a being who must follow reason or who stands first of all in need of grace and salvation?

3. Kierkegaard's Religion of
Paradoxicalness

The feeling of a genuine difference between Christianity and its philosophic interpretation by the school of identity led in the nineteenth century to protest under the leadership of the Dane, Sören Kierkegaard. There is a striking similarity between Luther's fight against the absorption of Aristotle's philosophy by the Scholastics and Kierkegaard's opposition to Hegel, whom he regarded as the strongest representative of the idealistic distortion of Christianity. But there is, however, a fundamental difference. Luther not only believed in the essential other-worldliness of faith but was also prescientific, untouched by modern empirical thinking. Kierkegaard and his followers, on the other hand, though likewise believing in the other-worldliness of faith, took account of the critical research that was going on in their day in framing their arguments in opposition to the prevalent "idealism." Moreover, Kierkegaard was equally opposed to the orthodoxy of his day. In a book with the strange title *Final Unscientific Postscript*,[1] he speaks of it as "the childlike form of Christianity, lovable in the small child, that becomes in the adult a childish orthodoxy, delighted with the fantastic, into which it arbitrarily introduces the name of Christ." He accuses orthodoxy of attempting to offset the neglect into which Christianity is falling by "raising its price" until "faith becomes something extraordinary and rare," easy only for those who possess the undesirable ca-

---

[1] Quoted from the German translation of the Danish original by H. Gottsched and Ch. Schrempf: *Abschliessende unwissenschaftliche Nachschrift.* 1925. Part II, p. 250. (Danish title: *Afsluttende Uvidenskabelig Efterskrift. . . .*) ·

pacity of applying fantastic and miraculous ideas to the real problems of religion, and "impossible for those lacking this capacity." In doing this the orthodox "confuse everything" and actually deny Christianity, which for everyone requires an equally difficult, but equally possible, act of faith.

From the point of view of Kierkegaard, the real Christian must be able to believe consciously against his reason, to be convinced of his guilt as an existing being, and to suffer joyfully under this feeling of guilt. But believing *against* reason is not the same as degrading reason. The very fact that reason must be considered as one of the greatest gifts of man and that faith is nevertheless greater requires the believer to accept the greatest of paradoxes and makes the decision for Christianity the important one that it is. To become a Christian is the positive answer to the most unreasonable and the most severe demand that can be made upon modern man: to estimate reason at its proper value and, nevertheless, to give it up in favor of revelation and salvation. Kierkegaard, therefore, gave to his kind of religion the name of the "religion of paradoxicalness."

In Kierkegaard's opinion the modern anthropological discoveries about the origin of religion might be true about other religions and even about Christianity in so far as it is expressed in human conceptual thinking and in human institutions. But the moment a man becomes possessed with the *Mysterium tremendum* of the "Numinous" or of the "Wholly Other," his mind is related to something incomparable to all human ideas. The "Wholly Other" is, so to speak, inclosed in brackets which shut it off from the logic of human thinking. It is not only beyond the categories of reason, it is also beyond the categories of history. Consequently, however much we may enjoy the progress of science and of all other human achievements, since they are human they are entirely irrelevant to the world beyond. Since this is so, our modern responsibility for truth and reason is real so long as we are acting in the sphere of reason or as scientists in any field, including the history of the Christian religion. But in relation to the "Wholly Other" we are responsible to another kind of truth.[1]

This modern, not pre- but post-rationalistic supernaturalism has won much ground during recent decades, not so much in the Anglo-Saxon countries, though it is beginning to arouse interest in England, as in the Scandinavian countries and in Central Europe. The disillusionment of the modern world with the capacities of man, the insight into the superficiality of an understanding of progress which simply identified a later stage of development with the better, and the self-delusion of modern civilization and science have supported this development. The old fundamentalism is probably doomed to die; but paradoxical theology will become the creed of many of the well-educated among the Protestant Christians, except perhaps among the Anglo-Saxon peoples, which succeeded better than the European continent to amalgamate the thought of the Enlightenment with their Christian tradition and which, in addition, enjoyed a comparative freedom from the most extreme disappointments in modern civilization.

[1] Important points of paradoxical theology are to be found during the whole course of Christian theology, especially in Chrysostom, St. Augustine, Luther, and the great mystics. But Kierkegaard was the first to place the idea of the paradoxical character of Christianity in the center of a coherent theological system.

4. Religious Symbolism

There is still another religious attitude, which is probably the most widespread in our times, though because of its completely untheological character and its evasiveness to logical argumentation it is given very little attention in theological treatises. It could be called "religious symbolism" because it finds the expression of the most valuable thoughts and emotions in images and symbols rather than in logical conceptions. But the artistic element in religious symbolism is in no way incompatible with radical scientific thinking. It can, for example, grow very well on the basis of any philosophy that resembles self-transcendent empiricism.

Symbolism does not pretend to know "what it is all about" in the transcendental sphere; it is more the sign of a fundamental doubt concerning the possibility of grasping the supernatural by human mental operations. It is not dissimilar to the religion of paradoxicalness inasmuch as it, too, feels the Absolute as the "Wholly Other." But just as it would deny Hegel's claim that human reason can define the categories according to which the Logos must operate, so it would also deny Kierkegaard's claim that testimony of the Absolute is to be found in the form of a paradoxical Christian experience. The true symbolist, therefore, may be called the most modest of all religious types.[1] On the other hand, he is far from being a relativist. He is also perhaps the most dynamic religious type,

---

[1] After completing the manuscript of this book, I came across the following sentences by Thomas Mann, which appeared in an article on "Living Philosophies: The Coming Humanism" in the *Nation* for December 10, 1938:

"I do, indeed, disclaim any doctrinaire attitude in spiritual matters. The ease with which some people let the word God fall from their lips—or even

since for him the transcendental is too powerful to be caught by the static concepts and the inadequate categories of the human intellect. Consequently, this type often betrays a decided disinclination for all the attempts of the theologians and philosophers to define what, to use a phrase of Plotinus's, the "eyes of the soul" may see; he is disgusted by the controversies of the theologians because he considers that arguments are only misleading and cannot make for true reverence.

The symbolic type, like all others, is never to be found in complete pureness. The Neoplatonist Plotinus is a symbolist when he speaks of the impossibility of determining the true nature of the One and the All otherwise than by saying what it is not, but he has also elements of the philosophy of identity and the philosophy of paradoxicalness. John Dewey in his recent writings on the problem of religion shows symbolic elements in combination with humanistic elements. Certainly one of the purest representatives of the symbolic attitude is Goethe. For him the only man who can love and understand the world—so far as we can understand it at all—is the one who looks at it not as an object at times so completely transparent that the divine light shines through it, but as something translucent through which we can imagine the Absolute in forms and ideas that elude description. In his "Proemium"[1] he

---

more extraordinarily from their pens—is always a great astonishment to me. A certain modesty, even embarrassment, in things of religion is clearly more fitting to me and my kind than any posture of bold self-confidence. It seems that only by indirection can we approach the subject—by the parable, the ethical symbolism in which, if I may so express myself, the concept becomes secularized, is temporarily divested of its priestly garment and contents itself with the humanly spiritual."

[1] Goethe's *Poems and Aphorisms*, edited for the Goethe Society of America by Friedrich Bruns. Oxford University Press. 1932.

gives expression to his religious attitude in the following
words:

To Him who from eternity, self-stirred,
Himself has made by His creative word;
To Him who, seek to name Him as we will,
Unknown within Himself abideth still:
To Him supreme who maketh faith to be,
Trust, hope, love, power, and endless energy.

Strain ear and eye till sight and sound be dim,
Thou'lt find but faint similitudes of Him;
Yea, and thy spirit in her flight of flame
Still tries to gauge the symbol and the name:
Charmed and compelled thou climb'st from height to height
And round thy path the world shines wondrous bright;
Time, space, and size and distance cease to be,
And every space is fresh infinity.

C. THE TRANSMISSION OF RELIGIOUS VALUES

If we examine the implications of these four religious
attitudes for the teaching of religion and the transmission
of religious values, we come to very different conclusions
with respect to each of them.

The fundamentalist will be inclined to regard the narratives of the Old and New Testaments as didactically well
suited for an introduction into the values of Christianity;
he will then, perhaps, go to the parables; at a later stage
he will show the system of Christian religion and morals
in a more abstract way; and perhaps he will end with a
comparative treatment of the great world religions, showing thereby the superiority of the Christian revelation.
The personal character of God and His Son will not be

disputed, nor the truth of the dogma be questioned. The alleged inseparability of Christian faith and proper human conduct will be emphasized, and much weight given to the child's early acquaintance with the religious traditions of the particular Christian community to which the child and his parents belong. Any yielding to other Christian ideas will be considered as apostasy, with evil consequences here and hereafter.

In contrast to the older kind of orthodox religious instruction which prevailed in many Protestant countries up to the twentieth century and which is dominant in some countries even today, the followers of the religious philosophy of identity try to base religious instruction largely on reason and on a careful observation of the psychological prerequisites for the conveyance of religious values. In consequence of this attitude they are open to all the doubts which have arisen with respect to the character of religious training. The problem of how to meet the conflict between science and faith, and modernity and religion is always with them. The difficulty is that the contributions of psychology, whether from the proreligious or the antireligious schools, have been of doubtful value. While orthodox religious education reckons upon the power of the Christian revelation to convince by means of its indwelling truth and authority, the religious humanist must lead the disciple through questioning and doubt to the acknowledgment of the central role of Christian faith in human life.

If this kind of religious education succeeds, the result is a broad-minded, elastic, and well-balanced personality. But the shortcomings of the method are many. In attempting to avoid the dangers of orthodox teaching and to awaken independent thinking it may fail to give the student inner certainty; and it makes the intended conveyance of religious values a prevailingly intellectual process, mixed with emotional appeals. But the result is not necessarily religion.

At this point the criticism of the followers of Kierkegaard is added to that of the orthodox Christians. How can the acceptance of the Christian paradox be taught through intellectual activities, through philosophy or the analysis of historical religions, which may lead men away from religious experience as well as toward it? But strong as Kierkegaard is in his criticism of both the humanistic and the orthodox way of teaching religion, accusing the latter of offering "idyllic mythologies," he himself does not suggest a practical educational method, and he cannot do so. In keeping with his assumptions he says:

> For the individual the same law applies as applied to the entrance of Christianity into the world: nobody can begin by being a Christian; a man becomes a Christian when the time is ripe, when he is doomed to become a Christian. A severe Christian education is a very risky enterprise. Christianity makes men whose strength lies in their weakness; but to force a child into a strict kind of Christian living will make a very unhappy young man. A rare exception is but a windfall.[1]

The fourth type of religious attitude, that of symbolism, has formulated no distinct theory of either Christian

---

[1] *Abschliessende unwissenschaftliche Nachschrift.* Part II, p. 245. Compare also Kierkegaard's *Einuebung in Christentum*, translated from the Danish into German by H. Gottsched and Ch. Schrempf.

religious education or education in general, though good
teachers and preachers of all religious convictions have always utilized its artistic possibilities. But they have done
so only incidentally and not on principle. The reason is
that our religious instruction and our religious services
have so far been too closely attached to the traditions of
particular churches and denominations to permit of the inclusion of the symbolic attitude as an inherent part of their
programs and methods. Furthermore, symbolism signifies
a general attitude of mind rather than the acceptance of
doctrines that can be singled out for direct transmission.
One could even say that symbolism does not strictly belong to the teachable parts of Christianity since in many
instances it lacks its important fundamentals. Yet it is
likely that symbolism is more fitted than the customary
ways to open the gates to religious experience.

The churches find some danger to organized religion in
both symbolism and the humanistic attitude. How will
the churches be able to hold congregations together if
Christian dogma is allowed to become as relative as these
liberal movements would have it? How can the minister
give reliable guidance if he himself doubts the reality of
the essential doctrines? The reality of this fear is shown
by the effectiveness with which the dogma integrated early
Christianity in spite of internal and external controversies
and the critical situation that has always arisen when the
dogma of a religion has disintegrated.

But it must be recognized that the number of ministers
today who do not believe in the literal meaning of the
dogmatic tradition is extremely large. And though the
dogma may be appreciated as the ritual created by the
community and sanctified by a long and sacred history, it

is clear that the layman can no longer be put off with ambiguous and evasive answers concerning the character and meaning of this tradition. We have already sufficiently emphasized the fact that nothing disturbs our religious life more than this uncertainty. Therefore, if the clergy wants both to preserve the dogma as a traditional form in the flux of ideas and to defend the Church against constant attacks from the rationalists, there is only one way out. It must clearly distinguish between the historical vestment of the dogma and its inherent meaning. The historical and ethnic setting in which the dogma originated was such that analogy and allegory were the forms in which the mind comprised religious truth. This was so even in the times of Thomas Aquinas, Luther, and Calvin. Even in our time of refined intellectual conceptions the profoundest that man can feel is still logically inexpressible. Man will probably always be obliged to speak in images, and in an ultimate sense all of our words are such. The medieval philosophers, debating the problem of realism and nominalism, saw this problem and consequently the whole issue of faith and reason with astounding clearness.

But while the image is not a reality, it signalizes a reality. Great works of art, though their fictions and their rhythms are but of allegorical value, contain as much and often more truth than scientific reports, though it is truth of another sort. We are right in speaking of the truth immanent in the *Divine Comedy*, in *Hamlet*, or in *Faust*, but we do not confuse the embodiment of this truth with the kind of reality that the artist is expressing.

The symbolic interpretation of the dogma would, on the one hand, allow us to respect its essential relation to the ultimate and its value as ritual. On the other hand, the dogma and the Christian doctrines would need constant reinterpretation in order that every generation might most easily find its own path to the infinite. The dogma, then, would be both a given certainty and a necessary task, both absolute and relative, static and dynamic. Progressive groups within the Church have already reached the stage of religious maturity when scientific thought and religion harmoniously flow together. With the general acknowledgment of the doctrinal tradition as a spiritual creation of man which retains its integrating power when it is interpreted symbolically, a new era of the reconciliation and co-operation of Christianity with an empirical culture would be reached, and the modern Christian could repeat with the same joyfulness what was said more than a thousand years ago by Hrabanus Maurus, one of the most amiable of Christian scholars: "*Immo vero quisquis bonus verusque christianus est, domini sui esse intelligat, ubicumque invenerit veritatem*"—"Every good and true Christian may know that wherever he finds truth it is the truth of the Lord."

D. CRITICAL EVALUATION OF RELIGIOUS EDUCATION

Until such an interpretation of Christianity has become established, shall we leave it to chance what form of instruction a teacher, more or less conditioned by circumstances and environment, shall follow?

With respect to the orthodox teaching of religion, the philosophy elaborated in this book permits only one reply. It may be that in some strongholds of Protestantism and Catholicism, among social groups with little scientific and empirical education, fundamentalism is still a vital force.

But with the development of public forms of enlightenment it must increasingly conflict with empirical knowledge and eventually give rise to the sort of situation that now exists in many countries: an increasing suspicion even in the remotest villages that the priest is either withholding the truth or isolating himself from the achievements of modern times. Events that have come to pass in many countries ought to warn us not to rely too much on the credulity of the common man. In some countries cultural and political life is now being shattered by the hostility of the population toward the churches because they have failed to fulfill their obligations to men seeking for truth.

Therefore, only those approaches to the problem of religious training can be discussed constructively that permit an understanding of Christianity in harmony with the modern quest for truth and that encourage a well-balanced development of the total person.

Of the three remaining schools, Kierkegaard's religion of paradoxicalness will hardly play a great part in popular education. He maintained, of course, that his form of Christianity is available to everyone. He would have said that it is not a special form of religion at all but the form that all true religion must take. The fact, nevertheless, remains that Kierkegaard's religious experience either befalls a person with irresistible power or can be understood vicariously through reason and knowledge only by a highly trained intellect. For Kierkegaard, as our quotations indicate, understood Christianity not only as something irrational and paralogical but as something completely paradoxical. His system is the result of a rigorously logical advance into the religious sphere that arrives finally at the negation of logic and reason. It became historically

possible only after the works of Kant and Hegel had permeated our philosophical thought and had sharpened the
intellectual tools required for the subtleties of the religion
of paradoxicalness. All that education can do with regard
to Kierkegaard's conception of religion is to take care that
routine, spiritual indifference, and intellectual compla-
cency do not shut off those depths of the soul from which
the realization of the paradoxical way to God may arise.

The religious philosophies of identity and symbolism are
constantly accused today both by the orthodox and the
followers of Kierkegaard of being unable to understand
the essence of religion, though it is from these schools
that some of the greatest modern religious philosophers—
namely, the humanistic and romantic philosophers, among
them Schleiermacher—have sprung. These critics support
their attack by referring to the supposedly excessive rationalism and individualism of these men. But, as a matter of historical fact, the humanists from the time of Erasmus on have been equally concerned with religious and
cosmological matters. Any kind of thought has, of course,
a tendency to lay stress upon the ideas called forth by the
needs of a particular period. During the many centuries in which humanism has been flourishing, freedom of
thought has needed emphasis as a prerequisite to the understanding of oneself and to the understanding of God.
An idea of such importance will never lose its value. The
danger is rather that orthodox and paradoxical theology
may conceal the sources of true humanity in all kinds of
vague romanticism and obscurantism, a danger to be no
more disregarded than the possible dangers of intellectualism hidden in the philosophy of religious identity. Even
Hegel, the most radical of the rational idealists and the

target of Kierkegaard's attacks, drew, according to his own testimony, the inspiration for his great philosophic efforts from the "pain of negativity," which is the longing for the "return to the Absolute" and for "the spirit infinite and nevertheless dynamic and omnipresent in the world." [1]

In this "pain of negativity"—in other words, in man's continual experience of the limits imposed upon his efforts to understand the secrets of the universe—lies also the source of religious symbolism. It is different from the philosophy of identity, however, in that it is less rationalistic and less desirous of compressing the universe into scientific categories and systems. It knows that the most we can hope for is to find the right symbol through which we can convey to ourselves and to others the meaning within and behind the phenomenal world.

The churches which, in spite of fundamental differences from the philosophy of symbolism, have always recognized the value of the artistic image for religious education are the Catholic and the Greek Orthodox, and to a lesser degree the High Church, while the Protestant churches, having come into existence through their opposition to ritualism and formalism—which really are the great dangers of the love for symbolism—have laid their emphasis upon individual experience. But within Protestantism there developed, as its unique symbolic expression of faith, the religious music of Bach. And many of the Protestant churches are beginning to show a concern for a more im-

---

[1] *Encyclopaedie der philosophischen Wissenschaften*, par. 569. As we cannot discuss this problem at length, we must simply refer to Hegel's discussion of the relation of philosophy and religion to the Absolute, especially his *Religionsphilosophie* and his *Encyclopaedie der philosophischen Wissenschaften*, pars. 482, 565, 571, and 573.

pressive presentation of religion. Reforms in ecclesiastical architecture and the conduct of services, as well as the style of religious youth movements, in many churches clearly reveal a growing desire to support the inward experience of religion by the power of imagination. Public performances of medieval religious drama—such as *Everyman*, *The Dance of Death*, and the *Passion Play*—and the works of such modern religious poets as Paul Claudel and Rainer Maria Rilke have had an effect upon the revitalization of Christian tradition which exceeds all that could be fairly expected in our rationalistic and technical age.

It is true that many of these factors do not leave any permanent effect; they stir up emotions without touching the roots of personality and, as the history of some churches shows, they easily degenerate into aestheticism. Nevertheless, they give sufficient witness of what could be done if our education could rely upon a civilization less incapable of expressing the deeper emotions than ours.

The inadequate development of the emotional capacities of modern man presents a serious cultural and educational problem. Sensationalism and sentimentality are always a substitute for a neglected, affective life. The emotions are appealed to and superficially satisfied by the excitements of many popular forms of entertainment. Or the need for a more active emotional self-expression may lead to political agitation, the devotion to a particular movement being offset by hatred of all others. Large numbers, in their desire for elevation above the daily routine, are misled by the religious offerings of modern prophets which are so shamefully below all great religious traditions that we are forced to question whether the churches and schools are giving the majority of the people any insight at all into the transcendental meaning of life. Only a complete lack of all understandable and embracing religious symbols can account for the despair that causes these emotionally impoverished people to reach for the obscurantism of the many modern substitute religions.

In many Protestant countries the only religious festival that has retained a symbolic value is Christmas, and even that has often been commercialized or has become a day for giving pleasure to the children and for the exchange of gifts. The majority of the public holidays commemorate battles or other occasions when one country or faction has defeated another. It is certainly doubtful whether these modern festivals direct our thoughts toward objects of comfort or moral stimulation as effectively as did the old Christian festivals. Most people would be richer and stronger to resist the many wasteful distractions and destructive elements of modern life if their education had given them a profounder experience of the artistic or religious creations dealing with the position of man in the natural and spiritual universe.

E. THE FUNDAMENTAL DIFFICULTY IN RELIGIOUS EDUCATION

In any discussion of the implications of the various religious schools for education we must not forget what Kierkegaard, with a fine feeling for the weakness inherent in all religious education, has pointed out: that no interpretation, no philosophy, no dialectical discussion is able to create the pure religious experience. It is the lack of appreciation of this fact that constitutes, unquestionably, one of the main reasons for the difficulty in the transmission of religion both to the young and to adults.

To illustrate, let us take an example from the field of art education. Many attempts to enrich the lives of men through art suffer from the teacher's opinion that it is enough to guide his students through a museum, analyze the beauty of a work of art, and perhaps encourage the buying of reproductions. He forgets that all this is useful only if he can presuppose in his students those inner qualities and capacities which make possible the transformation of merely intellectual operations into aesthetic experiences.

Just as there are many who speak of art without themselves having had an aesthetic experience, so there are undoubtedly many who speak of religion without having ever felt any actual religious response to the world. One can be orthodox in creed or convinced on the basis of philosophic deliberations that there is an Absolute beyond the world of the senses without being religious. Otherwise, religion would not be so often mistaken for morality just because the two are closely related to each other, or for regular attendance at church or adherence to a particular dogma. The experience of God is unthinkable without a personal act that can only be described in mystical terms. This act has nothing to do either with knowledge or with theurgy. In Greek philosophy it has best been characterized by Plotinus, in medieval mysticism by Master Eckhardt, and in Protestantism by Luther when he spoke of the solitary hours in the cloister of Wittenberg which led to the sudden relief of his inner troubles and his belief in the grace of God. It is much easier to explain to students of philosophy, theology, or education a difficult philosophic system than to explain to them the inner life of Luther or Pascal. For the understanding of Spinoza or Kant his education has given the intelligent student the necessary logical powers. But often he has never found, or has lost the power to experience, radical religious emotions, perhaps exactly because of his learning and his efforts to satisfy the intellectual requirements of the modern university.

This is the paradox of the religious experience, that it is logically inexplicable to both the learned and the unlearned unless they are disposed to it. But a simple man may have it without talking; it may quietly accompany his life and daily work, while the intellectual must conquer or reconquer it. Only with this understanding can we explain those sentences in St. Paul's letter to the Corinthians which, because they were interpreted as an attack upon the intellect, have brought so many disastrous consequences to Christianity:

> For it is written, I will destroy the wisdom of the wise, and will bring to nothing the understanding of the prudent. Where is the wise? Where is the scribe? Hath not God made foolish the wisdom of this world? For after that in the wisdom of God the world by wisdom knew not God, it pleased God by the foolishness of preaching to save them that believe.

It is on the basis of such considerations that some of the most serious religious educators and philosophers have expressed doubts as to whether even the best attempts at religious education can have the desired results. If the experience of the Absolute is not the result of conscious effort but of grace, an intuition and an event coming from above or from within, what can knowledge accomplish? Doubtless the more or less tacit acceptance of such a view has contributed greatly to the inferior role of religion in the modern curriculum, though this is due also to the difficulties of introducing religious instruction without arousing the opposition of competing denominations.

F. THE ROLE OF RELIGION IN MODERN CIVILIZATION

But since the end of the nineteenth century and increasingly since the World War, more and more people are beginning to realize that dependence upon science to the exclusion of religion will not lead us into an era of human freedom and happiness. Our progressive disillusionment has not been offset by new, more profound, and more comprehensive ideals but has resulted in disenchantment and psychic exhaustion. Man has been driven into a vacuum where he has nothing but himself, where all that he thinks and plans swings around himself alone; and that means that he is utterly impoverished. He necessarily misunderstands himself and can no longer possess himself in his potential totality, since for such self-possession he must know his place in the material and spiritual universe. The moment man attempts to derive the measures of his being and acting from himself alone, he is left without any measures at all; the freedom of an isolated being, torn out of *ordo* and Logos, has no transcendental meaning and attachment and thereby becomes a merely negative value; in other words, a nonvalue.

Man in this condition has only three ways to go. He may decide for virtue, as an individual act that will enable him to escape the feeling of absurdity that the world must impress upon him. This was the way of the Stoics and is again the attitude of some modern philosophers. Or he may be overpowered by the meaningless arbitrariness of his own existence and the complete relativity of all theoretical and practical doing. Or he may escape this conclusion and consider man—since he cannot see any regulative principle within or above himself—as dependent upon the surrounding circumstances, without being able to give these circumstances any coherent meaning. The result is then a philosophy of conditionalism or a so-called scientific attitude which forgets that a real science of man must see him not only in his individual wholeness but also in his relation to the universe.

The continuous peril of being overwhelmed by the barbarism to which the world is exposed and with which we are threatened in our own advanced times, the uselessness and the danger of all progress in knowledge without a corresponding increase in our responsibility for the dignity of man show us that education and culture cannot dispense with transcendent values. As we have said in earlier chapters, scientific methods cannot be used too much, but unless they are embedded in a meaningful general interpretation of man's role in the world they may be as easily used for his degradation as for his elevation, for destruction as well as for construction.

Here is to be found the value of all great religious and metaphysical systems for the continuation and advancement of civilization. They all proclaim that the civilizations of man exist only through *religio*, which means literally "being bound" to a Logos that determines man's relations to the rest of life and to the entire universe. In Christian mystical language it is the "Kingdom of God"; when we say in prayer "Thy Kingdom come," it is a request for connection with this source of peace and wisdom.

The decisive question in our present crisis, perhaps more so than at any time during the last few centuries, is whether we shall find *religio* again and through it a right appreciation of man, or whether the process of detaching man from the totality of the universe will go still further. If the latter is to be the case, the liberal and democratic forms of government, which themselves have contributed their full share to the disorder of the modern world, cannot continue. For, as we argued in our last chapter, they are based fundamentally upon a Christian humanism. The moment the social order ceases to spring from this natural source and, instead, is regulated by merely biological or materialistic doctrines, the democratic community must give way to organization by means of power. The individual will then no longer be a member of humanity but of a single nation with no criterion but itself. It would not be the first time that this has happened, but so far the result has always been disaster.

The question of religion is, therefore, much more momentous than we generally suppose, and the solution of the conflict between intellect and religious tradition is of crucial importance.

G. THE IDEA OF REVERENCE

Under these circumstances it is very unfortunate that religious instruction in modern times is, for the most part, less effective than any other kind of instruction. While the history and philosophy of religion have developed into independent sciences with considerable freedom of research, religious instruction has suffered from a general neglect. To the most thoughtful students of the problem it has seemed to offer insuperable psychological and philosophical difficulties, and, in addition, it has always been subject to the restraints imposed upon it by the interests of particular denominations or by the state, for which it is a useful form of indoctrination.

It is, therefore, a fundamental necessity for the development of a new religious spirit in modern society that religious education be lifted to the level of other fields of education and research. As long as conscientious parents must refuse to submit their children to the influence of inexperienced amateurs who teach in Sunday schools and give answers to which they do not even know the questions, the Christian heritage cannot be expected to renew itself.

It would betray a considerable lack of realism to believe that the goals alluded to can be reached before it is too late. The main handicap is the lack of unity in our religious life and the unwillingness of most denominations to open their specific doctrines to a general investigation of the essentials of Christianity. The situation may improve in Protestantism provided it does not lose still more of its influence among its followers; but in countries with a mixed Protestant and Catholic population there is no immediate hope for unified instruction unless Christianity, under the weight of immense catastrophes, is forced once again to go into the catacombs. And even in the catacombs the quarrels of the priests may continue.

But it may be that the problem is not one of the present religious denominations and their unity; it is a problem of the relation of religion to the total culture of a particular period. And this brings us back to our point of departure. If religion is not connected to the main arteries of civilization, it cannot have any lasting effect. For religion is either an inherent and permeating agent of civilization in its wholeness, or it is an artificial element cut off from the sources of its energy.

Hence, if, on the one hand, we are convinced that a renewed religion reconciled with the intellectual achievements of modernity is prerequisite to the recovery of our civilization and, on the other, that the churches alone cannot make the reconciliation, the immediate goal must be to instill into our general education a spirit that will open the way for a religious outlook upon the universe. This is possible under the auspices of the philosophy we have tried to expound in this book: the philosophy of self-transcendent empiricism. This philosophy of education takes the scientific and intellectual obligations of man as seriously as possible and, in addition, it leads us, through thinking, to the recognition of the fundamentally mystical nature of life. It leads to the creation of an attitude of mind which, whatever the final answer may be, is at least reverent toward the greatness of the universe and imaginatively aware of man's dependence upon it.

Reverence alone is not religion but simply an attitude of mind favorable to the reception of religious experience. On the other hand, no education is complete that fails to create an attitude of reverence in the student. The attainment of this immediate goal would, therefore, span the gap between these two great fields of human civilization. Intellectual training must not degenerate into logical exercises and the accumulation of knowledge but must encourage what the Greeks called a sense of wonder and what we have called reverence. Such a feeling stimulates the kind of thinking that is never satisfied with the results attained and presses on steadily toward profounder and more universal views and ultimately toward questions of a religious nature. Therefore, the three main fields of cultural education—the humanities, the natural sciences, and religion—must acknowledge reverence, in a creative and not a passive sense, as one of their common aims. All three of them must exist not only for their special purposes but also in order to inspire us with admiration for the universal powers that have created us and to which we shall be given back when the limitations of our human individuality are lost in death.

Already in those regions of civilization where a certain balance between empirical and religious thought has been achieved, the feeling of the insufficiency of a merely secular culture is awakening. Many of our leading thinkers have already driven their thinking beyond the old positivism and begun the search for those principles which will integrate the particularities of knowledge and experience into unity and universality.

Whether religious education will be part of the school curriculum or must remain outside of it, although it is a serious problem, depends largely upon the national educational tradition. Such problems cannot be solved in a merely administrative way. Their solution requires, first of all, the general acknowledgment of certain fundamental ideas such as we have advanced in this chapter and throughout this book and to which Wolfgang Goethe has given admirable expression in his "Pedagogical Province," a part of *Wilhelm Meister's Travels*. There Goethe records a conversation between Wilhelm, the hero of the novel, and three wise men, the leaders of the "Pedagogical Province," to whom he is going to entrust his son. This educational testament of Goethe has been rather

332 FUNDAMENTALS OF DEMOCRATIC EDUCATION

neglected during the modern empirical era, partly because of its combination of education with manual work and its emphasis on bodily gestures and partly because of its transcendental philosophy. During the last two decades, however, we not only have discovered, or rather rediscovered, the value of the co-operation of physical and mental training in eurhythmics and progressive forms of education, but also have become aware of the necessity of a new understanding of the problem of man, his culture, and his education. Therefore, at the conclusion of this attempt to construct a philosophy of education we may be pardoned for quoting at some length a part of Goethe's wisdom: [1]

"Well-formed, healthy children," replied the Three, "bring much into the world with them: Nature has given to each whatever he requires for time and duration; to unfold this is our duty; often it unfolds itself better of its own accord. One thing there is, however, which no child brings into the world with him; and yet it is on this one thing that all depends for making man in every point a man. . . .

"Three kinds of gestures you have seen: and we inculcate a three-fold Reverence, which, when commingled and formed into one whole, attains its highest force and effect. The first is Reverence for what is above us. That posture, the arms crossed over the breast, and look turned joyfully towards Heaven, that is what we have enjoined on young children;

---

[1] The quotation is taken from Carlyle's translation: *Wilhelm Meister's Apprenticeship and Travels.* Chapter X of the *Travels.* A new edition, revised, Boston, 1860. Vol. II, pp. 306 ff.

requiring thereby from them a testimony that there is a God above, who images and reveals himself in parents, teachers, superiors. Then comes the second; Reverence for what is under us. Those hands folded over the back, and, as it were, tied together; that down-turned, smiling look, announce that we are to regard the Earth with attention and cheerfulness: from the bounty of the Earth we are nourished; the Earth affords unutterable joys, but disproportionate sorrows she also brings us! . . .

"No religion that grounds itself on fear," said they, "is regarded among us. With the reverence to which a man should give dominion in his own mind, he can, in paying honor, keep his own honor: he is not disunited with himself, as in the former case. The Religion which depends on reverence for what is above us, we designate the Ethnic; it is the religion of the nations, and the first happy deliverance from a degrading fear: all Heathen religions, as we call them, are of this sort, whatsoever names they may bear. The Second Religion, which founds itself on reverence for what is around us, we designate the Philosophical: for the philosopher stations himself in the middle, and must draw down to him all that is higher, and up to him all that is lower: and only in this medium condition does he merit the title of Wise. Here, as he surveys with clear sight the relation to his equals, and therefore to the whole human race, his relations likewise to all other earthly circumstances and arrangements, necessary or accidental, he alone, in a cosmic sense, lives in Truth.

"But now we have to speak of the Third Religion,

grounded on reverence for what is beneath us; this we name the Christian, as in the Christian religion such a temper is with most distinctness manifested: it is a last step to which mankind were fitted and destined to attain. But what a task was it, not only to be patient with the Earth, and let it lie beneath us, we appealing to a higher birthplace; but also to recognize humility and poverty, mockery and despite, disgrace and wretchedness, suffering and death, to recognize these things as divine; nay even on sin and crime to look not as hinderances, but to honor and love them as furtherances, of what is holy. Of this, indeed, we find some traces in all ages: but the trace is not the goal; and, this being now attained, the human species cannot retrograde: and we may say, that the Christian religion having once appeared cannot again vanish; having once assumed its divine shape, can be subject to no dissolution."

"To which of these religions do you specially adhere?" inquired Wilhelm.

"To all the three," replied they; "for in their union they produce what may properly be called the true religion. Out of those Three Reverences springs the highest reverence,—reverence for oneself, and those again unfold themselves from this; so that man attains the highest elevation of which he is capable, that of being justified in reckoning himself the Best that God and Nature have produced; nay, of being able to continue on this lofty eminence, without being again by self-conceit and presumption drawn down from it into the vulgar level."

Chapter IX

THE MISSION OF AMERICAN EDUCATION

A. THE ESSENTIALS OF CIVILIZATION

If we consider philosophic thought not as something motivated simply by the desire for intellectual self-satisfaction but as responsible action the effectiveness of which depends upon its closeness to reality, then the philosopher of civilization is at present in a particularly precarious situation. He is trying to promote culture by revealing its essential functions and conditions; but, at the same time, the fate of the nations that are the main vehicles of civilization depends upon factors beyond his influence. The fate of civilization may be determined by the decisions of cabinets which themselves are entangled in a maze of unpredictable factors, and a wrong decision may send the world into cataclysms of hatred and bloodshed. He sees that even in rich countries unemployment is not overcome and that the best years of many of his fellow men are frustrated by the general economic helplessness. He sees that, in spite of all our knowledge and in spite of the shortage of goods essential for a dignified life, the production of armaments is still the most effective way of mobilizing human industry.

What is the use of philosophy in such a time? It can be

found only in the fact that without the constant struggle to come to clarity about himself man would have still less power to meet the challenge of disorganization. Speculation and abstract thinking are not necessarily aloofness in the sense of evasion, though sometimes they may be that. If they fulfill their mission, they will lead man some distance away from the scene of changing events and even from his own ego. They provide him with new resources, won through discrimination between the accidental and the essential, between what is and what ought to be, so that he may return into action and help humanity in its eternal task of mastering life through reason and understanding.

We may, therefore, dare to put aside for a while the diversity of the actual contents and daily responsibilities of civilization in order to ask for the unchanging prerequisites of its development. We find, then, that the progress of mankind depends upon the success with which seemingly contrasting components are brought into a constructive harmony. We may once more use the analogy of music and describe civilization as a counterpoint of a number of subordinate themes combined with a main melody.

In our fundamental philosophical chapters we found the relationship between growth and form to be one of the most urgent concerns of culture and education. In the chapters concerned with the more practical issues we found the right interaction of variety and unity to be a fundamental condition of a healthy society. The two combinations of growth and form and of variety and unity are not only essential for civilization, they are an inherent and, one may even say, an ontological condition of emerging

life. Wherever life advances, the dynamic principles—
growth and variety—and the ordering principles—form
and unity—become apparent.

But while in nature life functions organically, in the
human sphere it functions somewhat differently. In so
far as human life is still embedded in the more instinctive
phases of existence, unreflective forms of behavior prevail.
But the more man is able to use his reason, the more he
distinguishes and separates himself from the forces by
which the primitive is encompassed. As a result, an endless succession of new tasks and an increasing individualization in the face of complex political, social, and spiritual
forces cause man to become more and more devoted to
specialized purposes.

On the other hand, he can meet the challenge of freedom and civilization only if he does not lose sight of the
total conditions of his existence and of his relations to the
great powers of the human and cosmic universe. He can
develop into his own form only if, together with the cultivation of his own ego, he constantly transcends his empirical isolation into the whole of the components upon
which he and his civilization ultimately depend. For once
human powers have isolated themselves from their natural
relationships, they grow with an inexorable logic into
monsters that, instead of serving man for his full self-
realization, enslave him. Then machines, money, power,
and all our technical achievements no longer lead toward
progress but into a labyrinth of which the architect himself has lost the plan. Even in fields where man is less
driven by egoistic interests—in the intellectual fields—
he is inclined not to see his findings as part of an immense
cosmos but to identify tentative and partial findings with

ultimate and total results and to mistake these premature fixations of the reasoning process for living insights.

Here we meet another apparent conflict which has challenged man since the dawn of civilization, the conflict between reason and faith. Reason is, on the one hand, analytical and critical, fact-finding and specializing. It represents the ever-changing and restless element of the human soul. On the other hand, it has an inner tendency toward wholeness and permanence. But reason can arrive at wholeness and permanence only if it has the capacity for faith. Without faith as its background reason provides only variety; only with faith can it combine variety and unity, while faith alone leads to stagnation, dogmatism, and futile conflicts with reality. Therefore, all nations and periods with the capacity to synthesize growth and form possess also the power of uniting faith and reason. Peoples without faith are just as certainly doomed to fail as peoples without energy of thinking. All great discoveries result from the co-operative effort of these two qualities of the human mind.

Just as faith in a great aim, which, as with all great hopes, necessarily transcends mere empirical reality, is a condition of a productive interaction of unity and diversity, so it is also a prerequisite of a sound interaction of collective and individualistic trends in humanity. Sound collectivism in a social body is always more than its tangible reality. It springs from the unity of individuals who believe in their common future and who, because of this very faith, allow each other to act as free individuals. Collectivism without such faith resembles the uniformity of a prison, whereas individualism without the binding and forming power of a faith which allows the individual to transcend himself into the whole leads to atomism and chaos.

The inability of large parts of the modern world to find a dominating theme for civilization around which all the components of a full life may flourish is the cause of all great disturbances and in our time has again led to one of the most serious political and cultural crises in Western history. In politics it has resulted in a totalitarianism that mistakes imposed centralization for living form and thus leads eventually to impoverishment both physical and cultural. It would be more exact to designate such a system as particularism or partialism, since they express the very contrary of a total understanding of individual and social life.

Democracy, on the other hand, not as it is but as the ideal we are aiming at, is a process of increasingly humanizing society by absorbing into it as many constructive elements as possible. But how can we distinguish the constructive from the destructive? Whatever is constructive must, on the one hand, take into account the changing, pluralistic nature of life; it must not accept detailed recipes for living wisdom or fixed contents for directions of development. In this respect constructive action is always pragmatic. On the other hand, constructive action points to a totality of values; and it is from the vision of this totality that man has always drawn inspiration for the belief that his own self-realization means at the same time increasing responsibility for the whole of life and for the achievement of better conditions. Constructive action is therefore idealistic as well as pragmatic. But its idealism and its pragmatism form a single stream of living experience. According to the philosophy of self-transcendent empiricism, the week should not be divided into six days of discordant and bewildering experiences and one day of religion or recuperation; constantly more men and women must find an active and experimental life, along with the consciousness that its final significance depends upon voluntary loyalty to the permanent laws of humanity.

Because our thought is discursive, our conceptual language incapable of expressing everything at once, and because our action must have an immediate focus, we are always in danger of emphasizing one side of life at the expense of the other: growth and variety to the disadvantage of form and unity, or faith to the disadvantage of reason, and the reverse. History is full of partial thinking and fixations upon isolated trends. Even the greater minds, though they have seen both the dynamic character of life and its need for form, have not always avoided the danger of overemphasizing one side or the other. Hegel tried to combine form and dynamics in his dialectical principle of thesis, antithesis, and synthesis, as a principle immanent in the evolution of "spirit." But the aprioristic character of his philosophy caused him to be too forgetful of empirical and individual realities, and some of his followers gave much more weight to what is static and institutional than to what is dynamic in his thought. William James tried to combine his conception of the pluralistic universe with a deeper and uniting logos, but the two parts of his philosophy remain disjoined and the lack of interaction between the two principles of growth and form, reason and faith, is even plainer than in Hegel's system.

Perhaps Kant, by denying the competence of thought to arrive at strict conclusions about the ultimate form of life, has seen the problem most clearly. According to him, only the total personality, in apprehending the "moral law" through the ethical will and through responsible action, can grasp intuitively the regulating principles behind the surface of the phenomenal world. Not that this great master of rational thought intended to advocate mysticism to the disadvantage of reason. On the contrary, his often misunderstood purpose was to show man the validity of his mental instruments in both the changing empirical world and the world of regulating principles so that he might progress more directly toward a harmonious and self-conscious civilization.

But however much the understanding of civilization as a constant attempt at synthesis has been confused by the controversial development of side issues, the understanding itself and the reality behind it exist. James is not so far from Hegel or Kant as he himself sometimes believed; and no civilization has so far been able to thrive by cultivating one of its essential components at the expense of another.

B. THE AMERICAN RESPONSIBILITY

The United States, like every other country, has witnessed the interplay of form and growth, faith and reason, individualism and collectivism, and has also had occasion to see how the isolation of one trend from the totality of life leads either to aimless experimentation or to static uniformity. But so far the United States has never completely succumbed to the danger; its special character as an enterprising nation in a continent of unexploited possibilities provided for a wholesome diversity and balance of components. When the dissenters from Europe tended to become the conformists and inquisitors of America, the spirit of the frontier and new waves of immigration forced them either to retreat or to develop. The mind of this country, also, could not allow itself to slacken for long in a single line of thought. Cotton Mather was offset by Anne Hutchinson; the transcendentalism of Emerson and Josiah Royce by the pragmatism of Charles Peirce and William James. In addition, political and economic progress, greater than any ever experienced in other countries, helped the United States to maintain the necessary degree of unity in spite of all its diversity. But now, not only because of economic and political conflicts throughout the world but because of what is essentially a moral crisis in Western civilization, America has passed into another stage of its existence. It is not detracting from the courage and wisdom of the founders and great leaders of the United States to say that during the eighteenth and nineteenth centuries this country drew its most generative ideas from the European store created by ancient and Christian civilizations. Whether this source has now been exhausted or whether constructive ideas will still break through the uncertainty of Europe it is impossible to say. In any case, America can no longer rely on the Old World. Noah Webster and Emerson spoke of the task of the new continent to create its own civilization. Whether welcome or not, this task must now be accepted, and to assist in that task an education is needed which will not only convey knowledge but will aim at a full and cultured life resulting from creative insight into the entire life and all the needs of humanity.

To the accomplishment of this task education by itself can contribute only modestly. Yet since it is the business of the educator to clarify the contents and functions of civilization in the minds of the younger generation and to ally the essential and persistent prerequisites of culture to the changing diversity of daily life, he is first compelled to clarify these matters in his own mind. For this purpose a quantitative and merely "scientific" understanding of education, psychology, and the processes of learning, much though they may contribute to the clarification of partial problems, will not suffice. Education will betray mankind if it yields to its increasing tendency to run away from its greatest responsibilities into the deceiving illusions of the foreground. Without deep roots the individual, the nation, or education itself cannot reach its full maturity or withstand the difficult times ahead. Problems of measurement and evaluation, the difficult administrative tasks of adapting education to the needs of society and to vocational and professional requirements are of the highest importance. But these and similar pursuits will find the answers to their own immanent questions only if their special problems and methods are viewed in the light of a profound conception of humanity in its psychophysical completeness. Therefore, education, to offset the danger of increasing specialization, must come to understand itself as the cultural conscience of man. In this understanding education will find its best means of guiding humanity toward the enduring sources of regeneration.

CHAPTER I: WHY DO WE EDUCATE?

Bogoslovsky, B. B., *The Technique of Controversy; Principles of Dynamic Logic*. 1928

Healy, W., *Personality in Formation and Action*. 1938

Human Affairs: An Exposition of What Science Can Do for Man. Edited by R. B. Catell, J. Cohen, and R. M. W. Travers. 1938

Locke, John, *Some Thoughts concerning Education*. With introduction and notes by the Reverend R. H. Quick. 1902

MacIver, R. M., *Community, A Sociological Study. Being an Attempt to Set out the Nature and Fundamental Laws of Social Life*. 1931

McDougall, W., *An Introduction to Social Psychology*. Sixteenth edition, 1923

Mill, J. S., *On Liberty*. 1859

———, *Utilitarianism*. 1863

Montaigne, Michel Eyquem de, *The Education of Children*. Selected by L. E. Rector. 1899

Nietzsche, F. W., *The Complete Works*. The first complete and authorized English translation. Edited by O. Levy. 1909–1913

Nunn, T. P., *Education: Its Data and First Principles*. 1930

Perry, R. B., *Present Philosophical Tendencies*. A Critical Survey of Naturalism, Idealism, Pragmatism, and Realism, together with a Synopsis of the Philosophy of William James. 1929

Pestalozzi, *Selections*. Edited by L. F. Anderson. 1931

Plato, *Gorgias*

———, *Protagoras*

Plato, *The Republic*

Spencer, H., *Education, Intellectual, Moral, and Physical.* 1861

Wenzl, A., *Metaphysik der Biologie von Heute.* 1937

Willis, W. D., *Culture and Progress.* 1930

Woodworth, R. S., *Contemporary Schools of Psychology.* 1931

CHAPTER II: WHOM DO WE EDUCATE?

Allport, G. W., *Personality, A Psychological Interpretation.* 1937

Boring, E. G., *A History of Experimental Psychology.* 1929

Brett, G. S., *A History of Psychology.* Vol. I, Ancient and Patristic; Vol. II, Mediaeval and Early Modern Period; Vol. III, Modern Psychology. 1912–1921

Campbell, C. M., *Human Personality and the Environment.* 1934

Cannon, W. B., *The Wisdom of the Body.* 1932

Goldstein, K., *The Organism.* *A Holistic Approach to Biology Derived from Pathological Data in Man.* With a Foreword by K. S. Lashley. 1939

Hartmann, G. W., *Gestalt Psychology.* *A Survey of Facts and Principles.* 1935

Heiss, R., *Die Lehre vom Charakter.* 1936

Herbart, J. F., *The Aesthetic Revelation of the World.* In Herbart, J. F., *The Science of Education, etc.,* translated by H. M. and E. Felkin. 1892

Hocking, W. E., *Human Nature and Its Remaking.* New printing, 1929

———, *The Self; Its Body and Freedom.* 1928

James, W., *The Principles of Psychology.* 1896

———, *Talks to Teachers on Psychology: And to Students on Some of Life's Ideals.* 1923

Katz, D., *Animals and Men.* *Studies in Comparative Psychology.* 1937

Köhler, W., *Gestalt Psychology.* Fifth printing, 1930

Koffka, K., *The Growth of the Mind.* *An Introduction to Child-Psychology.* Second printing, 1925

Lewin, K., *A Dynamic Theory of Personality, Selected Papers.* 1935

McDougall, W., *The Energies of Man; A Study of the Fundamentals of Dynamic Psychology.* 1933

———, *The Frontiers of Psychology.* 1935

———, *The Riddle of Life.* 1938

Perry, R. B., *In the Spirit of William James.* 1938

Prescott, D. A., *Emotion and the Educative Process.* 1938

Sandiford, P., *Foundations of Educational Psychology. Nature's Gifts to Man.* 1938

Stern, W., *General Psychology from the Personalistic Standpoint.* 1938

Watson, J. B., *Psychology from the Standpoint of a Behaviorist.* Third edition, revised, 1929

CHAPTER III: TOWARD WHAT ENDS DO WE EDUCATE?

Adams, J., *The Evolution of Educational Theory.* 1912

Bagley, W. C., *Education and Emergent Man; A Theory of Education with Particular Application to Public Education in the United States.* 1934

Demiashkevich, M., *An Introduction to the Philosophy of Education.* 1935

Dewey, J., *A Common Faith.* 1934

———, *Democracy and Education. An Introduction to the Philosophy of Education.* 1916

———, *Experience and Education.* 1938

———, *Human Nature and Conduct. An Introduction to Social Psychology.* 1922

Herbart, J. F., *The Science of Education.* Translated from the German by H. M. and E. Felkin. 1896

Herder, J. G., *Outlines of a Philosophy of the History of Man.* Translated from the German by T. Churchill (*Ideen zur Philosophie der Geschichte der Menschheit, 1784-91*). 1800

Horne, H. H., *The Philosophy of Education. Being the Foundation of Education in the Related Natural and Mental Sciences.* Revised edition with special references to the educational philosophy of Dr. John Dewey. 1927

Huxley, A., *Ends and Means.* 1937

Irsay, S. d', *Histoire des Universités Françaises et Étrangères, des Origines à nos Jours.* 1933–1935

James, W., *Collected Essays and Reviews.* 1920

———, *Pragmatism, a New Name for Some Old Ways of Thinking.* 1907

———, *Psychology, Briefer Course.* 1892

Kant, I., *Fundamental Principles of the Metaphysic of Ethics.* Translated by Th. K. Abbott. Tenth edition, 1934

———, *Critique of Practical Reason*

———, *Critique of Pure Reason*

Köhler, W., *The Place of Value in a World of Facts.* 1938

Lippmann, W., *A Preface to Morals.* 1929

Perry, R. B., *In the Spirit of William James.* 1938

Royce, J., *The Philosophy of Loyalty.* 1920

CHAPTER IV: THE STRUGGLE OF THE EDUCATOR WITH THE PROBLEM OF VALUES

Alexander Hamilton and Thomas Jefferson. Representative Selections. Edited by F. C. Prescott. 1934

Beard, C. A., *A Charter for the Social Sciences in the Schools.* Drafted by Charles A. Beard. 1932

———, *The Nature of the Social Sciences in Relation to Objectives of Instruction.* 1934

Bogoslovsky, B. B., *The Ideal School.* 1936

Chesterfield, P. D. Stanhope, Earl of, *Letters Written to His Son, Philip Stanhope.* London. 1774

Comenius, J. A., *The Great Didactic.* With introductions, etc., by Keatinge. 1896

The Community School. Edited by S. Everett. 1938

Herbart, J. F., *The Application of Psychology to the Science of Education.* Translated by B. C. Mulliner. 1898

———, *The Science of Education.* Translated by H. and E. Felkin. 1892

Horne, H. H., *The Teacher as Artist. An Essay in Education as an Aesthetic Process.* 1917

Huizinga, J., *In the Shadow of Tomorrow.* Translated from the Dutch by J. H. Huizinga. 1936

Kohn, H., *Force and Reason.* 1937

Pestalozzi, J. H., *Leonard and Gertrude.* Translated and abridged by Eva Channing. 1901

———, *Selections.* Edited by L. F. Anderson. 1931

Publications of the Regents' Inquiry into the Character and Cost of Public Education in the State of New York, 1938–1939. General Report, *Education for American Life. A New Program for the State of New York.*
Studies

   1. *High School and Life,* F. T. Spaulding

   2. *When Youth Leave School,* R. Eckert and T. O. Marshall

   3. *Education for Citizenship,* H. E. Wilson

   4. *Education for Work,* T. L. Norton

   5. *School and Community,* J. B. Maller

Sigerist, H. E., *Man and Medicine. An Introduction to Medical Knowledge.* Translated by M. G. Boise. 1932

Whitehead, A. N., *Adventures of Ideas.* 1933

———, *The Aims of Education and Other Essays.* 1929

CHAPTER V: POSTULATES OF TEACHING

Bode, B. H., *Modern Educational Theories.* 1927

Burton, H., *The Nature and Direction of Learning.* 1930

Comenius, J. A., *The Great Didactic.* With introductions, etc., by Keatinge. 1896

Dewey, J., *How We Think.* 1910. Revised edition, 1933

Emerson, R. W., *The Conduct of Life.* New and revised edition, 1889

———, *Education, An Essay, and Other Selections.* 1909

Froebel, F., *Education by Development. Essays from the Second Part of the Pedagogics of the Kindergarten.* Translated by Josephine Garvis. 1899

———, *The Education of Man.* Translated by W. N. Hailmann. 1900

———, *Letters on the Kindergarten.* Translated by E. Michaelis and H. K. Moore. 1891

Goethe, J. W., *Wilhelm Meister's Apprenticeship and Travels.* Translated by Carlyle. A new edition, 1860

Herbart, J. F., *The Science of Education.* Translated from the German by H. M. and E. Felkin. 1896

———, *Outlines of Educational Doctrine.* Translated by A. F. Lange, etc. 1901

James, W., *Talks to Teachers on Psychology; And to Students on Some of Life's Ideals.* 1921

Kandel, I. L., *Comparative Education.* 1933

———, *Conflicting Theories of Education.* 1938

———, *The Dilemma of Democracy.* 1934

Klapper, P., *Contemporary Education. Its Principles and Practices.* 1929

Locke, J., *Some Thoughts concerning Education.* Edited by R. H. Quick. 1902

Monroe, W. S., *Directing Learning in the High School.* 1927

Morrison, H. C., *The Practice of Teaching in the Secondary School.* 1939

Mumford, L., *The Culture of Cities.* 1938

———, *Technics and Civilization.* 1934

Pestalozzi, J. H., *How Gertrude Teaches Her Children.* Translated by L. E. Holland and F. C. Turner. 1898

Plato, *The Laws*

———, *The Republic*

Rousseau, J. J., *Emile, or Treatise on Education*. Translated by W. H. Payne. 1901

Secondary Education. With Special Reference to Grammar Schools, etc. English Report. London, His Majesty's Stationery Office, 1939

CHAPTER VI: EDUCATION AND SOCIETY

Bury, J. B., *The Idea of Progress. An Inquiry into Its Origin and Growth.* 1920

Carlyle, T., *Chartism. Collected Works*, Library Edition, Vol. X, pp. 323–423

Cook, L. A., *Community Backgrounds of Education. A Textbook in Educational Sociology.* 1938

Counts, George S., *The American Road to Culture. A Social Interpretation of Education in the United States.* Third printing, 1932

Hocking, W. E., *The Lasting Elements of Individualism.* 1937

Löwe, A., *The Price of Liberty.* A German on Contemporary Britain. Second edition, 1937

Lynd, R. S. and H. M., *Middletown, A Study in Contemporary American Culture.* 1937

————, *Middletown in Transition.* 1937

Mead, G. H., *Mind, Self and Society. From the Standpoint of a Social Behaviorist.* Edited by C. W. Morris. 1935

Peters, C. C., *Foundations of Educational Sociology.* 1930

Political and Economic Democracy. Edited by M. Ascoli and F. Lehmann. 1937

Sumner, W. G., *Folkways. A Study of the Sociological Importance of Usages, Manners, Customs, Mores and Morals.* 1911

Sumner, W. G., and Keller, A. G., *The Science of Society.* 1927. Vols. I and II

Tuttle, H. W., *A Social Basis of Education.* 1934

Wallas, G., *The Great Society. A Psychological Analysis.* 1920

Whitehead, T. N., *Leadership in a Free Society. A Study in Human Relations Based on an Analysis of Present-Day Industrial Civilization.* 1936

CHAPTER VII: EDUCATION AND THE STATE

Alexander Hamilton and Thomas Jefferson. Representative Selections. Edited by F. C. Prescott. 1934

Beard, C. A., *The Unique Function of Education in American Democracy.* 1937

Counts, G. S., *The Prospects of American Democracy.* 1938

Educational Freedom and Democracy. Edited by H. B. Alberty and Boyd H. Bode. The Second Yearbook, John Dewey Society. 1938

Heimann, E., *Communism, Fascism, or Democracy?* 1938

Hocking, W. E., *Man and the State.* 1926

Humboldt, W. van, *The Sphere and Duties of Government.* Translated from the German by J. Coulthard, 1854 (*Ideen zu einen Versuch, die Grenzen der Wirksamkeit des Staates zu bestimmen.* 1791)

Kandel, T. L., *Comparative Education.* 1933

McCallister, W., *The Growth of Freedom in Education. A Critical Interpretation of Some Historical Views.* 1931

Ritchie, D. G., *Natural Rights. A Criticism of Some Political and Ethical Conceptions.* Third edition, 1916

Rugg, H., *Culture and Education in America.* 1931

Smith, A., *An Inquiry into the Nature and Causes of the Wealth of Nations.* New edition, 1904. Book V, "Of the Revenue of the Sovereign or Commonwealth"; Part III, "Of the Expense of Public Works and Public Institutions"

CHAPTER VIII: EDUCATION AND RELIGION

Harkness, G., *The Resources of Religion.* 1936

Harnack, A., *What Is Christianity?* Sixteen lectures delivered in the University of Berlin, 1899–1900. Translated by T. B. Saunders. 1901

Hocking, W. E., *The Meaning of God in Human Experience.* 1924

Inge, W. R., *The Philosophy of Plotinus.* Third edition, two vols., 1929

James, W., *The Varieties of Religious Experience.* 1902

Kierkegaard, S., *Sören Kierkegaards samlede vaerker.* Published by A. B. Drachmann, J. L. Heiberg, and H. O. Lange. 1901–1906

————, *Einübung im Christentum.* Translated from the Danish into German by H. Gottsched and Ch. Schrempf. Third edition, 1933

————, *Philosophische Brocken. Abschliessende unwissenschaftliche Nachschrift.* Translated from Danish into German by H. Gottsched and Ch. Schrempf. 1925

————, *Selections from the Writings of Kierkegaard.* Translated by L. M. Hollander. 1923

McDougall, W., *Religion and the Sciences of Life. With Other Essays on Allied Topics.* 1934

Niebuhr, R., *Does Civilization Need Religion? A Study in the Social Resources and Limitations of Religion in Modern Life.* 1929

————, *Moral Man and Immoral Society. A Study in Ethics and Politics.* New edition, 1934

Otto, R., *The Idea of the Holy. An Inquiry into the Non-Rational Factor in the Idea of the Divine and Its Relation to the Rational.* Translated by John W. Harvey. 1923

Tillich, P., *Interpretation of History.* 1937

————, *The Religious Situation.* Translated by H. R. Niebuhr. 1932

Whitehead, A. N., *Religion in the Making.* 1926

INDEX

A

Abilities, 74–77
Action, 151, 229
Adams, G. P., 126n.
Adams, J., 169
Adams, Sir John, 149, 347
Adamson, J. W., 10
Adequateness, postulate of, 223–225
Admonition, verbal, 240
Adult education, 18
Aims, 112. (*See also* Growth.)
Alberty, H. B., 352
Alcuin, 301
Allport, G. W., 60–62, 79, 346
Altruism, 40, 110
Analysis, 49
Anderson, L. F., 34n., 174, 345
Antagonism, between religion and reason, 295–302
Anthropology, 59, 97, 134, 164
Antiquity, 186, 199–202, 299. (*See also* Greeks, Romans.)
Antirationalism, 49
Apperceptive mass, 235
Apprenticeship, 11–17, 248
Aquinas, Thomas, 35, 60, 187, 228, 317
Arabic philosophers, 51
Arbeitsschule, 236
Aristocracy, 24, 27
    artificial, 170
    natural, 170
Aristotle, 51, 60, 94, 134, 154, 197, 228, 301, 307
Artes liberales, 300
Ascoli, M., 351
"As if," 69
Assimilation, 230
Association, 229
Attachment-detachment, 289
Attention, 229
Attentiveness, 58
Augustine, St., 299, 306, 310n.

Aurelius, Marcus, 51
Austria, 160, 166

B

Bagley, W.C., 347
Beard, C. A., 348
Behaviorism, 58, 61, 63–70
Bergson, H., 35
Berkeley, G., 305
Bible, 45, 138, 275, 277, 294, 303, 305, 313
Bill of Rights, 35
Biological point of view, 3, 4–9
Bode, B. H., 232, 349, 352
Boehme, J., 305
Boethius, 51
Bogoslovsky, B. B., 236n., 345, 348
Boise, M. G., 349
Bolshevism, 171
Borgia, Cesare, 22, 24
Boring, E. G., 346
Breasted, J. H., 122
Brett, G. S., 346
Bruno, Giordano, 76, 305
Bruns, F., 312
Buckoll, H. J., 272n.
Buddhists, 289
Burton, W. H., 232, 349
Bury, J. B., 351

C

Calvinism, 278, 317
Campbell, C. M., 346
Cannon, W. B., 346
Carlyle, T., 222n., 248, 332, 350, **351**
Carus, W., 60
Catell, R. B., 345
Chaptal, J. A. C., 130, 133
Character. (*See* Personality.)
Character education, 238–241
Chesterfield, Earl of, 168, 483
China, 241–242

355

Christian education, 124, 295–343
Christian mythology, 43
Christianity, 20–22, 24–25, 38, 43, 52, 124, 135, 146, 259, 263, 276–277, 290, 295–343. (*See also* Church, Religion.)
Chrysostom, 310n.
Church, 18, 48, 158–159, 162, 186–187, 271, 278, 318, 324. (*See also* Christianity, Religion.)
Church Fathers, 299
Churchill, T., 347
Ciceronian style, 199
Citizenship, problem of, 238–240
Civilization, economic foundations of, 170–171
  and education, 3, 153–171
  essentials of, 335–343
  religious foundations of, 326–328
  social foundations of, 165–170
Classical training, 163. (*See also* Antiquity, Humanism, Languages.)
Claudel, P., 322
Clearness, 229
Cohen, J., 345
Coincidentia oppositorum, 76
Collectivism, 17, 338–341
Comenius, J. A., 60, 112, 156, 171–172, 175, 180, 185, 219, 228, 231, 348–349
Common sense, 116
Community, school and, 14–15
Components, social, 243–270
Comte, A., 280
Concentration, 230
Conceptual thinking, 67
Conditioning, 83, 86–87
Condorcet, M. J., 60, 143
Configurational school, 55
Conflict, moral, 189. (*See also* Components, social.)
Congress, Continental, 278
Contrast. (*See* Components, social; Education; Personality.)
Controversies, 41
Cook, L. A., 351
Copernicus, N., 143
Correlation of subject matter, 234
Cosmos, 9, 276. (*See also* Personality, Religion.)
Coulthard, J., 283n., 352
Counter Reformation, 172, 183
Counts, G. S., 351–352
Craftsmanship, 248
Crime, 136–138
Criteria, ethical, 134–151
Curriculum, 203–216
Cusanus, Nicholas, 76, 305

D

Dante, 164, 317
Darwin, C., 5, 158, 280
Daunou, P. L. F., 133
Decision, necessity of, 185–190
Decorations, 224
Defects in reading, individual, 58
Demand, 229
Demiashkevich, M., 347
Democracy, 27, 212, 243–293
  and freedom, 282–294
  and utilitarianism, 25, 27, 121
Democrats, 199
Departmentalization, 202, 211
Depersonalization, 17
Descartes, R., 197, 245
Desire, 229
Detachment, attachment-, 289
Determinism, 76, 120, 140, 256
Dewey, J., 111–151, 231, 312, 347–349
Dimension in being, deeper, 134, 148
Directional character of personality, 85–89
Directionalism, 128, 149
Discipline, mental, 195
Diversity of subject matter, postulate of, 225–227
Divine Comedy, 317
Division of labor, 13
Doctrines, political, 41
Dogmatism, 49
Drachmann, A. B., 353
Driesch, J., 35
Drives, 32. (*See also* Propensities, Urges.)
Dschuang Dsi, 241–242
Dualism, 19, 33, 38, 41, 147

E

Eckert, R., 349
Eckhart, Master, 117, 305, 324
Eclecticism, 183–185
École active, 236
Economic foundations of civilization, 165–170
Education, as adaptation, 239
  adult, 18
  aims, 101–152. (*See also* Education and ethics, Values.)
  and biology, 3, 4–9
  character, 238–241
  Christian, 124, 295–343
  and civilization, 3, 153–171
  as cultural conscience of man, 343
  and emotion, 3, 42–49
  and environment, 10, 70–72
  and ethics, 3, 19–42, 101–152, 153–215
  formal, 14

Education, higher level of, 256
  and historical periods, 153–171
  idealism in, 102–151
  major factors, 153–185
  mission of American, 334–343
  natural conditions of, 6
  as organic growth, 203
  practice of, 185–215, 217–241
  progressive, 103, 124, 185–238, 255–270
  and religion, 295–343
  responsibility and freedom in, 266–269
  science of, 57, 343
  selective systems of, 225
  and society, 243–270
  and sociology, 3, 10–18
  and survival, 6, 7
  technical, 163
  traditional, 103, 124
  and utilitarianism, 28
  vocational, 198, 240–242, 343
Educator, 97. (*See also* Teacher.)
Ego, 68
Egoism, 40, 110
Élan vital, 35
Eliot, C. W., 28
Emerson, R. W., 125, 127, 242, 342, 350
Emotional point of view, 3, 42–49
Empiricism, 101, 184, 282, 318. (*See also* Idealism, Materialism, Pragmatism, Relativism, Self-transcendent empiricism, Utilitarianism.)
Endowment, constitutional, 77–80
Ends. (*See* Aims.)
Energy, 72. (*See also* Personality.)
Engels, F., 248
England, 132, 163, 166, 176, 181, 183, 245–246, 278, 310
Enlightenment, 52, 131, 143, 159, 285, 310. (*See also* Rationalism.)
Environment, 10, 70–72. (*See also* Education, Personality, School.)
Equality, 186
Erasmus of Rotterdam, 162
Escapism, 288–289
Ethical criteria, 134–151
Ethical direction, postulate of, 238–242
Ethical rigorism, 147
Ethics, and the aims of education, 101–152
  and educational policy, 153–215
  and the motives of education, 19–42
  Nietzsche's inversion of values, 21–29
  sources of ethical behavior, 31–38
  (*See also* Values.)

Europe, 60, 130, 341–343. (*See also the individual European countries.*)
Evaluation, 343
Everett, S., 348
Existence, human, 30
Expectation, 229
Experience, 101–139, 236–238
  religious, 303–312, 323–325
Experimentalist, 240

F

Factors, major, in education, 153–185
Faith, 338–341. (*See also* Reason.)
Faraday, M., 49
Fascism, 69, 171, 184
Fatigue, 58
Faust, 317
Feeling, 80–85
Felkin, H. M., and E., 350
Festival, 323
Feudalism, 223
Fichte, J. G., 127, 176, 282
Folklore, 250–252
Folk songs, 48
Form, 54–98, 114, 187, 289, 336–341
France, 130–134, 158, 163, 166, 183–186, 245, 273, 285, 294, 302
Franklin, B., 143
Frederick the Great, 302
Freedom, 31, 42, 73, 75–77, 79, 94, 101, 129, 139–141, 206, 256, 266–294, 337–343
Froebel, F., 219, 235, 242, 272–294, 350
Fundamentalism, 303–304, 313, 314

G

Galilei, Galileo, 143
Generalization, 4, 39–41
Gentleman ideal, 163
Germany, 70, 160, 166, 176, 245–246, 294. (*See also* Herbart.)
Gestalt psychology, 35. (*See also* Configurational school.)
Glayre, French councilor, 175
Goethe, J. W., 41, 60, 79, 197, 222, 238, 312, 317, 331, 350
Goldstein, K., 64, 136, 346
Gottsched, H., 308n., 315n., 353
Grace, idea of, 19
Greek mythology, 43
Greek orthodox church, 324
Greek philosophy, 21, 40, 51, 222, 275–277, 289, 290, 324
Greeks, 146, 223, 330
Gregory I, Pope, 301
Gregory VII, Pope, 301
Grotius, H., 35, 60
Groundwork of social life, 250–252

Growth, 112–151, 164–165, 187, 203, 226, 336–341
Guide words, 272–275
Gymnasium, German, 163

H

Habituation, 83, 86–87, 111
Haeckel, E., 122
Haldane, J. B. S., 9
Haller, A. von, 177
Hamilton, A., 348, 352
Hamlet, 189, 317
Happiness, 27, 29, 139, 224, 290
Hapsburg, 172
Harkness, G., 352
Harnack, A., 307, 352
Harris, W. T., 126
Hartmann, G. W., 346
Harvard University, 201
Harvey, J. W., 353
Healey, W., 4, 345
Hegel, 105, 126–128, 243, 250, 305, 311, 320, 324, 340–341
Heiberg, J. L., 353
Heimann, E., 352
Heiss, R., 346
Herbart, J. F., 69, 83, 112, 156, 176–183, 185, 194, 202–203, 219, 228–241, 346–347, 349–350
Herbartianism, 127, 176–183, 185, 229
Hercules, 43
Herder, J. G., 143, 347
High Church, 321
Hippeau, C., 132n., 133n.
Hippocrates, 51, 54
Historical periods and education, 153–171
History, 10–18, 51–58, 126, 171–185, 243–250, 272–278, 295–302, 335–344
  dialectical character of, 189
Hobbes, T., 60, 212, 271
Hocking, W. E., 346, 351–353
Holland, L. E., 228, 350
Hollander, L. M., 353
Holmes, H. W., 201
Homer, 43
Horace, 168
Horne, H. H., 348–349
Huizinga, J., 349
Hultzsch, E., 108n.
Human existence, 30. (*See also* Personality.)
Humanism, 104, 146, 199, 239
  disintegration of, 162–164, 184
  religious, 304–307, 328
Humanist education, 124, 198, 263
Humanities, 56, 196–202, 205
  new, 215

Humboldt, W. von, 282–287, 293–294, 352
Hungary, 166
Hunger, 32
Husserl, E., 56n.
Hutchinson, A., 342
Huxley, A., 289, 348
Huygens, C., 143
Hygiene, 37
  mental, 55, 60, 201
Hypothesis, 231

I

Idealism, 30, 40, 113, 125, 128–129, 135, 140, 142, 149, 288, 304, 339
Idealism in education, 102–151
Identity, religious philosophy of, 304–307
Ideologies, 22, 255–265, 272–274
Imagination, 230
Imperialism, 290
Indeterminism, 76. (*See also* Determinism.)
India, 181
Individualism, 17, 23, 257, 279
  of method, 220–221
Individuality, human, 138
Indoctrination, 28, 184, 255–269
Inge, W. R., 353
Inquisition, 53
Instincts, 31–32. (*See also* Drives, Propensities, Urges.)
Instruction, organization of, 202–205. (*See also* Postulate.)
  stages of, 230
Instrumentalism, 99. (*See also* Dewey, J., Empiricism; Pragmatism.)
Integralism, theory of, 35–38, 41–42, 76, 148
Intellectual, 16, 164
Intellectualization, 231
Intelligence, 80–85
Interest, 229. (*See also* Postulate.)
Interests, many-sidedness of, 202
Intuition, 230
Intuitionalism, 142
Ireland, 181
Irrationalism, 52
d'Irsay, S., 130–134, 348
Italy, 69, 161
Ius naturale, 35

J

James, W., 99–100, 102–151, 241, 275, 340, 346, 348, 350, 358
Jefferson, T., 167–170, 282, 348, 352
Jesus, 44–48, 132, 135, 163, 245, 251, 272, 303, 305, 307
Jews, 245
John, St., 277, 290

K

Kallikles, 21, 26
Kandel, I. L., 350, 352
Kant, I., 30, 49, 68, 104–105, 110, 143, 147, 151, 178, 320, 340–341, 348
Katz, D., 74, 346
Keatinge, M. W., 231n., 349
Keller, A. G., 351
Kepler, J., 143
Kierkegaard, S., 306, 308–313, 315, 319, 323, 353
Klapper, P., 232, 350
Köhler, W., 62, 346, 348
Koffka, K., 346
Kohn, H., 161, 349
Kotschnig, W. M., 16n.

L

Labor, division of, 13
Lange, A. F., 350
Lange, H. O., 353
Language, 4, 81–85
Languages, ancient, 163, 199–202
  modern, 200
Lashley, K. S., 64
Lawrence, Colonel, 139n.
Laws inherent in life, 8, 143–151
Leadership, 23
Learning by doing, 236
Lehmann, F., 351
Leibnitz, W., 69, 128, 305
Leigh, O. L., 168n.
Leo X, Pope, 298
Lewin, K., 347
Liberal arts, faculties of, 57
Liberal education, 199–202, 240–242. (See also Humanism.)
Liberalism, 158, 181, 247, 257, 279, 286, 295
  in religion, 304–307
Liberty, 115, 164, 186, 272–294. (See also Freedom.)
Liebert, A., 56n.
Life. (See Education, Personality, Social life.)
Life plan, 88
Lippmann, W., 348
Locke, J., 18, 228, 345, 350
Lodge, R. C., 102n.
Logical systems, 40
Logos, 275–280, 289, 326–327
Löwe, A., 351
Lowell Lectures, 103
Luke, St., 46
Luther, M., 187, 272, 307–308, 310n., 317, 324
Lykophon, 26
Lynd, R. S., and H. M., 351

M

McCallister, W., 352
McDougall, W., 72–75, 84–85, 345, 347, 353
Machiavelli, N., 271
MacIver, R. M., 345
Maller, J. B., 349
Mann, T., 311
Marshall, T. O., 349
Marsilius of Padua, 271
Marx, K., 248
Mary, St., 44–48
Materialism, 30, 38, 40, 128–129
Mathematics, 208
Mather, C., 342
Matter, 40, 141
Maturation, 5, 75
Maurus, Hrabanus, 301, 318
Mead, G. H., 351
Means, 289. (See also Aims.)
Measurement, 343
Medicine, 18, 53, 63–64
Melanchthon, P., 162
Memory, 4. (See also Personality.)
Mendel, J. G., 78
Mental discipline, 195
Mental functions, "higher," 84
Mental order, postulate of, 227–234
Metaphysics, 118. (See also Idealism, Religion.)
Method, 104, 117–118, 217–238
  postulate of individualism of, 220–221
Methodology
  in psychology, 66–70
  in teaching. (See Postulate.)
Mexico, 160
Middle Ages, 18, 51–52, 166, 183, 199, 205, 228, 301
Mill, J. S., 285, 292, 345
Mind, 4
  and body and brain, 4
  and matter, 141
Misera plebs, 21
Monism, 19, 33, 38, 114
Monroe, W. S., 232, 350
Montague, W. P., 126n.
Montaigne, M. E. de, 18, 345
Moral conflict, 189
Morris, C. W., 351
Morrison, H. C., 232, 350
Motherhood, 44–48
Mumford, L., 233n., 350
Mussolini, B., 161
Mythology, 43

N

Napoleon, 22, 24, 28, 92, 133, 184
Nation, school and, 10

Nationalism, 183
National-Socialism, 70
Natural rights, 290, 292
Natural sciences, 58, 210–213
Naturalism, 27–29, 34, 102–151, 256. (*See also* Materialism, Pragmatism.)
Necessity, of decision, 185–190
Needs, 32, 73–74
Negativity, pain of, 324
Neo-Kantianism, 57
Neoplatonism, 43
Neovitalism, 35
Netherlands, 278
Neurology, 63
New Education Fellowship, the, 192, 237
Newton, I., 69, 143, 277
Niebuhr, R., 353
Nietzsche, 20–42, 106, 345
Norton, T. L., 349
Nunn, T. P., 345

O

Oedipus, 43
Ontology, 38
Operationalism, 99
Ordo, 326
Organic curriculum, 213–216
Organic growth, education as, 203
Organism, human, 63
Organization, of instruction, 202–205
Original sin, 19
Otto, R., 353

P

Papacy, 187
Paradoxicalness, religion of, 308–311
Parents, 6, 49
Participation, desire for active, 230
Pascal, B., 140, 324
Paul, St., 137, 277, 325
Peirce, C., 342
Periods, mental, 228
Perry, R. B., 99, 102n., 104n., 325, 347–348
Personality, 51–94
    conflicts, 89–94
    directional character, 85–89
    form, 94–98
    goal-directedness, 85–94
    growth, 94–98
    metaphysics, 94–98
    structure, 70–94
    symmetry, 93
    traits in, 86–88
    (*See also* Total explanation of human being.)
Pessimism, 115

Pestalozzi, J. H., 34, 54, 103, 112, 156, 172–176, 180, 185, 190–191, 194, 213, 219, 228, 233, 345, 349–350
Peters, C. C., 351
Phases. (*See* Instruction.)
Phenomenology, 56n.
Philosophers, Arabic, 51
Philosophy, 2, 70, 335–343
    of identity, 304–307
    Stoic, 35, 146, 326
Physiology, 63–64
Plato, 26, 51, 197, 217, 222n., 238, 242, 345–346, 350
Plotinus, 51, 197, 305, 312, 324
Pluralism, 114, 150, 339. (*See also* James, W.; Dewey, J.; Pragmatism.)
Pneuma, 277
Political doctrines, 41
Postulate, of adequateness, 223–225
    of correlation of subject matter, 234–236
    of diversity of subject matter, 225–227
    of ethical direction, 238–242
    of individualism of method, 220–221
    of mental order, 227–234
    of self-activity, 236–238
    of totality, 221–223
Potsdam, spirit of, 246
Practice, educational, 185–215, 217–241
Pragmatism, 103–151, 183, 339. (*See also* Empiricism; Naturalism; James, W.; Dewey, J.; Peirce, C.)
Predicaments of psychology, 66–70
Prescott, D. A., 347
Prescott, F. C., 167, 348, 352
Prescientific, 69
Primitiveness, 11, 297
Private school, 17
Progressive education, 103, 124, 185–238, 255–270
Propensities, 32, 72–74
Protestantism, 278, 310, 318, 324. (*See also* Christian education, Christianity, Church.)
Prussia, 180–181, 294
Psychiatry, 63–66
Psychoanalysis, 55
Psychology, 51–100
    Gestalt, 35
    and metaphysics, 118
    remedial, 55
Psychophysical development, stages in, 88–89
Public schools, in England, 163
Pufendorf, S., 35
Purpose, 298. (*See also* Growth, Personality.)

Q

Quakers, 289
Quick, R. H., 345

R

Racine, J., 190
Radicals, 199
Rationalism, 157. (*See also* Enlightenment.)
Reading, defects in, 58
Reason, practical, 151
 pure, 151
Reason and religion, 295, 304, 338–341
Reasoning, 231
Reflection, 230
Reflexes, 58, 63–66, 70–71
Reformation, 156, 183, 186, 272
 Counter, 172, 183
Regents' Inquiry, 349
Relativism, 142, 144–151, 164–165.
 (*See also* Empiricism, Materialism,
 Pragmatism, Self-transcendent
 empiricism, Utilitarianism.)
Religion, disintegration of, 157–162,
 184
 and education, 295–343
 and emotional interpretation of education, 42–49
 Herbart on, 179–180
 and modern civilization, 326–328
 and pragmatism, 106–108
 and reason, 295–304, 338–341
 and truth, 106–108, 294–303.
 (*See also* Christianity, Church.)
Religious symbolism, 45, 311–313
Religious values, 313
Renaissance, 19, 53–54, 134, 158, 162,
 188, 223, 301, 304, 306
Responsibility, American, 341–344
Reverence, 328–334
Rights, natural, 290, 292
Rigorism, ethical, 147
Rilke, R. M., 322
Ritchie, D. C., 352
Robespierre, M., 133
Romans, 51, 163
Romanticism, 302
Rommen, H., 35n.
Rosenkranz, K., 126–127
Rosenstock, E., 298
Ross, W. D., 154
Rousseau, J. J., 112, 175, 228, 285, 351
Royce, J., 108–111, 114, 126, 342, 348
Rugg, H., 352
Russia, 70, 160, 245

S

Saint-Simon, C. H., 298
Sandiford, P., 347

Scandinavia, 291, 310
Schelling, F. W. J., 219
Schiller, F. C. S., 104–105
Schiller, J. C. F., 190
Schleiermacher, F. D. E., 305, 320
Scholasticism, 35, 87, 132, 228, 301,
 307
School, common, 227
 and community, 14–15
 and nation, 10
 as place of instruction, 194–196
 and private tutoring, 18
 remoteness of, 17
 as selective agency, 15–17
 as social environment, 190–194
 as social equalizer, 15–17
 as a world for itself, 11
Schrempf, C., 308n., 315n., 353
Sciences, 296
 exact, 55, 158
 natural, 58, 207, 210–215
Secretory system, 55
Selective systems of education, 225
Self-activity, postulate of, 236–238
Self-identity, 71–72
Self-preservation, 5–10, 19–50
Self-transcendent empiricism, 134–
 151, 238, 289, 339–343
Seneca, 51
Sermon on the Mount, 163
Shakespeare, W., 190, 317
Sherrington, C. S., 5
Sigerist, H. E., 213, 349
Sin, "against God," 136–138
 original, 19
Sinai, Mount, 157
Skepticism, 128, 132, 142
Smith, A., 282, 292, 352
Social components, 243–270
Social environment, 190–194
Social foundations of civilization, 165–
 170
Social Frontier, 121
Social life, groundwork of, 250–252
 unconscious and conscious, 252–254
Social studies, 207–215
Society, 10–18
 and education, 243–270
 and religion, 295–302, 326–328
 and the state, 271–294
Sociological point of view, 3, 10–18
Socrates, 26, 51, 132, 238
Sombart, H., 60
Sophists, 21, 51
South America, 13
Spaulding, F. T., 349
Specializations, 1, 202, 227
Spencer, H., 5, 280, 346
Spinoza, B., 48, 197, 324

Spirit, 31, 41, 275
Stages in psychophysical development, 88–89
State, the, 23–29, 239, 271–294, 296, 301
Stern, W., 347
Stimulus-response bonds, 58
Stoic philosophy, 35, 146, 326
Subconscious, 65–66
Subject matter, correlation of, 234–236
  diversity of, 225–227
Suggestion, 231
Summum bonum, 117
Sumner, W. G., 351
Survival. (*See* Self-preservation.)
Symbolism, religious, 45, 311–313
Sympathy, 230. (*See also* Participation.)
System, 229
Systems, logical, 40

T

Talent, waste of, 17
Teacher, 12, 17–18, 97, 201, 256–269, 294
Teaching, 217–241
Technical education, 163
Testing, 231
Theocritus, 168
Theology, 158, 298, 300, 304. (*See also* Religion.)
Thing-in-itself, 68, 144
Thinking, conceptual, 67
Thought, phases or aspects, 231
Thrasymachos, 21, 26
Tillich, P., 353
Total explanation of human being, 59–66, 85–101, 221–223, 275–279, 328–335
Totalitarianism, 339
Totality, postulate of, 221–223
Traits in personality, 86–88
Transmission of religious values, 313
Travers, R. M. W., 345
Truth, 105–134, 290, 294–303, 318
Turner, F. C., 228, 350
Tutoring, 18
Tuttle, H. W., 351

U

Ulich, R., 201
Unitas multiplex, 71

United States of America, 60, 158, 166, 176, 181, 207, 248, 263, 278, 286, 290, 334–343
Unity, of spiritual and practical, 275
Université imperiale, 184
Universities, 280
Uomo universale, 162
Urges, vital or motivational, 32, 72–74, 141. (*See also* Drives, Instincts, Propensities.)
Usefulness, 110
Utilitarianism, 25–27, 38, 113. (*See also* Pragmatism.)

V

Vaihinger, K., 69
Values, 19–49, 85–213, 238–294, 313–318, 326–334. (*See also* Education, Ethics.)
Vegio, Matteo, 306
Vesalius, Andreas, 53
Victorian era, 181
Vives, L., 53, 228
Vocational education, 198, 240–242, 343
Voltaire, F., 143, 254, 302

W

Wallas, G., 351
Walsh, J. J., 159
Washington, G., 108
Watson, J. B., 56, 347
Webster, N., 342
Weightman, R. C., 167
Weimar, Spirit of, 246
Welfare agencies, 18
Wenzl, A., 346
Whitehead, A. N., 188, 349, 353
Whitehead, T. N., 352
Will, 80–85
Willis, W. D., 346
Wilson, H. E., 349
Woelfel, N., 102n.
Woodworth, R. S., 346
Words, 82
Wordsworth, W., 90
World War, 52, 182, 237, 246, 257, 279, 302, 326

Y

Youth movement, 292

Z

Ziller, T., 229